Fabulous Feasts
Medieval Cookery and Ceremony

Fabulous Feasts
Medieval Cookery and Ceremony

by

Madeleine Pelner Cosman

George Braziller   New York

Published in the United States in 1976 by George Braziller, Inc.
Copyright © 1976 by Madeleine Pelner Cosman
Fifth printing 1992

Library of Congress Cataloging in Publication Data
Cosman, Madeleine Pelner.
  Fabulous Feasts.
  Bibliography:
  1. Food habits—Europe—History.
  2. Cookery, European—History.
  3. Civilization, Medieval. I. Title.
  GT2853.E8C67   394.1′2′094   76-15909
  ISBN 0-8076-0832-7
Printed in Japan

Illustration: Title Page
I: Fig. 13 *With wind instruments accompanying service of food. a noble banqueter eats from rectangular bread trenchers served by the Panter, using three special knives. Wine flagons cool in a footed cumelin; an elaborate, crowned drinking vessel is on the high table. At two long sideboards, twenty feast from round trenchers using an occasional spoon. An aumbry for displaying cups and plates completes the spare furnishings of the banquet hall. (Woodcut by M. Wohlgemuth, from Der Schatzbehalter, A. Koberger, Nuremberg, 1491. New York, The Metropolitan Museum of Art, Rogers Fund, 1919)*

Illustration: Facing Page
I: Fig. 14 *Mounted servitors carry large, covered tureens and elaborate drinking and pouring vessels. The covered dish on the left has an animal-shaped mouth; the large hanap held by the Cupbearer on the right is surmounted by a cross. On the table, footed drinking vessels and filled and wide-lipped serving platters share space with several knives of special design as well as small, sliced breads. Wielding the wand of his office is the Steward, who directs the food service in the hall. (From a portrait of Archbishop of Triers feasting, Germany, 1330. Koblenz, Landeshauptarchiv, Ms. IcI, p.3)*

Gratitude

My passion for medieval cookery dates from 1958: that year I became a medievalist, a wife, and—somewhat hesitantly—a cook. Indirectly, I had earlier learned the cooking techniques of a southern-plantation slave kitchen. My affectionate instructor, granddaughter of a Virginia slave, ran my parents' pantry with her proud inherited philosophy: taste with hand, test with smell. No written, measured, orderly recipes but oral lists of fragrant natural ingredients mixed by hand and spiced by "pinch" were her culinary legacy. Watching her was excellent preparation for understanding the treasury of medieval recipes—in which quantities are not mentioned, preparations and timing are ambiguous or absent—which I discovered by accident.

Medieval medicine is my profession. In the course of research I found beautiful recipes in such unexpected sources as medical manuscripts, public-health laws, and flyleaves of fourteenth-century scientific and astrological texts. Experimenting with intriguing snippets, I inflicted the tasty results on family and friends. Ultimately, I examined and translated most extant medieval manuscript cookery texts, particularly those in England and America.

Fabulous Feasts became inevitable after three pleasing circumstances: articles in *The New York Times* concerning my eccentric culinary interests; my professional appearances on stage and television; and the learned, enthusiastic contributions of my faculty, staff, and students of the Institute for Medieval and Renaissance Studies.

Craig Claiborne's delightful *Times* excursion with me into the wilds of medieval banqueting followed by several years Lisa Hammel's congenial view of my medieval habitat depicting one who not only thinks medieval but also lives it. Both articles elicited requests for menus, recipes, information on etiquette, ceremony, and festivity of feasting. My lecturing around the country and my "Medieval Daily Life" series at the Metropolitan Museum, initiated by Hilde Limondjian, confirmed that an intelligent audience appreciates a complex historical period through such commonplaces as its foodlore. As Dr. Florens Deuchler, former Curator of the Cloisters, remarked after a pleasant response to our medieval feast for the International Center for Medieval Art, clever people have taste as well as ideas. That the serious and the beautiful presented with their inherent exuberance will be popular was suggested amusingly by various radio and television programs; I taped "To Tell the Truth" in the same studio with football hero Joe Namath.

While there are many perils in academic administrative posts, there are more privileges. As Director of the Institute for Medieval and Renaissance Studies, City College of City University of New York, which coordinates fifteen departments, 153 undergraduate and 101 graduate courses, I have welcomed the ideas of many remarkable beings. Few scholars are so blessed as to have on their staffs a Benedictine-trained Israeli encyclopedia editor, printer, Foreign Legionnaire, historian, and linguist in the person of Daniel Furman. In appointing Dr. George Szabo (Curator of the Lehman Collection of the Metropolitan Museum) as Distinguished Visiting Scholar of the Institute, I had not anticipated his gracious enthusiasm for this subject. Nancy Sheiry Glaister, who coordinated the Institute's Cloisters Museum program, aided my work as did Professors Louis Sas, Robert Hajdu, Israel Schepansky, art-historian Annette Blaugrund, and Lore Schirokauer, art photographer extraordinary.

Contributions of my office staff were demonstrations of devotion, intelligence, and ingenuity. In times of crisis, Marion Fegan always has been arbiter of order, uniting gentle authority with nimble fingers. Miriam Mandelbaum typed mightily during an illness of Mrs. Hilda Fuhrman who otherwise transcribed the manuscript with personal taste and professional finesse.

Graduate and undergraduate students delighting with me in examinations of food and medieval science, literature, philosophy, theology, or art history include Robert Zoller, Frank Zirpolo, Lynne Bobenhausen, Susan Scholes, Joseph Scholar, David Hill, Joni Ditzig, Shari Hollender, Derek Norvell, Anne Mallon, Brian Unger, Laura Ann Johnston, Ellen-Jane Pader, Michael Harvey, Michael Hodder, Christine Ruggere, Jane Villon, Mark Mandel, and Rene Szafir Mandel. A mere listing, this includes Ellen's dash to London to check a manuscript reading, Laura's compilation of a glossary of culinary terms, Robert's researching, and Michael's pursuit of twelfth-century Latin kitchen and sewage documents.

Conversations happily affected my interpretations of texts. Sir Niklaus Pevsner, as guest in my home, inspired a new view of familiar manuscripts. Robert S. Lopez of Yale University reminded me, as we sat in my office rocking chairs, of important medieval Mediterranean culinary characteristics; Dom Jean Leclercq gave valuable references as did Paul Meyvaert of the Medieval Academy of America. Dr. Curt Bühler offered use of his wonderful fifteenth-century recipe roll. Since the National Endowment for the Humanities supports the Institute with a particularly generous grant, various friends from Washington have participated in academic aspects of this project: Doctors Ronald Berman, Roger Rosenblatt, Susan Cole, and Miss Floy Brown, as well as Professors Fridjof Bergmann, and Kenneth Wilson.

Lady Irene Roth shared with me medieval Jewish recipes from Sir Cecil Roth's unpublished manuscripts. Dr. Carlton Chapman, president of the Commonwealth Fund; Jeffrey Hoffeld, curator of the Newberger Museum, State University of New York at Purchase; Drs. Audrey and Clifford Davidson, John Sommerfeldt, and Otto Gründler of the University of Western Michigan; Professors Maristella Lorch, Columbia University, and Helen R. Downes, chemistry professor emerita of Barnard College, commented at significant moments upon aspects of this academic adventure; so did Drs. Cyril and Esther Adler, the Adler Museum of the History of Medicine, Johannesburg; Dr. Thomas Vesce, Mercy College; Dr. and Mrs. Gurston Goldin, New York; Nathan Goldstein of the New York Philharmonic, and Steve Reichlan. Bruce La Sala generously aided. Dr. Bern Dibner, The Burndy Library, shared welcome bibliographies.

I have delighted in the enthusiasm of such gourmets as Jacob Rosenthal, retired president of the Culinary Institute of America, Helene Bennett of the Wine and Food Society, and Hedy Giusti-Lanham of the America-Italy Society.

Beyond those with whom I consulted or exulted in things medieval culinary are libraries and museums whose treasures I studied and whose reproductions I borrowed for publication. Librarians, curators, and personnel of all of these institutions were both knowledgeable and gracious. At the *Pierpont Morgan Library* Dr. William Voelkle, Dr. Charles Ryskamp, Dr. John Plummer, and Miss Christine Stenstrom; the *Metropolitan Museum*'s Mr. Brad Kelleher, Miss Suzanne Boorsch, Miss Emma Papert, Mrs. Mary Dougherty, and Mr. Fredd Gordon aided greatly. Mr. George LaBalme, vice-president of the *New York Public Library*, its Spencer Collection's curator Mr. Joseph Rankin, as well as Dr. Jeffrey Kaimowitz and Bernard McTigue; the Research Division's Miss Faye Simkin; Mrs. Cole, the Rare Book Room; Eric Kopf, and Walter Zervas; the *New York Academy of Medicine*: Mrs. Weaver and Mrs. Soli Morgenstern; and *Jewish Theological Seminary*: Dr. Menachem Schmelzer—each made some memorable gesture of friendship. The *Cleveland Museum of Art* and the *Folger Shakespeare Library* in Washington are the final American public institutions which augmented manuscripts graciously lent by the private collectors of *Galeria Medievalia* and *The Camelot Collection*. The map showing trade routes in A.D. 1478 has been reprinted by permission of Penguin Books, Ltd., from Colin McEvedy's publication, *The Penguin Atlas of Medieval History* (1961), p. 89, Copyright © Colin McEvedy, 1961.

Most original manuscript material comes from England. At *The London Guildhall* Miss Betty Masters ever has been generous with the manuscripts under her aegis. At Oxford University, *Bodleian Library*, I am grateful for good words of C. G. Cordeaux and E. J. S. Parsons; and to Mr. Charles Morgenstern of *St. John's College Library*. From Cambridge's *Trinity College Library* I am thankful to Mr. Trevor Kaye, sublibrarian; and to Mr. Philip Gaskell, Librarian. *Canterbury Cathedral* and the *British Museum* allowed use of their superb materials as did the *Barber-Surgeons Guildhall*, Mr. Arthur Chamberlain offering both cordial welcome and excellent tea.

Across the Channel, the *Bibliothèque Nationale*'s courtesy was thanks to M. Marcel Thomas; the *Bibliothèque de l'Arsenal*'s, M. Lalance; the Musée Condé's, M. Raymond Cazelles; at the United States Information Service, librarian Christianne Laude aided in my need. In Germany and Czechoslovakia, *Landeshauptarchiv*, Koblenz, under Dr. Böhn, and *Archives of the City of Prague* lent interesting materials.

Working with George Braziller, Inc., has been both education and pleasure. Mr. Braziller's own enthusiasm for beautiful books (and fine fish) guided the work from beginning to conclusion; Adele Westbrook was editor, Monica Fischbach, editorial and production assistant; Claire Sanford, copy editor; Helen Dressner, Carol Hackett, and Fran Yablonsky, publicity; John Lynch designed this volume.

Last thanks, though simplest, are most fervent. Ruth Pelner Donnelly, my sister, cooks, types, and thinks: a formidable trio. I hope my parents, Dr. and Mrs. Louis Pelner, enjoy this book. My daughter Marin knows its contents well, having transcribed manuscript references and chosen illustrations; my son Clifford tracked manuscript illuminations with a birder's keen eye. The ultimate thanks are the dedication.

TO BARD,

T. G. B.

HARSHEST CRITIC   MONOLITHIC MIND   TRUEST FRIEND

Contents

VI MEDIEVAL FEASTS FOR THE MODERN TABLE:

A Practical Prelude to the Recipes

1. The Modern Medieval Banquet Hall. 2. The Table. 3. The Table Setting and Accoutrements. 4. The Serving Board. 5. Assembling the Rare, Raw Ingredients. 6. Wines. 7. Servitors and Service. 8. Music. 9. Costumes. 10. Emboldening the Feasters. 11. Making Menus for Fabulous Feasts. 12. Modern Re-creations of the Medieval Recipes.

OVER 100 RECIPES FROM MEDIEVAL MANUSCRIPTS

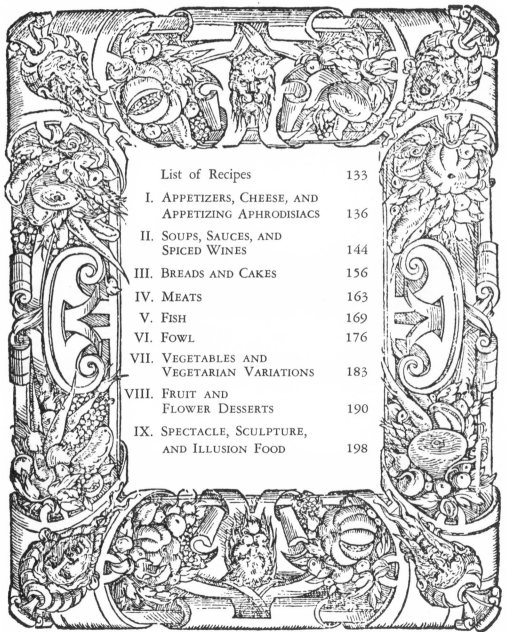

Fabulous Feasts

SETTINGS, SERVINGS, SUBTLETIES, MENUS, AND MARVELS

OODS are cultural insignia. Few indicators define a people so well as its foodlore. Food taboos and food celebrations are important to a culture's notions of sacrament and sin, praise and punishment, deprivation and indulgence, vigilant discipline and sustained extravagance. Medieval England's courtly appetites for splendor are evident in cookery books, courtesy manuals, household and court documents, legal records, medieval texts, and, in surprising profusion, in works of art ranging from marginalia of prayer books through literary romances. Details of medieval food habits in menu, service, table manners, and courtly magnificence adorn depictions of feasts of such diverse heroes as Belshazzar, Jesus, and King Arthur.[1] An excellent literary source for medieval culinary ideas is that exquisite repository of rich revel, *Sir Gawain and the Green Knight*.[2]

A brief culinary excursion into this romance will introduce the English banquet hall, its furnishings, its table adornments, and its noble servitors. The menus of the feasts attended by Sir Gawain are impressive literary food documents outmarveled however by historical banquet rec-

I: Fig. 1 *A man is served at the round table set before an impressive fireplace; another man warms himself while sitting in a large* barrel chair. *The white-coifed servitor from the kitchen beyond, in which a caldron hangs suspended by a chain within a large open hearth, serves a hearty haunch of meat.* (From the Da Costa Hours, *Bruges, 1520. New York, The Pierpont Morgan Library, M399, f.2v)*

1. Since the references are voluminous, see the BIBLIOGRAPHY under the special classifications *Art, Literature,* and *Music.*

2. Ed. J. R. R. Tolkien and E. V. Gordon (Oxford, 1967)

1

ords. In its foodlore, medieval life seems to have been even more dramatic than its portrait in medieval art.

Feast Itinerary of Sir Gawain

Medieval ceremonials of feasts are portrayed in more than twenty food episodes in *Sir Gawain:* there are hasty breakfasts, short repasts, elaborate formal festivities, quiet culinary gallantries in bed chambers, post-prandial wine scenes, and carousing wine parties through the night. A gamut of food settings, services, manners, and menus is run between one Christmas at King Arthur's court at Camelot and the next year's holiday season at Bercilak's castle. Here follows Gawain's culinary itinerary.

A high point of the Christmas season's court feasts, the particularly elaborate New Year's Day banquet, is interrupted by the rude intrusion of the green-garbed, green-mounted giant knight who challenges King Arthur to an exchange of beheadings. Having accepted this task as proxy for Arthur and successfully cleaved the green head from the green neck, Sir Gawain promises to submit to a return blow one year hence. He stays at Camelot through the spring, summer, and fall to November's All Saints' Day when a farewell feast is held in his honor. After much wandering in the wilds, Gawain arrives on Christmas eve at the Knight Bercilak's castle and is welcomed with a sumptuous dinner. An elegant spiced-wine service follows in the bedchamber on this first day of the nine he shares Bercilak's hospitality, winnings of the hunt, and—were Gawain as willing as she—his wife.

Succulent foods and festivities on Christmas day are followed by feasting and fine wines the next day and the one thereafter, St. John's Day, when revelry lasts till dawn. Gawain's fifth day as castle guest, he and his host seal a bargain over wine to exchange Bercilak's trophies of the coming hunt with Gawain's winnings in indoor courtly-love sports. Next morning, avid Bercilak breakfasts before his hunt at dawn; late-sleeping Gawain eats a meal later; both join for gala supper with the seductive mistress; they had exchanged the day's trophies: Bercilak's deer for the kiss Gawain received from Bercilak's wife; they conclude the evening with after dinner wines in the host's chamber.

Next day Bercilak again breakfasts briefly; Gawain dines after the lady's second attempt to seduce him; supper follows with elegant cheer in the hall; this meal is capped by yet another intimate wine ceremony where a last draught seals the pledge for exchanging winnings on New Year's Eve. As this eighth day dawns, Bercilak hunts after breakfast; Gawain, who accepted from the lady not her favors but her magic circlet, spends his merriest day before joining his host for dinner, having exchanged the fox-hunt trophy for three kisses. With laughter, music, and foods of their choice, they celebrate Gawain's final evening in Bercilak's harborage, making elaborate farewells before the morrow's parting. The next, and ninth, day is Sir Gawain's grievous test with the Green Knight; no food is there described.

This gastronomic itinerary suggests the multiplicity of food reference in *Sir Gawain and the Green Knight* but not its magnitude. Two particularly elaborate feasts in this same romance provide details for generalizations about medieval ceremonials of cookery. The first at Arthur's Camelot[3] and the second at Bercilak's castle[4] depict the Great Hall, the order of service, the courtesies of table, and the types, qualities, and por-

3. Lines 60–150.

4. Lines 884–900.

I: Fig. 2

I: Fig. 3

tions of various meats, fishes, stews, and beverages. They describe feast, melody, and humor, ritual graciousness, and niceties of seating.

Two Romance Feasts

New Year's Day at Camelot is celebrated with merriment at a great banquet. The King and his knights make their entrance after prayers in the chapel. Laughter, joy, gift-giving, and much mirth last until time for dinner. After washing their hands, they go to their appointed seats, the noblest sitting the highest; Queen Guinevere's chair is a canopied seat in the middle of the dais, at the elevated table of honor. The most important knights sit at the high table; there all guests are served double portions. King Arthur, however, refuses to eat until he hears of some adventure or marvel.

The first course comes with a flourish of trumpets, with many bright banners hanging from them; the noise of drums and the fine pipes make wild warbles that delight the eye and cheer the heart. Dainty dishes of exotic foods are served; abundant, fresh, so many and various that it is difficult to find place before the guests to set the silver platters. Everyone helps himself without stint. Each two guests have twelve dishes between them and good beer and bright wine. There is no lack of anything that could be wished. A new fanfare signals the start of eating. Scarcely has the sound ceased when there appears at the door the awesome giant, gorgeously garbed in green from his green-haired head to his green horse's hooves.

The second notable banquet in the romance is the welcoming feast at Bercilak's, set in an elegant chamber hung with rich carpets and tapestries. The servants, having brought trestles, set up the table and put a sparkling white cloth on it, then an overcloth, a saltcellar, and silver spoons. Gawain washes his hands, and the well-trained servants offer him many excellent stews, well seasoned, and double portions of them, and various kinds of fish, some baked in pastry, some grilled on embers, some boiled, and some in piquant spiced stews and many cunningly wrought sauces. Gawain constantly and courteously says that this is as fine a feast as ever he had eaten. But all reply that this meal was fit for a fast; a real feast soon will come.

The Great Hall

Usually a high-ceilinged, spacious room, the banquet hall generally had a balcony or gallery or special raised-floor section for musicians whose fanfares and entertainments were part of courtly food service. Not only used for banquets, the Great Hall also was living room, parlor, audience chamber, and social center of the court or noble household.[5] Furnishings thus were spare and multipurpose. Its walls hung with banners and tapestries, and the floors polished stone or wood or tile, the hall was furnished with a special table or a cupboard called an *aumbry* upon whose open shelves elegant platters and ewers could be displayed. A *surveying board* or *dresser* was another table to which foods were brought for final preparation, decoration, "dressing," and "saucing" before service. A third type of furniture, found either in hall or pantry, was the *trencher board* upon which special breads were cut with a prescribed array of knives and ceremonies. Most carving of meats was done by noble servitors at the banquet table itself.

I: Fig. 3 *Drinking from transparent crystal stemware, the wedding guests are served by a kneeling* Carver, *who is disjointing a bird, and* Butler, *supervising six stoneware wine flagons. Several knives and a loaf complete the setting on the* trestle table. *("Wedding at Cana" from the* Grandes Heures, *15th century, French. Paris, Bibliothèque Nationale, Ms. Latin 919, f.41)*

5. See T. Wright, *A History of Domestic Manners* (London, 1862); H. Braun, "The Hall," and "Private Houses," in *An Introduction to English Medieval Architecture* (New York, 1968); and the BIBLIOGRAPHY classifications *The Times* and *Art.*

15

6. For representations of tables in medieval art and life see G. Schiedlausky, *Essen und Trinken* (Munich, 1956); and the BIBLIOGRAPHY classification *Gastronomy*.

7. In Chapter V, see "Characterization by Food Habit."

8. See Charles Oman, *Medieval Silver Nefs* (London, 1963).

9. Fascinating illustrations are found in W. H. Hope's "On the English Medieval Drinking Bowls Called Mazers," *Archaeologia* 50 (1887), 129–93; M. and C. Quennell, *A History of Everyday Things in England: 1066–1179* (New York, n.d.); E. H. Pinto, *Treen and Other Wooden Bygones* (London, 1969); G. Savage, *English Pottery and Porcelain* (New York, 1961); and the BIBLIOGRAPHY classification *Gu, utensils*.

10. See C. J. Jackson, "The Spoon and Its History," *Archaeologia* 53 (1892); N. Cask, *Old Silver Spoons of England* (London, 1926); C. G. Rupert, *Apostle Spoons* (London, 1929); F. G. H. Price, *Old Base Metal Spoons* (London, 1908).

11. See J. F. Hayward, *English Cutlery* (London, 1956).

Pl. 1   *The bride, seated beneath* a baldaquin, *and her maids of honor are served by a* Carver *and regaled by musicians blowing horns from their gallery. Servants enter from the kitchen behind the dining hall to serve guests seated at the long table, the* sideboard. *Opposite them is an ornamental* aumbry *upon which platters and ewers are displayed, one of which is being offered by the* Cupbearer *or* Surveyor *to a table servitor. (From* Histoire de Renaud de Montauban, France, 1468–70. Paris, Bibliothèque de l'Arsenal, Ms. 5073)

The Table

Special guests and the hosts sat at the *high table,* literally raised above the level of all other tables by a *dais,* and perpendicular to them.[6] Sitting along one long side of this high table, the honored could see and be seen by all others who sat in descending order of social rank on benches or stools at long tables parallel to the side walls of the hall, called *sideboards.* Medieval tables were of two basic types, the "permanent" and the "temporary." Always ready for setting was the permanent *stable table* that, like the *table dormant* of Chaucer's Franklin,[7] carried foods at most hours. Generally made of- oak, it was a massive piece of furniture. The second type was the *trestle table* or *horse-and-saddle table*—such as Sir Gawain feasted from in Bercilak's castle—consisting of boards laid atop trestles or saw horses, set up for meals and taken down between. Usually these removable table tops had carrying handles, oftentimes decorated. Though long rectangles are most frequently depicted, other medieval table shapes included round, oval, and square.

On the Table

Upon the table a white cloth, covered with an overcloth called a *sanap,* was background for few table adornments and less cutlery. A *salt,* an open, embellished container, stood before the seat of the most honored—thus others sat "below the salt." One type of saltcellar more popular on the continent than in England was the boat-shaped *nef*[8] whose often elaborate rigging and jewel-encrusted bow made it more ornament than utensil. *Table fountains,* either on the main tables or centrally situated in the hall, spouted wines or fragrant waters. The more complex their pipings, the more varieties of drinks they served from their turrets, spigots, and sculptured terminals.

Goblets or tankards made of glass or metal, or double cups called *hanaps*—in which the cup's cover itself was another cup—were used for drinking. So too was transparent crystal stemware. *Mazers* were bowls, sometimes footed, used as drinking vessels. Wooden, porcelain, glass, or metal, the mazers often had elaborate rim embellishments.[9] Both open and covered pitchers and flagons with decorated finials and handles were used to pour wine, ale, and mulled ciders. Gold, silver, pewter, or the popular bronze-colored copper and zinc alloy, *dinanderie,* were the metals most frequent for ewers and pitchers, though others were fashioned from rock crystal, glass, stoneware, wood, or ivory. Silver or gold spoons and a few sharp knives completed the table settings.[10] Guests often carried their own knives, encased with other necessaries, such as a pair of scissors or a file, in a *chatelaine.* Forks, though known in European kitchens and used on Byzantine tables as early as the twelfth century, nevertheless were not fashionable in England until the late Renaissance.[11] English visitors to Italy reported the peculiar, finicky table habits of the fork-wielding Italian nobility and avoided such superfluous encumbrance.

Individual plates at place settings were only rarely used. Foods conveyed from kitchen to table on serving platters called *chargers*—such as the twelve silver dishes set before Sir Gawain—were selected by guests and then placed before them upon large slices of bread, round in shape or, more usually, square, called *trenchers.* Often colored and spiced green with parsley, or yellow with saffron, or pink with *saunders* (san-

1

2

dalwood), trenchers served as edible platters. Furthermore, once gravies and sauces were absorbed by the bread, it was kept for the morrow as a nutritious *sop* in wine or milk; or as food for the dogs; or as culinary aims for the poor at the gate.

Table Manners

Elaborate rituals were observed for finger-eating. Spoons were used for soups and puddings; knives, some with serrated tips, lifted meats from platters and sometimes to the mouth.[12] But all else was picked, balanced, and conveyed by those most portable, manipulable, graceful terminals of the hands. Certain fingers were extended while eating specific foods to allow grease-free fingers available for the next dish, as well as for dipping fingers into condiments and spices. (Some among us still maintain an atavistic extension of a pinky-finger at a teacup.) This primacy of finger implements explains in part the prevalence of easily handled foods at feasts, the meat- and fish- and fruit-filled pastries, breads, sweet tarts (called *doucettes*), and individual pies or *coffyns*. However, since much food was served with piquant sauces, gravies, stuffings, and creams, punctilious dexterity (such as Chaucer's Prioress's)[13] was necessary grace:

> At mete wel ytaught was she with alle:
> She leet no morsel from hir lippes falle,
> Ne wette hir fyngres in hir sauce depe;
> Wel koude she carie a morsel and wel kepe
> That no drope ne fille upon hire brest.
> In curteisie was set ful muchel hir lest.
> Hir over-lippe wyped she so clene
> That in hir coppe ther was no ferthyng sene
> Of grece, whan she dronken hadde hire draughte.
> Ful semely after hir mete she raught.[14]

Fingers were washed between courses and at the meal's end.

Service of Feasts

After prayers in chapel or at table, guests washed hands with warm water—oftentimes fragrant with herbs or flower petals—poured by servants called *Ewerers* from a *laver* or *aquamanile*.[15] The first to wash was the host or the most honored guest; social hierarchy was significant even in courtly cleaning ceremonies. The place of honor at the high table was not the "head" but the center; the seat or *settle* of honor was often covered by a canopy, a *baldaquin*. Service started here, with all subsequently served according to rank.

Trumpet fanfares, rollings of drums, and shrill pipe tunes signaled the service of specific courses and dishes within the feast.[16] On silver platters or in covered tureens, individual foods were served to each pair of guests who then shared that plate. Food after food was thus brought to the table with each pair helping themselves to delicacies of choice. Double portions were appropriate for honored guests (according to laws of hospitality and harborage) and for special occasions (according to ecclesiastical calendars and sumptuary regulations).[17] Social propriety and custom demanded culinary notice of important people and events.

12. See C. T. P. Bailey, *Knives and Forks* (London, 1927).

13. *The Canterbury Tales*, ed. F. N. Robinson, *The Works of Geoffrey Chaucer* (Boston, 1957). Chaucer's depictions of foods and feasting as related to character and hypocrisy are discussed in detail in Chapter V.

14. *Prologue* to the *Canterbury Tales*, ll. 127–36.

15. See the BIBLIOGRAPHY classification *Art;* and A. Wagner, *Heralds and Heraldry in the Middle Ages* (London, 1956).

16. See E. A. Bowles, "Musical Instruments at the Medieval Banquet," *Revue Belge de musicologie* 12 (1958); and the BIBLIOGRAPHY classification *Music*.

17. See F. E. Baldwin, *Sumptuary Legislation and Personal Regulation in England* (Baltimore, 1926); also, Chapter V.

Pl. 2   *Richly costumed servants attend the Duke of Berry feasting. A* Carver *poises his knife, small live dogs walk near the elaborate gold salt-cellar, the* nef. *A* Butler *pours wine from a covered flagon while a blue-robed attendant holds a* mazer; *an* aumbry *displays gold plate. The Duke's* banquette *is raised above table-level by a carpeted* dais. *(From the* Très Riches Heures *of Jean, Duke of Berry. Chantilly, Musée Condé f.2r)*

I: Fig. 4 *Guests drink from footed or plain* mazers, *convey fruit or bread to their mouths in bite-sized portions, finger whole fish, and wield notched fish knives. Other guests hold their double-cupped* hanaps *or round loaves from some of which the "upper crust" has been carved. Dogs join the feast. (From Gregory's* Moralia, *12th century. Paris, Bibliothèque Nationale, Ms. Latin 15675, f.8v)*

18. See H. De Lafontaine, *The King's Musick* (New York, 1973); A. Baines, *Woodwind Instruments and Their History* (New York, 1963); and A. Carse, *Musical Wind Instruments* (London, 1965).

19. See E. J. Dent, "Social Aspects of Music in the Middle Ages," *Oxford History of Music* (London, 1929); W. H. Mellers, *Music and Society* (London, 1948); R. Withington, *English Pageantry* (London, 1920); E. Meyer, *English Chamber Music* (New York, 1946).

20. G. P. Krapp and E. V. K. Dobbie (eds.), *Anglo-Saxon Poetical Records* (New York, 1931–42).

21. See Thomas Morley, *A Plaine and Easie Introduction To Practicall Musicke,* ed. R. Harman (New York, 1952).

22. A delightful set made for Queen Elizabeth is discussed by Curt Bühler, *Renaissance News* 9 (1956), 146f.

23. See W. Gundesheimer (ed.), *Art and Life at the Court of Ercole I* (Geneva, 1972); E. Winternitz, *Musical Instruments* (New York, 1967); W. Woodfill, *Musicians in English Society* (Princeton, 1953); and the BIBLIOGRAPHY classification *Music*.

24. *Banchetti Compositioni di Vivende* (Ferrara, 1549), ed. F. Bandini (Venice, 1960); L. Lockwood, "Music at Ferrara," *Studi musicali* 1 (1972); H. M. Brown, "A Cook's Tour of Ferrara in 1529."

Profusion of food brought by servants in procession made for visual splendor. This was complemented by stirring sound. Music was to be seen as well as heard; glittering banners on blaring trumpets were as important to pageantry as the fanfare sound.

Banquet Music

Music was other ways important during feasts. Instruments accompanied dancing by entertainers or guests; minstrels sang to lutes, harps, dulcimers, pipes, and shawms.[18] Feasters themselves performed part-songs, catches, and caroles.[19] Before and during service of dishes and courses, and especially after the feast, musical entertainments were significant in an English tradition traceable back through Anglo-Saxon lore to the Venerable Bede. His story of "the first English poet" Caedmon[20] depicts the meadhall custom of passing the harp at table from guest to guest for each to sing a traditional or extemporaneous song. Poor Caedmon, not knowing how to perform, left the hall in shame; soon thereafter a divine miracle gave him his requisite rhythm and tongue to sing praises of heaven and earth.

Throughout the Middle Ages and Renaissance all well-educated Englishmen and women were expected to know music well enough to read at sight a simple score and participate in banquet musicales.[21] Sometimes small flat platters called *roundels,* made of porcelaine or stiff paper, were served with the last course of a feast.[22] When the food was eaten, each guest turned over his roundel to find written on the reverse a text or poem or bawdy phrase which required an improvised setting and singing.

Banquet music performed by professional musicians was scrupulously planned for dramatic effect. The permanent court performers or those invited for specific occasions followed a musical menu as carefully crafted as the culinary.[23] Numbers of instruments, blendings of their sounds, appositions amongst lyrics of songs, alternations between solo and choral settings—such were balanced within the concert yet coordinated with the foods and their service. Remarkable programs for feast music are the banquet scores recorded by Cristoforo da Messisbugo, Cook for the Este court at Ferrara.[24] Each course, each fish dish, dessert, and wine was supplemented by viol, voice, and choir. While noble guests washed hands with perfumed water, a musical performance by six singers, six viols, a lira, lute, "citara," trombone, recorder, flute, "sordina," and keyboard instruments—*tanto bene concertata*—accompanied the seventeenth course.

Courses and Menus

The variety and multiplicity of foods at feasts, the tables laden so heavy—thus *groaning boards*—the long orders of courses and numbers of dishes within them suggest extravagant eating and gluttonous excess. Yet Gawain's twelve dishes at one sitting, and the menus for celebrating crownings of kings or investitures of archbishops document not what was eaten but, rather, profusion of choice. The often repeated phrases: "foods of their choice," "whatever dishes they desired," "select wines," are less likely simple epithets of excellence than actual references to the act of selection among proffered possibilities. Choice was more significant than food quantity. Liberality meant abundant offering.

Hunc uisunt cuncti paruiciciam sibi iuncti Huic conuiuante & eusua munera dantes.

Prophus ablatis tribus & septe sibi natis Iob recipit totideos meliorsit quã sit ideo.

I: Fig. 4

One esthetic enterprise of medieval courtly gastronomy was the sequential ordering of the prepared and decorated foods. The medieval "course" was closer than the modern to the Latin origins of the word *currere*, to run, a running, passing, flowing ordering in time. No mere appetizer–entree–dessert sequence made the medieval menu. Yet there was a tripartite configuration for most feast fares: each of three "courses" had seven or twelve or fifteen separate meat or poultry or fish or stew or sweet dishes—or, in the most elegant feasts, all. The medieval course, then, was an artful succession of foods in time.

Fruits or potages began the first course; and fruits, wafers, and wine, or confections such as *Strawberye* ended the last. The elements of each course, whose duration was many hours, were interspersed with music and entertainments, while noble men and boys carried elaborate, decorated dishes in a spectacular series of tastes and textures.

Allocation of dishes to a course, or their ordering within it, sometimes was governed by genre: numerous different meats followed by many varieties of fowl. Or gastronomic hygiene determined order: sweet then sour, "hot" then "cold" foods; or "moist" versus "dry" components or spices affecting digestion and health. Or a zoological hierarchy determined precedence; in the *Liber Cure Cocorum*[25] a suggested sequence is whole-footed birds first, and of these the largest, then on down to the smallest: swan before goose, drake before duck, in an animal social order. Or arrangements of food followed from obvious or recondite symbolism, or sheer exuberance of color or form: a four-course feast for which the sculptured food decorations, the *subtleties*, represented the four seasons of the year as well as the four ages of man's life, had foods appropriate to each.

Menus for a Coronation and a Funeral

Medieval bills of fare are startling documents. King Henry IV, whose fascinating medical history is bound with his food habits,[26] was crowned at Westminster in 1399; his coronation banquet, which Froissart chronicled[27] for political more than culinary record, followed this order:

First course   1. Meat in pepper sauce   2. *Viaund Ryal*   3. Boar's head and tusks   4. *Graund chare*   5. Cygnets   6. Fat capon   7. Pheasant   8. Heron   9. *Crustade Lumbarde*   10. Sturgeon, great luces   11. A Subtlety

Second course   1. Venison in frumenty   2. Jelly   3. Stuffed pig   4. Peacocks   5. Cranes   6. Roast venison   7. Coney   8. Bittern   9. Pullets   10. Great tarts   11. Fried meat   12. *Leche Lumbarde*   13. A Subtlety

Third course   1. *Blaundesorye*   2. Quince in comfit   3. Egrets   4. Curlews   5. Partridge   6. Pigeons   7. Quails   8. Snipes   9. *Smal Byrdys*   10. Rabbits   11. Glazed meat-apples   12. White meat *leche*   13. Glazed eggs   14. Fritters   15. Doucettes   16. *Pety perneux*   17. Eagle   18. *Pottys of lylye*   19. A Subtlety

Not all medieval feasts were triadic and not all celebrants ate the same food. At the funeral collation commemorating Nicholas Bibbes-

25. Ed. Richard Morris, from the Sloane MS 1986 (London, 1862).

26. See M. P. Cosman and L. Pelner, "Elias Sabat and King Henry IV," *New York State Journal of Medicine* 69:18 (1969), 2482–90.

27. For a congenial account, see Thomas Austin's introduction to his *Two Fifteenth Century Cookery Books* (London, 1888); compare Froissart's *Chronicles*, eds. Gillian and William Anderson (Carbondale, 1963).

I: Fig. 5 *This fastidiously garbed couple sitting beneath a* baldaquin *is regaled by a woman harpist. Two knives, two transparent glass drinking bowls, an oval platter, and two small loaves complete the service on the white-clothed* trestle table. *(15th century, French. Oxford, Bodleian Library, Ms. Rawl. Liturg. E36 f.90v)*

I: Fig. 5

I: Fig. 6

I: Fig. 6 *Seated* al fresco on a parapeted balcony (or a hall painted for illusion of "outdoors"), a regal pair share a wine chalice; on the table, dishes of bird heads, fish, and roasts simultaneously are set for selection. On the right are two covered wine pitchers and an elaborate spire-covered drinking vessel, a hanap. A musician plays her vielle. The short tablecloth displays the lady's fur-trimmed gown, and the lord's fashionable 15th century pointed slippers. (By the "Spanish Forger," 19th century. New York, New York Private Collection, SL68)

I: Fig. 7 Roundels *were dessert "platters" of wood or porcelain or tile, decorated and inscribed with a poem or ditty, often risqué, that the feaster was expected to sing to improvised or popular melody. Made for Queen Elizabeth, this set bears the English coat of arms as a central boss; all nest neatly in an embellished wooden box. Messages, here more moral than racy, exhort embracing virtue, eschewing sin, and following the golden rule—even in marriage. (Dated 1595. New York, The Pierpont Morgan Library, M681)*

I: Fig. 7

I: Fig. 8 *While some peacocks were served whole, refeathered and gilded, others were plucked bare save for their heads and tails. In this humorously crude portrait of a peacock, the bird's crest and tail are gold, its bare skin a contrasting pink. A Carver kneels before the trestle table covered by a white cloth with a diamond-faceted design. Two gold cups, three knives, three breads, and two spice vessels are the only table accoutrements. (From Jacques de Longuyon,* Voeux de Paon, *France or Flanders, 1350. New York, Pierpont Morgan Library, Glazier 24, f.52)*

worth, Bishop of Bath and Wells, on December 4th, 1424, laymen ate meat, his clerical colleagues, fish.

First meat course 1. *Nomblys de Roo* 2. *Blamangere* 3. Meat with mustard 4. Pork chop 5. Roast capon 6. Roast swan 7. Roast heron 8. *Aloes do Roo* 9. Swan neck pudding 10. *Un Lechemete* 11. *Un bake*

Second meat course 1. *Ro Styuyd* 2. *Mammenye* 3. Roast coney 4. Curlew 5. Roast pheasant 6. Roast woodcock 7. Roast partridge 8. Roast plover 9. Roast snipe 10. *Grete byrdys Rosted* 11. Roast larks 12. *Vennysoun de Ro Rostyd* 13. *Yrchouns* 14. *Un leche* 15. *Payn puffe* 16. *Colde bakemete*

First fish course 1. Eels in saffron sauce 2. *Blamangere* 3. Baked herring 4. Milwell tails 5. Ling tails 6. *Jollys* of salmon 7. Boiled merling 8. Pike 9. Great plaice 10. *Leche barry* 11. *Crustade Ryal*

Second fish course 1. *Mammenye* 2. Almond cream 3. Codling 4. Haddock 5. Fresh hake 6. Boiled sole 7. Broiled gurnard with syrup 8. Bream 9. Roche 10. Perch 11. Fried minnows 12. *Yrchouns* 13. Roast eels 14. *Leche Lumbarde* 15. Great crabs 16. *A cold bakemete*

A Sample Courtly Menu

While King Henry's and the bishop's menus were historical feasts for political occasions, sample menus exist for meat dinners or fish feasts for

other noble tables. For the Duke of Gloucester's household, his Chamberlain John Russell suggested such a fish dinner as this:[28]

First course   1. *Musclade* of minnows   2. Salmon belly or *sounds*   3. Eels   4. Porpoise and peas   5. Baked herring with sugar   6. Green milwell   7. Pike   8. Roast lamprey   9. Roast sole   10. Roast porpoise   11. Gurnard   12. Baked lamprey   13. *Leche*   14. A fritter   15. A Subtlety representing Spring, A Youthful Figure, *Sanguineus*.

Second course   1. Dates in comfit   2. Red and white jelly   3. Conger, salmon, doree in syrup   4. Brett, turbot, or halibut   5. Carp, bass, millet, or trout   6. *Chevin* and bream   7. Seal   8. Roast eels and lampreys   9. A *leche*   10. A fritter   11. A Subtlety: Summer, A Warrior, *Colericus*.

Third course   1. Almond cream *Iardyne*   2. *Mawmenny* potages   3. Fresh sturgeon   4. Breme   5. Perch in jelly   6. Whelks, minnows   7. Shrimps   8. Fresh broiled herring   9. *Pety perueis*   10. *Leche* fritter   11. A tansy   12. A Subtlety: Autumn, A Weary Man, *Fleumaticus*.

Fourth course   1. Hot apples and pears with *sugar candy*   2. Ginger *Columbyne*   3. Wafers   4. *Hypocras*   5. A Subtlety: Winter, An Old Man, *Melancolicus*.

Gargantuan Gorging?

A few enumerated foods, such as in the second course, may represent the cook's choices among several dishes rather than preparation of all. But such occasional manuscript equivocation notwithstanding, the bills of

28. John Russell's *Boke of Nurture,* ed. F. Furnivall, *Early English Meals and Manners* (London, 1868; reprint Detroit, 1969).

fare are no less prodigious. Even for the less-well born but epicurean in taste, sample menus exist which are historical analogues for the Franklin's table in Chaucer, well laid with finest bread, ale, wines, fish, flesh, dainties, and seasonal delights.

Such menus, however, document what was prepared for service, not what was eaten. The instructions for carving foods for great lords in the household manuals such as the *Boke of Kervyng*,[29] and the depiction of their favorite dainties—wings and necks of fowl, spiced liver of whale— suggest that prescribed and small portions were considered "correct" for the most noble, discriminating palates. Boar served the whole household, but specific anatomical portions were proper for certain classes of diners. Most medieval culinary treatises indicate food selection was as much cultivated an art as hunting or music-making. Careful choice, elegant ritual, and fastidious tasting separated the noble from the hungry.

Most modern commentators upon medieval cookery have reasoned, teleologically, that if huge quantities of food were listed in the texts, then all foods must have been consumed. However, medieval banquet records deny such conclusion; modern analogies in the rich buffet menus of a wedding or a Bar Mitzvah feast—in which ostentation supersedes feeding—also suggest that ambient tasting was more likely the amenity than gorging. Unless armor covered portly paunches while the high-waisted gowns disguised fat waistlines; or noble courtiers were all hearty, hard-riding, adolescent physiological specimens; or medieval metabolisms were faster than the modern—then medieval commentary and modern reason suggest that gigantic quantities of food were not consumed regularly. Gargantuan menus the household documents certainly attest to; but they do not delineate Pantagruelian appetites. Grand feasts created an impression of plenitude. Splendor of selection, opulence of presentation—proof therefore of noble wealth or Divine plenty—made the medieval feast an esthetic and, doubtlessly, political spectacle.

Noble Servitors Between the Kitchen and the Hall

A noble cadre transferred such spectacles from kitchen to hall. While rough kitchen work was done by hired scullions, varlets, and *quistrons* (kitchen boys), the titles, responsibilities, and implements of the food service were carried by noblemen and the sons of gentlemen. At King Henry's inaugural banquet, for example, Thomas Beauchamp, Earl of Warwick, was Panter, serving the king's bread; the Earl of Somerset, as Carver, disjointed pheasant wing from breast. Others equally important served as Ewerer carrying washing water and towel, and Cupbearer fetching wine.

These titles were not merely ceremonial. Noblemen in medieval England usually were served by noble youths sent to their courts for education in domestic service in addition to other chivalric or courtly accomplishments. To serve well in a significant household was superb means for political and professional advancement for the second sons and others who could not inherit their fathers' estates. Hearing the politics of the table, seeing, meeting, and serving the great, the potentially illustrious thus learned the decorum of court and there presaged their own futures. Sir Thomas More as a youth waited at table for Cardinal Morton,[30] who predicted that boy would prove a marvelous man. The

29. Wynkyn de Word's *Boke*, ed. F. Furnivall, *Early English Meals*.

30. See John Roper, *Life of Sir Thomas More*, ed. Singer (London, 1822).

31. See M. P. Cosman, *The
Education of the Hero in
Arthurian Romance* (Chapel
Hill, 1966, Oxford, 1967).

32. The *Prologue* to the *Canterbury Tales*, l. 100.

medieval courtly food services were settings for the educations of heroes.[31]

Each such domestic station had its title and its tools. One of the most exalted positions was the *Carver's*. A son might so serve his father (as did Chaucer's Knight's),[32] the most trusted squire so cater to the lord his employer. A prodigious number of rules and technical terms pertain to carving, preparing, and presenting fowl, flesh, and fish. After "unlacing a capon," the Carver served only the left wing to the lord, mincing it with wine and spiced sauce. Baked meat pies were to be cut only at top of the crust if hot, in the middle if cold. The kidney of fawn, kid, or lamb was the delicacy served first; only then, one rib. To "depart a crayfish," the Carver slit the "belly of the hindpart," cleaned the "gowt," sliced the flesh, broke the claws, and stuffed the shell with bread. For each technique for each animal, special knives, levers, and hand positions—most knives were held by two fingers and thumb—were specified exactly. Splendid serving ceremony is recommended in Wynkyn de Worde's *Boke of Kervyng* for alaying a pheasant, winging a partridge, displaying a crane, breaking an egret, untaching a curlew, and unlacing a coney.

The *Panter*, guardian of the lord's bread (from the French word *pain*), ceremoniously rolled the *portpayne*, the special cloth for carrying bread. He used three knives at his own breadboard: a *chaffer* for large loaves, a *parer*, and a *trencher knife* for smoothing the edges of the specially sliced bread that served as platters. Trenchers in England generally consisted of four small bread squares, sides abutted, forming a larger square upon which selected foods later would be placed; a fifth

28

I: Fig. 10 *Demonstrating the genuflections of courtly service, two food servitors present a bowl and the "upper crust" from a round loaf, cut for the noble feasters, here holding footed drinking vessels before their trestle table whose embellished carrying handles are visible beyond the folds of the tablecloth. King David, here feasting with Abner, welcomes his guest in the right-hand panel before regaling him and his party at left. (Old Testament, 13th century, French. New York, The Pierpont Morgan Library, M638, f.37v)*

square covered the central seams of the joining of the four. Sometimes, however, trenchers were single rectangles or circles. The Panter's fourth knife, the *mensal knife*, cut the choice "upper crust" from rolls and breads for presentation to the master. From this bread custom comes our modern appellation for the mighty. Bread baked the day of service was for the lord alone; from the pantry other guests received day-old bread; the household, three-days' bread, and for their trenchers, bread four days old. The Panter also controlled the salt; he was required to carry his ivory salt planer—2 inches by 3 inches in dimensions.

The *Butler* supervised butts of wine and ale, with responsibility for checking and cleaning all cellar casks, funnels, and spigots as well as for avoiding spoilage and pilfering. He ameliorated weakened or discolored wines by adding the requisite spices or wine mixings; *Romeney* was to be added to a sick and pallid wine, and *coloure de rose* to overboiled wine. (In the market place such tempering of wines was considered adulteration, prohibited by law.)[33] Armed with wine augers, gimlets, adzes, pipes, and stopples of his office, he not only kept wines in condition but made such spiced-wine mixtures as ended most feasts and lesser lordly meals, *Hippocras.* A drink, yet a digestive, it was named for the Greek physician Hippocrates and his garment's "sleeve"—the name of the special strainer bags of "sleeve" shape in which the ginger, cinnamon, pepper, sugar, and other spicery were mixed with red wine. The Butler determined proper spice balance by tasting "with mouth and tongue."[34]

"To prove by mouth" was a technique not only to establish correct taste but to avoid accidental or political poisonings. Good servants were

33. See Chapter III, on Wine and Ale, for laws, court cases, and ingenious drink malefactions.

34. See John Russell, *Boke of Nurture,* in F. J. Furnivall's *Early English Meals,* ll. 162, 561, 646, 829.

I: Fig. 11

taught *credence,* the procedure for discovering by taste any dangerous foods and drinks.[35] The court *Steward,* who supervised the food service, and *Chamberlain* tasted or instructed others in the delicate craft.

Other gentlemen of the household included the *Sewer,* charged with arranging dishes before and after they reached the table; the *Almoner,* guardian of the Alms Dish in which first crusts cut from bread as well as left-over foods were placed for distribution to the poor; the *Surveyor,* who controlled the *surveying board* to which the *Cook* directed the bringing of individual serving platters; the *Marshalls, Squires, Ushers,* and *Sergeants-at-Arms,* who carried the platters and tureens to the noble feasters. Dressed in the costume of the noble house, these members of the catering staff augmented feast ceremony by their patterned routines for service and by the ritual genuflections and choreography of their movements.

Fumositées and Health

While a noble kitchen cadre served the lord's pleasure, it was also a major force for his protection. Servitors were charged not only with *credence,* but with avoiding for their sovereign those foods (or their bony or hairy excrescences) which might annoy, injure, or otherwise discommode him. A charming mnemonic by John Russell counseled avoiding the undigestibles, called *Fumositées,* by thrice three concentrations upon the letters *F, R,* and *S.*

F is the furst/that is Fatt, Farsed & Fried;
R, raw/resty and rechy, of comberous undefied;
S/salt/soure/and sowse/alle such thous set aside.[36]

So also sinews, skins, hair, crops, feathers, heads, pinions, and bones must be prevented from reaching the master's mouth; his health disturbed, so also might be his domain. Yet each of those trinal triplicities of F, R, S was a quality of some favored ingredient, or popular cookery technique, or quality of food decoration. To balance appetite with health, and to achieve equilibrium between ceremony and safety, the final act of courtly catering was testing by tasting. From this visceral viewpoint, esthetics and politics converged at the courtly table.

Marvelous Entertainment

Culinary spectacles were marvelous entertainment. The best medieval feasts united the sumptuous with shocking, "unnatural," and incredible events. Foods themselves were sculptures or games.[37] Cooked peacocks were served resplendent in their iridescent feathers. Tethered live birds were baked into pies; the crust cut, they sang. Bestiary animals such as the *Cockentrice* were created by ingenious cooks sewing the uppers of a baked chicken with the nethers of a pig. Armorial devices and heraldic emblems were reproduced in pastry and in aspic. The banners of great houses with their ancestral quarterings were represented by capons or conies in colored jellies.

Jugglers or acrobats sometimes were served *in* enormous puddings such as the *allemain* and leapt out to amaze guests into admiration. Dwarfs, jesters, "wildmen," and "freaks" performed during feasts to entertain by shocking, to delight noble feasters by their own marveling.

I: Fig. 11 *Games of chance were frequent between dishes or courses. In this allegorical feast the* Prodigal Son, *sharing a mazer with buxom* Flesh, *plays backgammon with vainglorious* World *whose right foot trammels the head of* Conscience, *while aged* Avarice *quaffs a glass poured from a pitcher with lion-mouthed handle. To bagpipe tunes played by* Reason, Avarice *hands her accomplice,* Selfishness, *a stolen money bag. (Woodcut by Cornelis Anthonisz, Germany, ca. 1540. New York, The Metropolitan Museum of Art)*

35. The technique is graphically depicted in Chapter IV, Fig. 2.

36. Lines 357 f.

37. To prepare such, see the RECIPES, section 9, *Spectacle, Sculpture, and Illusion Foods.* On games played *at* and *on* banquet tables see F. N. David, *Games, Gods, and Gambling* (Griffin, 1962); N. Rabinovitch, *Probability and Statistical Inference in Ancient and Medieval Jewish Literature* (Toronto, 1973); and Charles Cotton, *The Compleat Gamester* [1674] (Bane, Mass., 1970).

I: Fig. 12 *Attending this sumptuous feast are seven pairs of royal crowned couples served peacock resplendent in its feathers, and rabbits, birds, and roasts by graceful genuflecting servitors. The hooded Surveyor, standing near the open-shelved* aumbry *which displays ewers and chargers, hands a wine flagon to a Butler who will serve in the center of the table. Dogs gnaw bones behind the* banquettes. *The honored pair sitting beneath the* baldaquin *have numerous soldiers for sergeants–at–arms at hand. (By the "Spanish Forger," 19th century. New York, The Pierpont Morgan Library, SL77)*

Pl. 3 *This ladies' feast features the* settle of honor *beneath an embroidered* baldaquin. *The Panter stands ready to cut the* trenchers *with his three special knives:* chaffer, parer, *and* trencher knife *for smoothing the edges of the small square bread slices. Salt containers with peaked covers and small round loaves or buns are on the sparsely set table. A food platter is carried by another gentleman of the household, perhaps the* Carver. *(15th century, Flemish. Oxford, Bodleian Library, Western Mss., Ms. Douce 374, f.17)*

I: Fig. 12

3

4

At one banquet, a sculptured castle with beasts—deer, boar, goats, and hares—was borne into the hall by squires. It had a fountain in whose center a tower spouted wine in five directions, each wine of a different quality: Vernaccia, Greek, Bielna, Sanporciano, and Sienese. Around the fountain were cooked peacocks that seemed to be alive, pheasants, partridges, and other wild birds. There followed ten white horses, mounted by armed knights: but the horses were made of wicker, covered with cloth, concealing six men each. At the last course, two large trees were presented, one green and one silver, with pendant pears, peaches, apples, figs, and other fruits of many colors, all candied.[38]

While the literary King Arthur's demand for marvels before meals and the figure of the Green Knight both have long heritages in legend, folklore, and fertility myth,[39] command for the incredible and its appearance were typical of the feast entertainments of the day. Two of the more outlandish elements of the appearance of the Green Knight—his riding horseback into the hall and his arrogant boisterous challenge mid-feast—are paralleled by chronicles of medieval life. At the banquet celebrating Baldwin, Archbishop of Triers, for example, all courses were carried by mounted servitors, ceremonially passing from stable to table. At the coronation festivity for King Henry IV in 1399, a knight on a horse barded with crimson interrupted the feasting to challenge any who denied the King's right to rule. This Champion thereby reaffirmed it by startling the audience to reassert its loyalty in public display. Entertainment and public policy thus joined in the Winchester banquet hall.

Feast pageantry introduced costumed courtiers and servitors parading on horseback in the hall; presentations of elaborate, symbolic, or mechanical gifts at table; allegorical reminiscences of classical or Biblical or political events in sculpture or mummery or dumbshow or dramatic vignette.[40] All these suggest the medieval fascination with things being seldom what they seem. They depict the medieval taste for the incredible, for the illusion beyond mere magnificence. Illusion was necessary corollary to medieval cookery.

Subtleties

Large, sometimes edible sculptures called *subtleties* or *warners* decorated the dining hall. Elaborate, gigantic, often spun-sugar or pastry or marzipan creations, these were paraded through the hall between courses or situated on platforms for viewing. They simulated individual human or animal figures: Saint Andrew, Father Time, a Lawyer, Winter and Old Age, an eagle, a tiger, a dragon *flambé*. They imitated many-towered castles or rigged ships or hunters riding to hounds or cathedrals glistening with altars. Occasionally made of wax or papier mâché, or cut from heavy paper board, such sculptures with their extravagant architecture and allegorical motifs contributed to the ceremony of the hall and its theater of feasts.

French Romance Feasts

Much courtly art in England was French in origin, and much culinary technique and banquet pageantry was inspired by French or Burgundian models; a brief glance at medieval French literature reveals surprising food scenes.

38. Compare the banquet festivities in Olivier de la Marche, *Mémoires* in C. Petitot (ed.), *Collection complète des mémoires relatifs à l'histoire de la France* (Paris, 1820).

39. See Larry Benson, *Art and Tradition in Sir Gawain and the Green Knight* (New Brunswick, 1965); R. S. Loomis (ed.), *Arthurian Literature in the Middle Ages* (Oxford, 1959).

40. See L. H. Loomis, *Adventures in the Middle Ages* (New York, 1962), 274–81, On "tragetours" and magic at feasts, banquet-hall festivities, see Roy Strong, *Splendour at Court* (Boston, 1973); Sydney Anglo, *Spectacle, Pageantry and Early Tudor Policy* (London, 1969); and references in the BIBLIOGRAPHY classification *Literature*.

Pl. 4 *A fish dinner is served to three diners holding knife or* mazer. *King Saul attempts to end the feast by violence and is only temporarily interrupted by the kneeling* Cupbearer *who presents a gold double cup with trefoil finial to his royal master being "corrupted" by the advice of a small green devil whispering into his ear.* (Old Testament, *13th century, French. New York, The Pierpont Morgan Library, M638, f.31v)*

I: Fig. 13

I: Fig. 14

Chrétien de Troyes' romance *Perceval*[41] (ancestor by two hundred years to *Sir Gawain and the Green Knight*) seems unlikely comparison, for it is an unfinished biographical romance of a callow, foolish, Dümmling youth whose educational adventures lead to his questing for the Holy Grail. Amazingly, Perceval's every major adventure but one is inextricably bound with food. Some are amusing precedents to scenes in *Sir Gawain*.[42]

Ingenuous Perceval, purposely kept ignorant of chivalry and courtliness, left his mother's isolated forest and met his first adventure with a beautiful Lady in a Tent. Behaving absurdly with this courtly damsel because of his literal interpretation of misunderstood advice, and ravenously hungry, he spied a wine bottle and three venison pastries; he devoured, gulped, kissed, and left. The knight whose lady, food, and drink he had thus insulted returned to his tent, rashly threatened and punished his lady—and then calmly sat down to eat the remnants of his meal. After Perceval bumptiously entered King Arthur's court, then the castle of the Knight Gornemant with whom he shared an excellent meal from the same dish, his next adventure was with a lady and food. Her besieged castle town, so desolated that therein was little bread, pastry, wine, cider, or ale, nevertheless provided Perceval with a trestle table laid with a meager dinner of bread, boiled wine, and buck, which he ate eagerly. After vanquishing the besieger, Perceval spent time with the lady in love-making since there were no provisions for drinking or eating! Soon a merchant's barge came up the river; cooks and kitchen boys swung fast into action to feed the neediest, hungriest first.

I: Fig. 13 *With wind instruments accompanying service, a noble banqueter eats from rectangular* trenchers *served by the* Panter. *Wine flagons cool in a footed* cumelin. *At two long* sideboards, *twenty feast from round* trenchers, *using an occasional spoon. (Woodcut by M. Wohlgemuth, from* Der Schatzbehalter, *A. Koberger, Nuremberg, 1491. New York, The Metropolitan Museum of Art. Rogers Fund, 1919)*

I: Fig. 14 *Mounted servitors carry large, covered tureens and elaborate drinking and pouring vessels. The covered dish on the left has an animal-shaped mouth; the large* hanap *held by the* Cupbearer *on the right is surmounted by a cross. (Germany, 1330. Koblenz, Landeshauptarchiv, Ms. 1 c I, p.3)*

remierement sist laurenet
de Reins. Apres seoit
lempriss. Apres seoit
le Roy ainsi come ou milieu
du front de la sale. Apres
le Roy de france seoit le roy

des romains. Et auoit autant de distance
du Roy au Roy des romains come du
Roy a lempereur. Et auoient lempereur
le Roy et le Roy des romains chascun se
purement vn ciel de drap dor torse de velu
au aus armes de france. et par dessus ceulx

I: Fig. 15

At King Arthur's court, Perceval arrived during the high feast of Pentecost at which the King refused to eat until he had heard a marvel. Perceval then visited the Fisher King's castle where he shared an extraordinary banquet served upon an ivory table top set upon wood trestles. Venison, well seasoned and cooked, was carved by a squire at table with slices of meat placed on bread trenchers. Clear wine and grape juice Perceval drank from a gold cup. The mysterious Grail passed; delicate foods and fine wines followed. After the repast came beautiful fruits and spices: dates, figs, nutmegs, cloves, pomegranates, electuaries, Alexandrian gingerbread, aromatic jellies. Spiced piment, mulberry wine, clear syrups were all drunk before Perceval and his gallant host retired for the night. Without asking the compassionate questions pertaining to the mysterious Grail that he was supposed to, Perceval left the Fisher King and arrived at a holy hermit's hut. There—told enigmatically that the Holy Grail was not a vessel which holds a pike, lamprey, or salmon —Perceval ate penance food of such herbs as lettuce, chevril, and cress, bread of barley and oat, and drank only clear spring water.

Food and Medieval Life

Whatever the tradition of food scenes in Arthurian matter—the heritage doubtlessly reaches back through Celtic and classical sources to sympathetic magic—clearly poets used such scenes to create specific effects, and literary banquets contributed to the audience's judgment of the poet's art. Medieval life was many ways regulated by food laws of church and monastery, civil statutes regulating food and drink in the towns, medical uses of foods, religious theories of piety or deadly sin, representations in art of culinary temptations in saints' lives, philosophical pronouncements on moderation and restraint, and economic circumstances of harvest or famine. All these amalgamated foods with health of the body or the body politic or the soul.

The medieval Christian calendar alternated culinary correlatives: feast and fast, fast and feast. New Year's festivals, St. John's Day, or the Feast of Fools gave ecclesiastical sanctions as well as public structure to excess.[43] Beneficent psychological effects of such "play" in the Middle Ages were complemented by medieval theological justifications for festival;[44] these ethical and dogmatic concerns conjoined in the subject of food. Feast released restraint; excess was salutory since it reaffirmed boundaries of control; self-control was justified between these festivals. Feasting also ratified distinctions among virtues: to taste sin is to know and crave it; depriving the self of the desired is sterner test and keener triumph than ignoring the forbidden without tasting it. Food celebrations and food festivals also were affirmations of God's plenty—the variety, multiplicity, and sundryness of the world's order.

Secular powers utilized festivity for political purpose. Beyond the practical necessities for the care and feeding of a gathered household or court, opulent feasts were assertions of political might. Mustering exotic expensive foods and ancillaries to service—all of which once expended were consumed and, appetites renewed, required yet again—demonstrated control over purse or people. Even the seating and service at feasts re-emphasized social ranks; here ostentation itself was ordered.

An impression of medieval culture is obtained by reviewing its culinary manners. To test a people, taste its food.

I: Fig. 15 *This elaborate feast spectacle simulates a rigged ship, scaling ladders at a turreted castle, and "water." The* interlude *actors* battle. On the table are three nefs, *two glasses, one* handled-and-covered tripod vessel, small rectangular trenchers, *and a half-loaf. This pantomime celebrating the Crusaders' capture of Jerusalem in 1099 depicts Godfrey of Bouillon (crosses on shield and gypon) and Richard the Lion-Hearted. The occasion was King Charles V's party (in 1378) for Emperor Charles IV. (From the* Grandes Chroniques. *Paris, Bibliothèque Nationale Ms. French, 2813, f.473v)*

41. Translated R. S. Loomis, *Medieval Romances* (New York, 1957); compare H. Mustard, *Parzival* (New York, 1961).

42. See R. S. Loomis, *Arthurian Tradition and Chrétien de Troyes* (New York, 1949); R. W. Linker, *The Story of the Grail* (Chapel Hill, 1952); U. T. Holmes, *Chrétien de Troyes* (New York, 1970).

43. See Harvey Cox, *The Feast of Fools* (Cambridge, 1969); and Barbara Swain, *Fools and Folly During the Middle Ages and Renaissance* (New York, 1932).

44. See J. Huizinga, *Homo Ludens* (Boston, 1955); Hugo Rahner, *Man at Play* (New York, 1967).

Peacocks, Parsley, Princely Pie

THE CHARACTERISTICS OF MEDIEVAL FOOD

 OURTLY medieval cookery was an esthetic enterprise. It is not simply that good gastronomy is as much art as it is craft. Medieval English kitchenry emphasized artful splendor at least three ways: in ingredients, preparation, and decoration. Raw ingredients consisting of exotic animals, fish, and birds were complemented by rare imported spices and herbs whose very presence in England represented prodigies of effort and expense. So too in cooking techniques which emphasized food texture, contrast between sweet and sour, and "ready mixers" prepared or bought in advance—such as *almond milk, verjuice, amyndoun, quinade,* and *eisel wine*—which tempered food out of blandness into piquancy.

Kitchen art was expressed dramatically in food decoration, in the astonishing concern with food painting and food sculpture. Coloring foods artificially, though with natural pigments, allowed for sauces, meats, breads, pastries, and confections tinted green with parsley, or amber with saffron, or red with sandalwood. The color best crafted to noble tastes was gold. Gilding with egg yolk, saffron, and dandelion embellished the roast crane or the aspic armorial.

II: Fig. 1 *This neat, modest farmyard contains both the cows and sheep whose milk, butters, and cheese are churned by the woman in the background. The picture depicts equally the domestic contributions of both men and women: one woman tends a cow in the far barn while another milks her bell-ringed animal; sheep are helped by the farmer out of a sheepcote into line following a shepherd, while another herder carries a young lamb. (From the* Da Costa Hours, *Bruges, 1520. New York, The Pierpont Morgan Library, M399, f.5v)*

11

1. For the common and "exotic" animals, see Topsell, *Fourfooted Beasts*, ed. Rowland (London, 1658); and F. E. Zeuner, *A History of Domesticated Animals* (London, 1963); Peter Ucko (ed.), *The Domestication and Exploitation of Plants and Animals* (London, 1969); and the BIBLIOGRAPHY classification *Ga*.

2. See W. Radcliffe, *Fishing from the Earliest Times* (London, 1926); and Yarrell's delightful *History of British Fish* (London, 1841).

3. Compare the medieval with the classical ideas in R. T. Günther, "The Oyster Culture of the Ancient Romans," *Journal of the Marine Biological Association* 4 (1897).

4. See H. Innis, *The Cod Fisheries* (New Haven, 1940); J. T. Jenkins, *The Herring and the Herring Fisheries* (London, 1927); A. Davidson, *Mediterranean Seafood* (Harmondsworth, 1972).

5. D. and P. Brothwell, *Food in Antiquity* (London, 1969); J. André, *L'Alimentation et la cuisine à Rome* (Paris, 1961); Reay Tannahill, *Food in History* (New York, 1973). The standard Ancient Roman text is Apicius, *De re culinaria*. See BIBLIOGRAPHY classification *G*.

Pl. 5 *Two rural gentlemen and a woman with* distaff *watch the horn-blowing herder drive cattle through the castle gates. The clock or dial on the manor house registers the hours of farm chores. (From* Petrus Crescentius, *15th century. New York, The Pierpont Morgan Library, M232, f.212)*

(Overleaf)

Pl. 6 *A falconer carries his eager bird on his left wrist while his hunting hounds bay at the foot of a pheasant-laden tree. (From the* Tacuinum Sanitatis, *15th century, Italian. The New York Public Library, Spencer Collection, Ms. 65, f.86v)*

Kitchen sculpture created "illusion food." Shaped for semblances, fruits were disguised to emulate meat *Haslet*. Roast peacocks, refeathered, bones reset and armatured, were fashioned to look alive. Huge, crenellated castle-shaped pies were so imitative of real architecture that strolling musicians or jugglers might leap from pastry towers; they did, playing pipe and tabor. Sometimes meant to be eaten, these food sculptures otherwise were to shock feasters into admiration.

RAW INGREDIENTS

Take a pecok, breke his necke,
and kutte his throte, and fle him ...

Flesh, Fish, and Fowl

For a modern re-creation of a medieval feast, the more sophisticated city food merchants easily will produce cow, pig, deer, rabbit, goose, chicken, lobster, and eel. Less eagerly they will find the more exotic pheasants and shellfish. But they would be jailed, rightly, if they produced animals gracing a medieval cookboard which now are endangered species. Their names and the detailed recipes for their preparation attest to the incredible variety of animal foods available to the noble medieval palate.

Interlarded amongst recipes for use of calf, fawn, mutton, kid, pork, coney, rabbit, and ox are recipes for beaver and bear.[1] Walrus, seal, porpoise, dolphin, and various whales, though mammals, were classified as fish in the Middle Ages and utilized for feasts along with the more prosaic cod and herrings.[2] Crustaceans and molluscs, also considered fish, included crayfish, crab, lobster, mussel, oyster, scallop, shrimp, and whelk.[3] The list of fish for which medieval recipes or special carving instructions exist resembles more a history of medieval water life than a provisions tally: bass, bream, and brett; carp, colin (sea cob), codling, and conger; dace, dogfish, doree, eel, and flounder; garfish, gurnard, haddock, hake, and halibut; keeling, lamprey, ling, loach, and luce; mackerel, minnow, and mulvel (or milwell); perch, pickerel, pike, plaice, ray, and roach; salmon, smelts, sole, sturgeon, and swordfish; tench, thornback, thurlpole, torrentyne, trout, turbot, and whiting.[4] These and multiple other *fyssches* and *flessches* allowed for the Christian calendar's alternation between meat and fish days. Certainly courtly food did not suffer from the monotony of taste generally ascribed to it.

In these lists, several entries represent different stages of growth of the same animal. The cookery tomes so distinguish them, with special recipes for their preparation. Codfish, for example, was thought to be first a whiting, then a codling, then a cod. Pickerel was believed to grow to a pike and age to a luce. Rabbits are the young coneys; suckling or nursing infant rabbits, "suckers," were especially prized, as they had been in ancient Rome.[5]

Birds augmented this variety of feast ingredients. Beyond the expected hen, rooster, goose, gander, and young pullets of each, larger and smaller fowl were raised or caught or netted or shot by arrow or hunted by hawks: bittern, bustard, crane, curlew, and dove; eagle, egret, gull, heron, and lark; mallard, partridge, peacock, pheasant, pigeon, plover, and quail. These were as plentiful as sparrow, shoveler, snipe, sorcell,

7

8

stork, swan, teal, whimbrel, and woodcock.[6] Miscellaneous *smale byrdys* also were ingredients for stewing or baking into pies.

Despite this multiplicity of meat types—and because proper classification of raw foods was associated with sanctity and sin—clever or ingenuous clerics and laymen secured their favorite roasts by tampering with natural history. The well-favored "barnacle goose," forbidden succulent flesh if a mere goose, was often permitted during Lent because barnacles, as a seafaring nation knows, are fish! Fetal rabbits were adjudged "nonmeat." Though the beaver surely was "flesh," his toothsome tail was classified as a fish. Beaver tail is the answer to the medieval riddle: What swims like a fish, tastes like a fish, is a fish, and yet is not a fish?

Giblets, Wombs, "Garbage," and Dainties

Extraordinary diversity of animal type is matched by ingenious utilizations of parts of their anatomies. Recipes call for limbs, ribs, butts, haunches (or *cushions*), guts, and liver. Wings and necks were particularly important for several noble delicacies; yet others required entrails and genitalia.

Giblets such as liver, gizzard, gullet, gut, and heart were ingredients for stuffing the animals from which they came. *Wombs,* meaning stomachs, from pigs, sheep, or fish were stuffed with meats, eggs, and spices, making self-contained dishes reminiscent of modern sausage. The recipe for *An Entrayle,* for example, calls for stuffing a sheep's maw with chopped chicken, pork, cheese, eggs, and spicery. Pig's stomach, stuffed with ground pork, ginger, nuts, and spices, created a fanciful "hedgehog" or *Yrchoun,* well decorated with "spines" made from almonds. Swim bladders, called *sounds,* were removed from codfish or plaice, then cooked with stuffing and sauces. Livers of whale, sturgeon, and dolphin, when salted, smelled "like violets," tasted "most pleasantly," and gave "competent nourishment."[7] "Daintées," named in the hunting manuals as a particularly choice treat, were the testicles of deer, served with sweet-and-sour seasoning.

Other animal innards and excrescences were referred to as "garbage." Not a pejorative term then as it is now, it included all viscera and entrails. Considered leftovers, not detritus, from noble kitchens, it was given or sold to pie tradesmen for baking into pies sold to commoners in local markets.[8]

Hoofs and Feet, Animal Oil and Grease

A recipe beginning with feet of calves and hoofs of *vele* produces fine "gelatine" for fruits or meats or fish. Such "jellies" were particularly useful for artistic embellishments such as edible seascapes with cooked "live" fish swimming, or fabrication in food of heraldic emblems of noble houses. Jellies were cool contrasts to hot foods within the same feast, or within seasonal menus, prominent in outdoor spring and summer feasts.

Natural fats and oils from beasts, birds, and fish were preserved for frying, sautéing, and baking. Along with butter, they were used in medieval England free from most distinctions which otherwise separate the culinary worlds of oil and butter.

Butter was not only used in cooking but as a glaze, and simply a spread for bread. Numerous distinctions were made among types—such

6. See A. O. Cooke, *A Book of Dovecotes* (London, 1920); Henry Best, *Rural Economy in Yorkshire* (London, 1857); E. C. Curwen and G. Hatt, *Plough and Pasture: The Early History of Farming* (New York, 1953).

7. See Muffett, cited by John Russell in F. Furnivall (ed.), *Early English Meals,* 173.

8. See Chapter III for several ordinances of the pastry bakers as well as case histories of bread lawbreakers and their punishments; for manuscript references see the BIBLIOGRAPHY classification *Bread.*

(Preceding Page)
Pl. 7   *While boiling water is prepared in the slope-roofed hearth, and a woman approaches with a vessel for catching blood, a butcher prepares to slaughter the hog. Probably Europe's most frequent domestic animals, pigs were fattened on acorns before butchering.* (From the Rohan Hours, *15th century, French. Paris, Bibliothèque Nationale, Ms. Latin 9471, f.17v*)

Pl. 8   *Medieval sheep were as important for their milk as for their wool. Milk-drinks, butter, and cheeses were made from the nutritious fluid here drawn into a black, wide-rimmed milking vessel by a shepherdess regaled by pipe tunes of the gigantic shepherd nearby.* (From the Rohan Hours, *15th century, French. Paris, Bibliothèque Nationale, Ms. Latin 9471, f.85v*)

as butter of Claynos or Hakenay—according to whence it came or from which animal's milk it was churned.

Broth, Blood, and Marrow

Giblets, "garbage," feet, and bones also were used to prepare stocks and broths, reserved and ready for need. Fish sometimes were cooked in beef broth, fowl in fish broth. Half broth, half wine combinations were marinades or boiling stocks for restoring texture and tenderness to the long-lived, dried codfish, the *stockfish*. A fish for all seasons and classes (apparently hated by the poor who needed its protein—though Erasmus said it nourished no more than a stick did—yet enjoyed by the noble in elaborate recipes), soaked stockfish itself made broth used in cooking still other fish.

Blood as ingredient in various dishes was either undiluted or mixed with broth or wine, half blood, half other. Alone it was used for coloring sauces brown or black as well as for flavoring. With spices and herbs, blood was base for gravies and stuffings. For roasted swan, for example, the cook must kill the swan, making an incision through the mouth toward the brain—*kutte it in the rove of the mouthe toward the brayne enlonge*—and letting it bleed, reserving the blood for *Chaudwyn*, a giblet gravy utilizing gizzard, heart, liver, bread, broth, and blood.

An intriguing taste to the modern palate is bone marrow in all manner of medieval pies and tarts. Not only with meats but fruits, nuts, and eggs, marrow added nutriments as well as consistency to open pastries which otherwise might be too liquid to "set."

Milks and Eggs

Milks and eggs were used in medieval cookery in varieties of ways. Cow's milk, but especially sheep's and goat's, was used plain or skimmed or creamed or "crudded" or "clotted." Not only for making butters and cheeses (the so-called "white meat" or white food), milk curds were added to puddings and sauces. Milk heated, combined with wine or ale and spices, and so curdled, was known as *posset*, drunk alone or, in turn, added to other recipes. Ground nuts boiled in milk yielded both a drink and a stock for soups and sauces; one of the several forms of *almond milk* was so prepared.

Eggs in medieval cookery are best appreciated via one statistic in an awesome list of provisions for King Richard II's London larder in 1387. Among other foods for retinue and guests, it enumerates 14 boars, 14 salted oxen, 50 swans, 50 capons, 300 marrowbones, and 11,000 dozen eggs. Though medieval eggs doubtlessly were smaller than the modern, 132,000 eggs in one household in one year suggests the magnitude of the requisite hen coops. Not only chicken eggs were cultivated; other bird eggs, particularly the sparrow's, were thought to have aphrodisiac effects, and were gathered in quantity. Medieval recipes call for egg raw, whole, white, yolk, beaten, whisked, soft-boiled, hard-boiled, chopped, crumbed, flaked, shaved, poached, "dropped," fried, baked, broiled, roasted, blown, and stuffed. Eggs alone, with herbs, with or within sauces, stuffings, and garnishes, were balanced in importance by eggs used for *flourrishings*. These were embellishments and glazes on breads, pastries, meats, poultry, and fish in that culinary artistic phenomenon called gilding. For all meals, for all types of dishes—dairy, meat, and

II: Fig. 2

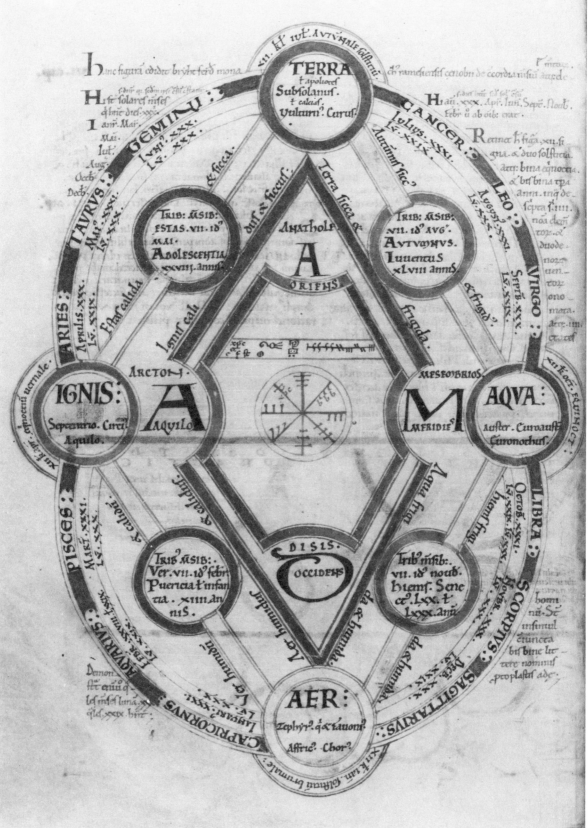

II: Fig. 3

dessert—the well-appointed medieval kitchen thus utilized prodigious numbers of eggs.

Herbs and Spices

To modern eye and taste, medieval spicery is probably the most startling aspect of the cookery. How tangy, sharp, and hot such common meat sauces as *sauce vert* must have been which combined parsley, mint, ditany, thyme, alecost, garlic, vinegar, pepper, salt, and *eisel wine*. How piquant might stewed and stuffed capons taste whose recipe begins: "take percelly, sauge, isoppe, rose mary, and thyme" and adds saffron, "good herbs," a pottel (2 quarts) of wine, raisins, sugar, and ginger. Gardens of fragrant leaves, foils, seeds, berries, and barks were used in medieval cookery—such as basil, borage, mallow, ditany, true love, oregano, fennel, ginger paris, cardamon," "grains of Paradise," galingale, clove, sorrel, pennyroyal, hyssop, mandragora, licorice, purslane, mustard seed, nutmeg, anise, mace, mint, peppercorns, pine seed, cubeb, sandalwood, and cinnamon.[9] Not only in sauces and stuffings, herbs and spices were used in pies and breads, in fruit tarts, and in wines. In the profusion of types but also the combinations of fragrances and tastes, medieval spicery now seems wildly aromatic.

Expensive, imported spices from the East were listed in recipes alongside those from the kitchen herb garden.[10] Special "powders" bought premixed, *white* or *black powder,* for example, united such spices as cinnamon, ginger, and nutmeg, some imported varieties of which were costly. These in turn were "pointed" with vinegars before being mixed with other ingredients. Spices were bought, and so called for in recipes, in various forms: whole cloves, powders, liquids, sticks, chunks, cakes, grains, coarse-ground, light-ground, and crystalline. Numerous varieties of each spice were available commercially; a recipe for a spiced wine suggests ginger *colombyne* rather than ginger *valadyne* or *magdelyne.* Such herbs and spices flavored and enfragranced ciders, ales, wines, rosewaters, and other fruit and flower juices. Furthermore, spices were strewn on, between, and around foods prepared with yet other condiments and herbs.

Why this medieval emphasis on spicery? What purposes beyond food "pickling" and preserving did spices serve? How "spicey" did foods actually taste?

Spices were superb insignia of conspicuous wealth. They were also indicators of ostentatious waste. Given the difficulties of transport, the very presence of imported exotica in a household demonstrated its owner's access to a copious treasury or a mercantile sea-lane or land route or, in some instances, a distant people.[11] While remarkable varieties of imported as well as domestic spices and herbs were sold in London's markets by the Spicers and Pepperers and Gardeners, some condiments were more expensive than others, and yet others were available only to the highest nobility, brought as gifts by ambassadors or bought on noble command by merchantmen. A particular odor or taste in food thus affirmed the political statement: power bought this.

Not only allied to wealth, herbs and spices were utilized because of ideals of health. Then, as now, some foods' effects upon the physiology had to be tempered, no matter what the pleasure of their taste. Particular spices were thought to aid digestion or avoid flatus or counteract heartburn

II: Fig. 3 *The totality of the created universe was seen as gloriously integrated. Just as the larger creation, the* macrocosm, *consisted of four elements (earth, air, fire, and water) possessing four "contraries" (hot, cold, moist, and dry) so man's body, the* microcosm, *possessed four vital fluids, the four humours (blood, phlegm, choler, and black bile). Humoural equilibrium determined physical demeanor, personality, and health. Food generated humours; diet determined or cured disease. (From Byrhtferth's Manual,* 12th century, English. Oxford, St. John's College Library, Ms. 17, f.7v)*

9. See J. W. Parry, *The Story of Spices* (New York, 1953); T. Stobart, *Herbs, Spices, and Flavorings* (London, 1970); and J. I. Miller, *The Spice Trade of the Roman Empire* (Oxford, 1969).

10. See L. F. Salzman, *English Industries of the Middle Ages* (Oxford, 1923); Alicia Cecil, *A History of Gardening in England* (London, 1895); and Frank Crisp, *Medieval Gardens* (London, 1924).

11. See C. M. Cipolla, *Money, Prices, and Civilization in the Mediterranean World* (Princeton, 1956); and R. S. Lopez and I. W. Raymond, *Medieval Trade in the Mediterranean World* (New York, 1968).

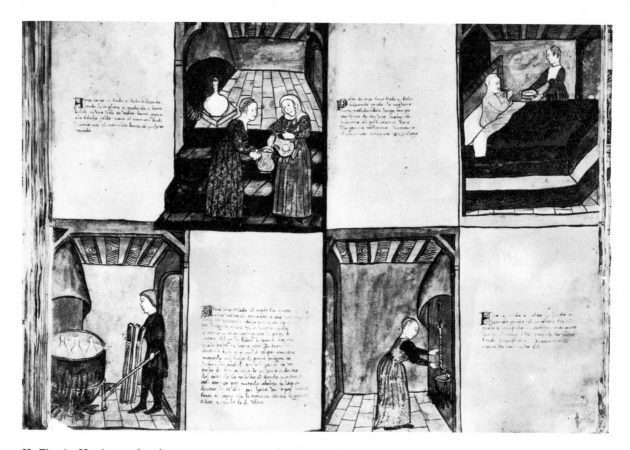

II: Fig. 4 *Various foods were used more for medicinal than culinary purposes. In this "medieval health handbook," medicinal foods and drinks include a brew in the upper left; lower left: chicken flesh and broth steeped in a "still" with quince juice; barley gruel served to a patient in a damask-covered bed; and spelt prepared in an open-hearth caldron. (From the* Tacuinum Sanitatis, *15th century, Italian. The New York Public Library, Spencer Collection, Ms. 65, f.88v–89r)*

12. Andrew Boorde, *A Dyetary of Helthe,* ed. F. Furnivall (London, 1870), 287. Boorde writes in a tradition older than that of the Greek physician Dioscorides; kept popular in such as 11th century Ibn Botlân's *Tacuinum Sanitatis,* medieval herbal lore is delightfully depicted in *A Medieval Health Handbook* (New York, 1975).

or compensate for overeating. Since all foods were understood to possess some balance amongst four contrary qualities: hot, cold, moist, and dry (which in turn were associated with the four bodily "humors" controlling health and disease), it was necessary to balance the "moist" quality of a food with a "dry" herb, or to balance a "hot" spice with a "cold" herb. Certain spices and foods therefore were mixed together not only to enhance taste but to complement one another. Modern nutritionists might find historical antecedents of protein complementarity and acid balances beautifully illustrated in the best medieval herbals.

Cinnamon (or canel), one of the most frequent spices in medieval cookery, was required for confections of apples, pears, and quince, dredges for beefsteak, caneline glazes for fish, and spicing of such wines as *Hippocras.* While some recipes may have been imported from the East along with the spice, there was an Anglo-Saxon folk tradition for canel's use as well as for other frequent spices such as ginger and nutmeg. This English tradition in turn was associated with Greek, Roman, and Arabic appreciations of cinnamon. Just as Pliny, Macer, Dioscorides, and other "olde aunceyent, and approbat Doctours" knew the best healing herbs, so the medieval herbalists believed that ginger "heats" the stomach and helps digestion; clove comforts the sinews; mace helps against colic and body fluxes and laxes; nutmegs are good for a cold in the head and beneficial for the spleen. Cinnamon is so important a *cordyall,* the question often asked was: "Why does a man die who can get cinnamon to eat?"[12] This but suggests the vast herblore and spice cunning of medieval cookery.

Though health and wealth considerations led to uses of spices and

46

herbs, it is astonishing to recognize that we have no reliable judgments of their quantities. Almost all medieval recipes indicate processes and ingredients but no measurements. One might simmer a hen in half broth, half wine with cloves, mace, pepper, and canel (the recipe is called *Gelyne in Dubbatte*) but there is no clue to how much of each. Absence of proportions coupled with multiplicities of spices has led to the assumption that all medieval food was heavily spice-laden. Impression, however, is not evidence. Those few recipes which enumerate quantity of spices suggest sparing amounts: a touch, a pinch, "to taste," $\frac{1}{2}$ oz. to 3 gallons of wine. More important, however, medieval medical texts detail dangers of overspicing and counsel moderation in use of herbs and spicery. Since most such medical books were popular rather than technical treatises—for example, Andrew Boorde's *A Dyetary of Helthe*, and Nares's *Haven of Helthe*[13]—more laymen's health manuals than professional instruction books, inference from their contents is compelling. Furthermore, even a modern list of all the condiments in a well-seasoned stew might seem excessively pungent if the minute quantities of the many and the mixed spices were not stated. Rather than wildly spiced, medieval foods were more likely mildly fragrant.

Sugar and Honey

Sweets, like spices, had multiple forms and uses. Sugar and honey alternated in popular favor, though most fifteenth-century cookery tomes suggest honey "in default of" sugar. Sugar was imported and sold in many types (black, white, brown, Alexandrian, Indian, or "Cyprus") or forms (powdered, crystalline, conical, block, "Sugar of Three Cute," or "Sugar Candy").[14] When too scarce or too expensive, honey was substituted. Not only was honey made in domestic hives but it was also imported, sometimes from Russia.[15] And honey often was required in recipes, plain or clarified, as the sweetener of choice. "Clarifying" sometimes liquefied an older, grainier, solid honey, heated to restore its clear translucent state and syrupy consistency; and other times apparently solidified it, as in *Leche Lumbarde*: *clarifi yt on the fyre tylle it wexe hard*. In breads and pastries, meat and fruit dishes, and in such confections as dates or quince "in comfit," sugar and honey were used in profusion of types. Yet again, their quantities rarely are specified.

Vegetables and Fruits

That medieval cookery frowned on fruits and vegetables and forbade them raw is, like the spicery shibboleth, an erroneous perception based on incomplete data. That fruits and vegetables were raised, picked, and sold is demonstrable by medieval maps of gardens and orchards, by graphic depictions of harvesting in manuscripts and tapestries, and by market laws regulating fruit-and-vegetable vending.[16] It is true, however, that most medieval English cookery manuals have few vegetable dishes; but almost all have some. Since many of these manuscripts are incomplete, their components having been separated or lost, they may once have contained vegetable recipes just as, in fact, a few medieval cookery volumes do.

Important extant sources for medieval lore of fruits and vegetables are the *herbals* and *dietaries*. Concerned not only with herbs but with much else otherwise considered *flora*, these volumes were as much medical

13. They incorporate advice on herbs and hygiene, meats and temperaments, diets for asthma, palsy, and gout, and instructions on healthful apparel and sleeping habits.

14. See N. Deerr, *The History of Sugar* (London, 1949).

15. The most comprehensive survey is E. Crane (ed.), *Honey* (New York, 1975). See also H. M. Fraser, *Beekeeping in Antiquity* (London, 1931); and J. Banchereau, "Travaux d'Apiculture," *Bulletin Monumental* 77 (1913), 403–11.

16. For an introduction to the extraordinarily large bibliography on medieval plants and nutrition see the BIBLIOGRAPHY classification *Gastronomy*, as well as A.M. Cecil, *A History of Gardening in England* (London, 1895); S. G. Harrison and G. B. Masefield, *The Oxford Book of Food Plants* (Oxford, 1969); P. C. Mangelsdorf, *Plants and Human Affairs* (Bloomington, 1952); V. R. Boswell "Our Vegetable Travelers," *The National Geographic Magazine* 96 (1949), 145–217; H. Helbaek, "Domestication of Food Plants in the Old World," *Science* 130 (1959), 365–72; particularly important are B. S. Dodge, *Plants that Changed the World* (London, 1962); G. Carefoot and E. Sprott, *Famine on the Wind: Plant Diseases and Human History* (New York, 1967).

17. Venice, 1475; ed. and trans. as *On Honest Indulgence and Good Health*, by Elizabeth B. Andrews, 1967.

18. Boorde's *Dyetary*, 289.

19. See J. Organ, *Gourds* (London, 1963); and A. Morettini, *Olivicultura* (Rome, 1950); as well as references in note 16, above.

20. See W. Younger, *Gods, Men and Wine* (Cleveland, 1966); and H. W. Allen, *A History of Wine* (London, 1961).

21. See W. D. Gray, *The Relation of Fungi to Human Affairs* (New York, 1959); W. Houghton, "Notices of Fungi in Greek and Latin Authors," *Annals and Magazine of Natural History* 5 (1885), 22–49.

Pl. 9 *Fruit, vegetable, and herb gardens were planted in country and town. On this manor's carefully tended individual plots, gardeners with spade, rake, and diamond-shaped grills (for supporting plants) work in the walled enclosure. Outside an open gate two men (one is the author Petrus Crescentius) discuss rural occupations. Watching through a window, a courtly lady wears the fifteenth-century hennin headdress as she sews. (From* Petrus Crescentius, *15th century. New York, The Pierpont Morgan Library, M232, f.157)*

as culinary treatises. Health-habit manuals might be the more accurate name for such as Boorde's *Dyetary* or Platina's *De honesta voluptate*.[17]

Plants for eating or distilling into juices, soups, and sauces are described botanically; their properties pertaining to health delineated; and recipes for their preparation suggested. In these treasuries of folk remedy and classical wisdom, certain vegetables indeed are said to be dangerous. But prohibitions are followed by "if . . ." with enumerations of disease or personal temperament which would preclude their use. Certain cabbages, peas, beans, and fruits ought not be eaten by those whose already "gassy" stomachs or troubled colons would produce inordinate flatulence. Asparagus would increase a bad odor of urine. Turnips and walnuts along with fatty foods and hard cheeses ought not be eaten by those with gout or epilepsy or rheumatism. Those with melancholy temperament must avoid fried meats and foods overly salted, burned, dried, or otherwise difficult to digest.[18] They ought to abstain from strong wine. They must emphasize in their diets: cow's milk, almond milk, egg yolks, "hot and moist" herbs, boiled meats, and easily digestible foods.

Such dietary restrictions are not condemnations of foods but recommendations against their use by particular people in special circumstances. Diet therapies for disease, based on observation and common experience, these might be dismissible as superstition were it not for some medieval medical notions now accepted as "scientific," chemically or clinically; the modern "ulcer diet" is not dissimilar from the medieval melancholic's.

Fruits and vegetables as well as nuts and flowers used in medieval cookery make a wholesome cornucopia. Amongst the popular vegetables were lettuce, cabbage, green beans, peas dried and fresh, carrot, celery, spinach, cucumber, parsnip, radish, leek, artichoke, chicory, endive, beets, olives, onions, lentils, and turnips.[19] Rice, which might be classified as grain rather than vegetable, was a menu staple. Fruits, used not only in compotes and pies but stews and stuffings, include numerous varieties of apple and pear, fresh and dried (costard and blaundrell apples and wardon pears were favorites), strawberry, orange, quince, melon, grape, hurtleberry, mulberry, "bogberry," cherry, plum, peach, medlar, service, pomegranate, and St. John's bread, the ubiquitous carob. So also, date, fig, raisin, currant, prune, and variations in type among them: "great grape" raisins versus the currant. Raw or stewed fruits preceded dinners and culminated them. They also were used in recipes plain or in such preserves as "dates in comfit" or "quince in quinade."

Grapes, though used for cooking, were more important to winery.[20] The stewing of fish, birds, or beasts in undiluted grape wine was varied sometimes with half broth or half blood. Wine dregs and lees had special uses in recipes. Even the "flours of red vyne," the nutritious skim of yeast fungi on fermenting wine,[21] was a raw ingredient of various foods.

Flowers and Nuts

Blooms other than fungi bound cooking to decoration. Sugared roses, violets, primroses, floscampies, and various tree blossoms made such delightful flower dishes as *Roseye*, *Vyolette*, *Prymerose*, and *Spyneye*, this last made from hawthorn flowers of that "spiney" tree. Once

9

cooked, these dishes were further colored with the flower's pigment—blossoms were boiled in wine and the "paint" applied with a feather-brush—and embellished with live sprigs or garlands.

As frequent for cooking as fruits and flowers were nuts.[22] Walnuts, chestnuts, and filberts were commonly used. No nuts equaled the significance of almonds; almost all households used astounding quantities of pounds per year. About one-third of all medieval court recipes use almonds in some form: slivered, crushed, ground, powdered, blanched, fried, boiled, broiled, or roasted. As components of numerous types of dishes, they added taste, texture, and decoration. An interesting dessert called *Malmens Bastard* (after the sweet Spanish wine, *Bastard*) required three pounds of pounded or ground almonds added to two quarts of clarified honey, one pound of fir-pine seeds, one pound of currant raisins, two gallons of *Bastard* wine (or ale), plus sandalwood, canel, ginger, salt, and saffron. Almonds in decorative artifice were used in slivers to counterfeit the prickly quills of a sheep's-maw "hedgehog" or "urchin." In sugar paste, almonds made marzipan, a confection easily molded into ornamental shapes. Also called by the name *Marchepane*, famous in later English cookery and court ceremony, the best variety was made from "Jordan" almonds. Finally, almonds formed the basis of one of the most significant "ready mixers" in medieval cookery, *almond milk.*

22. For astonishing varieties and usages, see F. Howes, *Nuts, the Production and Everyday Uses* (London, 1948).

COOKING PROCESSES

Take a Pecok, breke his necke, and kutte his throte, and fle him, the skyn and the ffethers togedre, and the hede still to the skyn of the nekke. And kepe the skyn and the ffethers hole togiders; draw him as an hen and kepe the bone of the necke hole, and roste him.

Chaucer's enumeration of the culinary virtues of the Cook on the Canterbury pilgrimage—he knows how to roast, boil, broil, fry, make stews, and bake pies—is a respectable summation of most medieval cookery techniques. These predictable methods for transforming ingredients into prepared foods would, with few emendations, characterize the modern as well as the medieval craft. A pair of techniques not mentioned by Chaucer, however, demonstrate a difference in approach as much to the cookery as to the instructions for it in the cookbooks: *aforcing* (or *afarsing*) and *alaying*. These processes, and the "ready mixers" which achieve them, are allied in most medieval English cookeries with a surprising allowance for flexible mixtures and vegetarian variations upon recipes. They are an invitation to gourmet initiative.

Aforcing and Alaying

Aforcing and *alaying* are opposite forms of *tempering* food, changing its consistency and its qualities by adding a particular prepared substance to the raw ingredients. Such tempering may be no more than thickening and thinning. But in most instances *aforcing* meant not simply thickening but augmenting the amount—as in "stretching" a dish to serve more people than the recipe intended; or increasing nutritive value—as in adding grain or eggs or cheese; or stuffing a bird or fish or fruit which could be cooked equally well without the "forsure." *Alay-*

Pl. 10 *This winter farm scene depicts sheepfold, bee-hives, and a tall stone dove-cote at the farther end of the wattle-enclosed farm-yard. A blue-garbed figure cuts firewood which he binds in bundles called* fesses, *which appear not only near his feet but also adjacent to the casks at the wall of the farmhouse in which three figures raise skirts and tunics to warm their ankles and legs before the roaring fire. The birds eating the feed on the ground were important sources of food. (From the* Très Riches Heures *of Jean, Duke of Berry, "February." Chantilly, Musée Condé)*

II: Fig. 5 *The four* humours *often were personified as possessing not only their "contrary" qualities but the essence of the seasons of life. These, in turn, corresponded to the seasons of the year. Sanguine youthful spring ages into phlegmatic winter of old age. (From the* Guild Book of the Barber-Surgeons of York, *15th century, English. London, British Museum)*

ing was the opposite: diluting the pungency; or, conversely, increasing the piquancy of a thick sweet mixture by adding such a liquid as vinegar. *Alaying* with sharp or sour fluid that had "sting" or "bite" was called *pointing*. While changing taste and texture, *alaying* also augmented quantity. Both procedures increased culinary interest.

Among common medieval aforcers and alayers were *almond milk, verjuice,* vinegar, *eisel,* and *amyndoun.* So also were kitchen-breads, certain spice powders, and flower–waters such as rosewater. Naturally, the same substance might either aforce or alay depending upon the nature of the mixture to which it was added. These medieval ready mixers were so prevalent in storeroom and kitchen that few questioned their components, or, alas, enumerated them before their adding to dishes. Imperfect modern analogies might be mayonnaise, mustard, or ketchup, rarely prepared "from scratch" for recipes which demand them. Classical analogies to the idea of "ready mixers" might include *liquamen* or *asafetida.*

Almond Milk

"Take good fair almond milk" or "thick fresh milk of almonds"—such appear so often in medieval cookery for such variety of dishes that it is exasperating to recognize that no one knows exactly what it was. Taken for granted by the manuscript composers, the components of something so basic simply were not stated. From references to it, it appears that almond milk was a decoction of simmered whole or ground almonds in either water or milk. Ever ready for use, it was prepared in advance or bought ready-made. This thick white fluid with almond taste could have been mildly fermented, as were most other prepared mixers; none knows for certain. (A comparable milk in traditional Ceylonese cooking, "coconut milk," made from coconut meat boiled in water, is a significant element of curries.)

Verjuice

Verious, vergeous, or *verjuice* is equally vexing, because though frequently used to alay a dish, its components are rarely described. Apparently, it was a semifermented fruit liquor. Italian writers, such as Platina, describe it as a pungent pork broth. One English source considers it a juice made from crabs. Most English and French cookeries, however, suggest interchangeability of *verjuice* with such acidic fruit substances as orange juice or crabapple juice, strongly suggesting therefore its own nature as a fruit fluid; several define it as juice of unripe grapes, or sour apples, or fennel.

Vinegar and Eisel

To sharpen taste, to make a dish pungent or "poignant," vinegar (*vin aigre*) or *eisel,* both sour-wine products, were added to sweet or "heavy" foods. In a recipe for the fruit dessert *Strawberye,* in which sugar appears plentifully, there is the instruction: *poynte it with vynegre.*

23. Accessible printed versions of such recipes in Middle English appear in Thomas Austin (ed.), *Two Fifteenth Century Cookery Books* (London, 1888).

Take strawberys, wash them in good red wine; strain them, and do hem in a potte with gode Almaunde mylke, a-lay it with Amyndoun, other with the floure of Rys, and make it chargeaunt, add currant raisins, saffron, peper, ginger, cinnamon, galengale and sugar grete plente.[23]

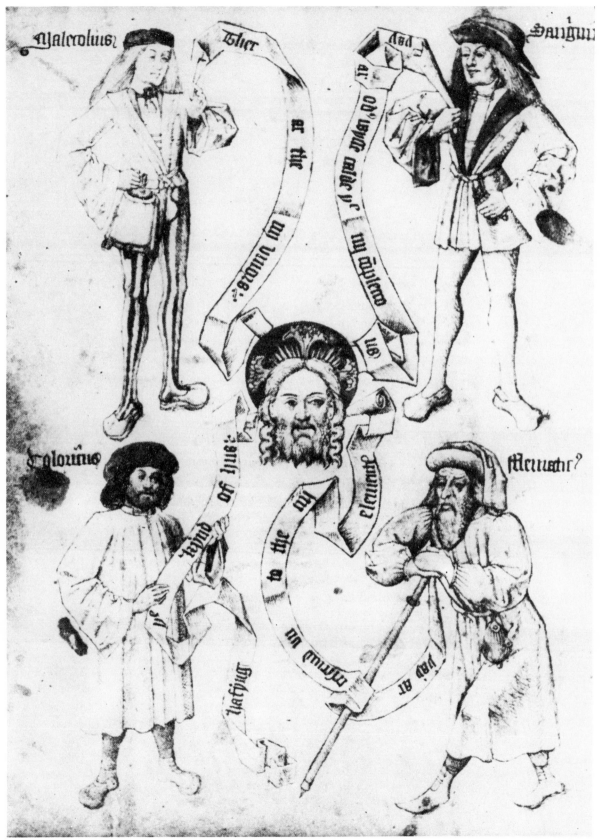

II: Fig. 6 *Honey was culti-vated in hives even on the smallest landholder's prop-erty, for it was an important sweetener in most foods, substituting for the expen-sive varieties of sugar that had to be imported from the Mediterranean. Honey was at times imported from Russia. (Woodcut by Hans Weiditz for Cicero's* Officia, *Augsburg, 1531. New York, The Metropolitan Museum of Art, Gift of Felix M. Warburg, 1918)*

This unification of opposites, this tempering of sweetness with sour "pointing," is remarkably frequent in medieval cookery: let it be *poynaunt an dowcet*, piquant and sweet, says a recipe for wardon pears in sugar syrup to which is added a *lytil venegre*. A recipe for *Egredouncye* (the word derived from the French phrase sour-and-sweet, *aigre-doux*) combines beef and venison, sweet and well herbed, alayed with bread, and pointed with *vynegre* or *eysel wyne*.

Amyndoun

Alay with Amyndoun, recommends the *Strawberye* recipe, and, happily, that ready mixer's nature is understandable exactly. Reminiscent of the "peas porridge hot" nursery rhyme, it takes nine days and nine nights to prepare this dry, salted, wheat thickener of texture but thinner of taste and stretcher of ingredients.

> *Nym whete at midsomer & salt & do it in a faire vessel do water thereto, that the whete by yheled let it stonde IX days and IX nyt, and everyeday whess wel thy whete & at ye IX days ende bray het wel in a morter and drie hit ta enst ye sonne do it in a faire vessel & kouere hit fort, thou wil it note.*

Kitchen-bread, flour, and yeast

Alaying with bread was more frequent than with amyndoun; some recipes allow cook's choice between them. Fascinating variety of bread uses in cooking corresponds with considerable numbers of bread types, such as *wastelbrede*, *payndemayne*, and *simnel*. Here considered is not

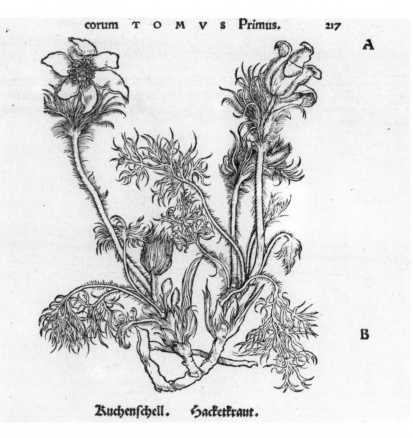

Kuchenschell.   Hackekraut.

II: Fig. 7 *Herbs were culti-vated for numerous culinary purposes in small kitchen gardens as well as large municipal plantings. Aug-menting the tastes of vari-ous foods, the herbs also served medicinal and san-itary purposes. Many were considered potent aphrodis-iacs. A florescence of early printed herbals in the late fifteenth and early sixteenth centuries shows their pop-ularity. (Woodcut by Hans Weiditz for Brunfel's Her-bal, Strassburg, 1530. New York, The Metropolitan Museum of Art, Gift of Mortimer L. Schiff, 1918)*

the hall-bread for plain eating or for cutting into edible platters, the *trenchers,* but the kitchen-bread, "tempered" to serve itself as "tem-perer" to other foods. Crumbed and combined with herbs, bread was used in stuffings, stews, and compotes. Bread soaked in wine or vinegar or almond milk was drawn through a strainer as a *pointed* thickener. Toasted, it was cut into *faire gobbits* and used crouton-style in soups and gravies to sop up juices.

"Sops," as such absorbent breadbits were called, were considered choice morsels to be saved and eaten at another meal. A sign that Chau-cer's Franklin is a proper epicurean is his fondness for a breakfast of a sop in wine. In fact, the hall-bread trenchers, when not used as culinary alms, were also saved for later meals, especially breakfasts, for which those tasty, protein-laden dainties were the bases of almond-milk por-ridges, gruels, and creations such as *Fennel Soppes* and *Slitte Soppes.* *Brewis* were breadpieces soaked in the drippings of roasts turned on spits, or, sometimes identical with sops, simply juice-engorged breads.

Saved "frugally," such sops or *brewis* were not, however, the retrieved and reused foods of the poor. They were lordly leavings. Another type of sop utilized new bread in leftover sauces to make a "noble dish." For a baked lamprey pie, served cold, the recipe has this conclusion: When the lamprey is removed from the pie shell (or *coffin*) and eaten, take the lamprey syrup, add wine and ginger, and boil:

Take fayre paynedemayne y-wette in wyne & ley the soppis in the cofynne of the lamprey, & lay the syrippe a-boue, & ete it so hot; for it is gode lordys-mete.

II: Fig. 8 *W h e a t   w a s   t h r e s h e d   w i t h   l o n g* flails *whose beating edges were connected to the handle by joints. Long-toothed rakes gathered the grain before its sheafing into* fesses. *Triangular-shaped* winnowing fans *separated grain from chaff.* (Old Testament, *13th century, French. New York, The Pierpont Morgan Library, M638, f.12v)*

Though there is a multiplicity of kitchen-bread's uses, and though household-ordinance accounts list prodigious grain purchases, there is a surprising paucity of bread recipes. Since professional bakers were distinct from cooks, baking manuals may have been kept separate from other cookery tomes, and now most are lost. But there is a plethora of bread laws in the *assisa panis*.[24] Perhaps even noble houses bought as much bread as they baked.

Flour, however, is often referred to in recipes for other than bread baking. One of the most frequent is not wheat, rye, or barley, but rice flour. *Take fayre flour of rys* begins many a recipe, some of which offer choice between rice flour and *amyndoun* for aforcing or alaying.

Yeast alayed by stretching bread and pastry in their risings. Called *berme* or *yezy,* yeast made light fritters, "breaded" foods, and tarts. It was even more important in fermenting fruit products.

Cook's Choice and the Experience Assumption

The cook's prerogative to choose between alternative "ready mixers" or raw ingredients—"take amyndoun or rice flour"; "use coney or chicken"; "aforce it with flesh of pig or cow"; "use sugar enough or honey 'in default' "—allowed several effects for any single recipe. Vegetarian variation was a form of cook's choice for many fish and fowl dishes to accommodate meatless days and seasons. Recipes containing "If it is Lent, then . . ." and substituting eggs for beef, or "If you would have it on a fish day" and offering a fruit for a bird, allowed favored dishes without forbidden components.

Beyond calendrical alternations, this freedom of cook's choice may

24. These rules, preserved in the London Guild Hall, are available in partial translation in *Calendars* of the various London archives; see the BIBLIOGRAPHY classifications *Archive Aids* and *Bread.*

derive from four other possibilities: first, seasonal restrictions in availability of fresh raw foods. English climate often required autumn slaughters of certain domestic animals so as to obviate the need to feed them through the winter.[25] Second, certain foods were thought safer or better according to seasons. Writers following Galen believed venison, "which engenders melancholy," better eaten in summer than winter; others recommended against summer venison because the meat—then "venomous" —caused liver and bile trouble. Third, divergencies in taste of particular patrons for whose households the cookbooks were written could thus be accounted for by suggested alternates. But the most important element in the prevalence of variations within recipes was the experience assumption: "do it as with a goose," "strayn it as you would *galentyne*," "mince it like venison." Those cooks or their surrogates or followers for whom the texts orginally were made required more suggestion than direction, more reminder than instruction. They were professional practitioners of a noble craft, apparently literate, oftentimes wealthy, and sometimes members of the gentry themselves. Like the court musicians for whom music manuscripts gave the outlines of melody with the requests for improvisation, the court cooks utilized fewer particulars and greater initiative and taste.

Measurements

The assumption of experience may also explain the absence of measurements in most recipes. To the neophyte, cooking rules such as "do it till it is done," "make it thick enough," "spice it sufficiently," are unsettling or infuriating. Timing as well as weighing and proportioning are

25. See G. C. Homans, "Men and the Land in the Middle Ages," *Speculum* 11 (1936), 338–51; E. S. Higgs and J. P. White, "Autumn Killing," *Antiquity* 37 (1963), 282–9.

II: Fig. 10 *Using long scythes, two field workers cut the grain for loading by the woman to the left. The heavily laden hay wagon is drawn by two horses; another wagon winds up a hill to a windmill. (From the* Da Costa Hours, *Bruges, 1520. New York, The Pierpont Morgan Library, M399, f.8v)*

absent from most medieval cookeries. However, omission of stated measurements need not mean that ingredients and times were unmeasured. Medieval kitchen utensil inventories suggest that ingredients were measured with care. In noble and in merchant-class kitchens, pantries, and storerooms there were numerous calibrated scales and measuring vessels for dry and liquid ingredients: "beams" with scales and weights; pairs of balances; brass *auncers,* very small balances for weighing. Reasonably, these must have been used for more than mere measurements of stored food. Furthermore, sand-glass timers and early clocks also were part of the kitchen equipment of the fourteenth and fifteenth centuries. Manuscript directions nebulous to the unknowing doubtlessly were sufficient to the expert whose past culinary exploits could be reproduced by aid of utensils at hand for accurate apportioning.

Various Kitchen Utensils

Requirements of the hearth signal a major difference between medieval and modern kitchen gear. Flints for fire lighting, bellows for aerat-

II: Fig. 11 *While pigs feed on acorns in the forest at left, a horse-drawn plow makes furrows in a well-fenced field for the autumn sowing. (From the* Da Costa Hours, *Bruges, 1520. New York, The Pierpont Morgan Library, M399, f.10v)*

ing, and iron pot rests, pot hooks, pot hangers, tongs, and fire fenders were standard equipment. Numerous pots and pans of graduated sizes and shapes were used, smaller and larger caldrons, kettles, gridirons, waffle irons, and griddles. Usually pots were fitted to tripod stands called *blandreths,* so as to be raised above the fire's coals, or the vessels themselves were three-footed. Stirrers, spoons, spatulas, skimmers, and slotted and pierced ladles required particularly long handles. So did the *pele,* the long paddle which removed breads, pies, and pastries from ovens. Kitchen shovels not only ordered coals of the fire but were cooking vessels themselves; an interesting egg concoction called *Potrous* was made in an iron shovel packed with salt. *Chauffers* were deep fryers; *posnets,* saucepans; and the *trappe,* another specialized pot, probably like a "Dutch oven."

Open-hearth spits in large kitchens usually were mechanized for automatic or easy turning by a series of gears, pulleys, and weights. Great caldrons were lifted by ratchet devices such as the *rachyncroke* or racking crook. Skewers, *broches,* and *pricks,* for reinforcing animals or meats

II: Fig. 12

on spits, were made of iron or metal alloys which, like those for cook pots, were assayed and controlled by civil ordinances of the guild of Brasiers. Brass, iron, and metal-alloy pots shared space with earthenware. Some clay cookware apparently was considered disposable, for several recipes call for long, slow stewing in sealed earthenware pots which were broken to remove their contents.

Flesh-hooks, axes, hatchets, and a large array of knives, each with special function, blade tempering, and size, served in the kitchen and locked-storage areas such as the *gardmanger* or *gardevyan.* Covered pitchers, covered platters, and storage vessels of metal, porcelain, and treen were more or less elaborate depending upon their owners' wealth. But most were some way embellished, with an animal-mouth spout or knopped finial or engraved coat of arms.

Rather impractical though elegant gold and silver kitchenware and table gear given to the Prince of Wales in 1371 in an elaborate presentation, complete with music, included 6 gold pots, 3 gold basins, 6 silver basins, 6 silver ewers, 10 dozen porringers, and 2 silver basins covered with white enamel. More practical metals such as *dinanderie,* brass, and bronze were frequent materials for *chargers,* pitchers, and other kitchen and hall utensils. Pewter, however, was even more usual in courtly households. Of this alloy whose proportions of copper, lead, and tin were controlled by ordinances of the Pewterers, pots, porringers, platters, pitchers, chargers, cruets, and kitchen candlesticks were made in round and square shapes, the square always the finer pewter with greater copper content.

Three kitchen utensils critical to the preparation of most medieval

58

foods were mortar, sieve, and strainer. Mortars and pestles in various sizes, and made of metals or woods or porcelains, ground, crushed, and pounded spices, herbs, almonds, bones, dried beans, fruits, vegetables, and animal flesh. Sieves, usually made of horsehair, were many-sized and variously meshed for coarser or finer sifting. The *wheterydoun*, for example, separated grain from chaff, a gross sifter for wheat and rye. Strainers, sometimes hairmeshes comparable to sieves, more often were fabric. A more loosely or more finely woven stuff, according to requirements of the kitchen, was used in open cloth or bag shape. Best strainer bags were composed of *boulting cloth;* these were made or bought in accurate liquid measurements. Making *Hippocras,* for example, required three straining bags, gallon or pottel size. Strainers, like sifters and mortars, were available in "nests" of graduated size as well as of "fineness."

Numerous kitchen mills were used for pulverizing grains, pepper, and spices.[26] Hand mills equipped with cranks, gears, and blades or stones ground dried fish, meal, and fruit. *Miers* crumbed stale bread.

Baskets in various weaves and sizes with and without handles were indispensable kitchen containers and carriers. Grasses, rushes, and horsehair were usual materials for their fabrication.

Feathers were kitchen ephemera serving at least three functions. They "refeathered" a cooked bird to create the lifelike illusion. They made good glazing brushes: "Take a feather and endore the stuff in the pastry with the curds." And quills were used to kill fowl. One roast partridge recipe has: "Slay him in the nape of the neck with a feather." Probably the sharp quill point penetrated a major vein; possibly a hollow quill channeled blood into collecting vessels for those recipes, such as roast swan, requiring blood for sauce and glaze.

Multiple Cookings, Mixings, and Princely Pies

A final triad of medieval cooking techniques arouses the curiosity of most adventurers into the medieval kitchen: multiple cookings for single dishes; marvelous mixings in stews of fragrant ingredients; and a prevalence of pastries. Numerous medieval recipes employ more steps than today seem necessary. A *Royal Crustade* requires three separate bakings; a veal stew, four changings of pot and five separate cookings. Some recipes look as though Chaucer's Cook's bake, boil, broil, fry, roast, and stew were all for a single dish.

Why such multiple cookings? Many medieval health manuals warn against the dangers of undercooked flesh. Given the uncertainties of food preservation, such was reasonable precaution. Furthermore, many preserved meats and fish required many cookings and changings of stocks and pots to plump the dried food or to eliminate the salt or spice curing or other residue of preservation. Certainly, however, such were not the necessities for freshly killed meats available to the wealthy in most seasons. As with absence of spice measurements, so with timings of multiple cookings: we cannot judge excess. Without indications of time, we cannot know how long was the initial boiling nor the final roasting; several techniques could have served one food without overcooking, as in some modern roasts, seared in fat to seal, baked till done, then briefly broiled to crispen. Unknown and unknowable also is how hot or intense was an open fire made with birch or oak or hickory or charcoal or yet other fuels.

II: Fig. 12 *Large caldrons suspended from* ratchyncrokes *can be adjusted above the flames in the open hearth during cooking for the community in this monastic kitchen. Other kitchen implements, a large crooked ladle and a water basket, are hung on the walls. (From the* Vita *of St. Benedict. New York, The Pierpont Morgan Library, M184, f.20)*

26. See W. L. Goodman, *The History of Woodworking Tools* (London, 1964); Lynn White, Jr., *Medieval Technology and Social Change* (Oxford, 1962); and J. M. Hoffeld, "The Art of the Medieval Blacksmith," *The Metropolitan Museum of Art Bulletin* (December, 1969).

Special delight of medieval cooking is the surprising mixture of tastes and fragrances. Unexpected juxtapositions are found in recipes uniting lamb with chicken, venison with fish, beef with pears, almonds, dates, and violets; mixed piquancies of herbs, wines, spiced fruits, eggs, and marrow; creams, herbed ales, lentils, cheese, and coney all in the same pot. Such mixtures were called *seaws* in Anglo-Saxon, whence the modern stew, or *mortrews* from the French word for mortar (*mortreuil*), in which ingredients were pounded. When not in the same caldron, all mixed ingredients were baked in the same pie. Varieties of pastries—small sweet tarts called *doucettes,* the uncovered pie shells and lidded *coffyns,* the *rastons, risshewes* or *rissoles,* crisps, and fritters, most all with aromatic stuffings or *forsures*—made splendidly self-contained foods for finger-eating.

Probably the most princely pie exemplifying the mixings and the pastries is this: Mince and mix beef, suet of mutton, salt and pepper. Make a *faire large cofyn,* and put in some of this meat. *Then take capons, hennes, mallardes, connynges . . . wodecokkes, teles, grete briddes and plom hem in a boiling potte; and then couch al this fowl in the coffyn.* Add more of the meat and mutton as well as marrow, hard egg yolks, dates, raisins, prunes, cloves, mace, cinnamon, and saffron. Close the pie with a top crust and bake . . . *but be ware, or thou close it, that there come no saffron nygh the brinkes therof, for then hit wol never close.* Spiced and colored saffron's gold, such a *grete pye* turned practical requirement (for serving the same dish to members of the same rank in a household), into theatrical plenitude. Vivid, commodious pastries were prodigies of courtly kitchenry.

II: Fig. 13 *Herbs were used in distilling sauces and brews in addition to medicines. This kitchen distillery employs three laborers at the sorting, the still, and the bottling of the vegetable broths which had been heated in two types of furnaces, one an open fire, on the left in the large open hearth, and the other an enclosed "furnace" over which the flask was boiled. (Woodcut by Hans Weiditz, Strassburg, c. 1530. New York, The Metropolitan Museum of Art)*

DECORATION: FOOD PAINTING AND FOOD SCULPTURE

Take a Pecok . . . and roste him, And set the bone of the necke aboue the broche, And abowe the legges to the body, as he was wonte to sitte a-lyve; and when he is rosted ynowe, take him of, And lete him kele; And then wynde the skyn with the fethurs and the taile abought the body, And serve him forthe as he were a-lyve.

Like the refeathered roast peacock, that princely pie was both food and spectacle. The astonishing quantity as well as variety must have been calculated less to feed than to amaze. So with most medieval kitchen art. Food painting and sculpture had little direct relationship to taste or to nutrition. Illusion food probably piqued appetite less than curiosity, stimulated as much wonderment as lust to eat.

Food Painting

Concluding numerous recipes for soups, sauces, jellies, pastries, breads, batter-encrusted meats, and fruit confections, there appear such phrases as: "if you would have it green, color it with parsley"; "to make it red, use saunders"; "add saffron to make a faire amber color." Natural dyes thus were added for art, not taste. Flowers or herbs were boiled in a white wine or other fluid which kept the color in solution. Among the most popular food colors and their agents, parsley, mint, mallows, and hazel leaves made most greens. Shades of blue were obtained from blue turnsole or heliotrope. Violets tinted foods toward purple. Pinks and reds through lavenders were created via *saunders*, the red sander or san-

Ruchenmaistrey.

Abb. 574. Inneres einer Küche mit Koch und Magd.

II: Fig. 14

dalwood; flosscampy, the red wild flower; red turnsole; as well as *alka-net,* the root dye from the boraginaceous plant sometimes called Dyer's Bugloss. Yellow, gold, and orange were made from saffron, yellow turnsole, dandelion, and egg yolk. Blood made almonds, sauces, and aspics brown or black. For sweet foods whose color was to remain white, sugar was used instead of amber honey.

Sometimes, one color was used alone; or several colors were mingled and marbled; or single foods were tricolored. Some soups, sauces, and sliced jellies, for example, were made white or natural, then separated in thirds, one section dyed red, another yellow, the third green. A triplecolored fruit dish called *Fygeye* utilized—"if you wil color it in three manners"—saunders, saffron, and the brown of the figs themselves.

Foods thus artificially colored with natural agents were often further painted on their surfaces. *Vyolette,* a sugared, boiled flower dessert tinted by the cooked violets, was then "enflorished" with the hue of the fresh flowers *y-peyntid a-bove.*

Gold was the color into which much dross food was transmuted. Like the alchemists working over their caldrons and brews, the kitchen colorists made gold semblances since they could not create the perfect "immortal" metal. Since aurifaction was impossible, they practiced aurifiction.[27] Egg yolk mixed with ginger powder and saffron painted or *endored* foods, gilded heraldic and bestiary creatures to a noble glory. The *Cockentrice*—upper capon, nether pig, or forepart pig and hinder capon, neatly sewn together after roasting—was painted gold highlighted by green.

Roast peacock, refeathered and beaked, appeared alive but giltbeaked, -clawed, and -plumed. Bread such as *Payn perdew,* birds, fruits, aspics, and glazes were gilded for ceremony and semblance.

Food Sculpture

Other illusion foods united color with shape. Fish roe tinted green with pea juice were made to appear (and taste) like peas. Choppedpork meatballs, *Pome doree,* were made hard and round, coated with batter, endored *with sum grene thing* such as parsley or hazel leaves, to make green apples. Apparently a water-pitcher, another food, appropriately called, for its appearance, *Appraylere,* was baked from lean chopped pork, aged cheese, bread, spices, and herbs, stuffed into a greased pitcher finally broken to reveal the sculpture it molded. Dried fruits, threaded and strung on a skewer in alternations of dates, figs, prunes, and whole almonds, disguised in golden batter and then roasted, counterfeited the brocheted meat of *Haslet,* the noble reward of the hunt, the entrails of wild boar. This is the delicacy given the knight in *Sir Gawain* and lauded in the *Craft of Venery.*

The roasted pig's-maw "hedgehog" (*Yrchoun*) or, with almond quills was colored partly green and black with blood. Here, as elsewhere, kitchen artists violating natural history acceded to heraldry and fancy.

Despite the emphasis on appearance and illusion, such sculpted and painted foods were meant to be eaten. These illusion foods were the *entremets,* or *entremesses,* the food entertainments and spectacles between other dishes in banquet courses. These differ from *subtleties,* the more dramatic food sculptures, which were *warners* between courses, and which sometimes were edible though oftentimes simply decorative.

II: Fig. 14 *In the courtly kitchen, footed caldrons stood above the fires' coals while heavier caldrons were raised by chains and pulleys. A pit roasting two birds was elaborately mechanized for self-turning or easy cranking. To the right of the cook, tasting from a ladle and stirring with a pierced skimmer, is a pair of long-handled, round-headed implements, probably peles used for inserting bread and pastries into ovens. (Woodcut printed by Froschauer in* Kuchenmeisterei, *1507, Augsburg, Germany. New York, The Metropolitan Museum of Art, Rogers Fund)*

27. The phrase is Dr. Joseph Needham's, noted during our conversations in Rome, October, 1973, at the International Academy of Legal Medicine.

Er tet auch manigen vmb swanth
Mit den andern di er gieng

II: Fig. 15 *Aggressive peacocks attack a crow pretending to be a peacock by "dressing" in peacock's feathers. (From Hugo von Trimberg's* Der Renner, *15th century, German. New York, The Pierpont Morgan Library, M763, f.34v)*

28. *Le Ménagier de Paris,* ed. and trans. Eileen Powers, *The Goodman of Paris* (London, 1928).

Pl. 11 *A vertical hearth sports a caldron with* ratchyncroke, *gridiron tongs, a stoneware pot on the coals, a small warming niche, and pot-resting hooks on the borders. Other kitchen gear includes platters, ewers, shears, bellows, pitchers, an herb basket, and a skimmer. (From the* Hours of Catherine of Cleves, *1440, Dutch. New York, The Pierpont Morgan Library, M917, p. 151)*

Subtleties were the prerogative of the most noble; *entremets* graced the tables of the wealthy including the nobility but also pervaded the culinary repertoire of the rich merchant households. The gentle Goodman of Paris, sagely instructing his young wife in foodlore,[28] judged *subtleties* beyond his station though *entremets* essentials for their finest dinners.

Sauces at Table

To excite attention and to stimulate admiration were the two purposes beyond the good taste of *entremets*. However, illusion foods, just as simpler roast fish, flesh, and fowl dishes, had one final appetizing accompaniment at table: sauce. Sometimes "sauce" simply meant seasoning; many a recipe for roast fowl suggests its serving with "no sauce but salt." However, sauce mixtures were often required in the cookery volumes, with rules attributing proper sauce to delicacy.[29] Sauces were to achieve dual effects: to pique the appetite and to please the palate.

The most elaborate households had a *Saucer* responsible for preparing these garnishes, the most common of which were variations upon white sauce, black sauce, or green sauce. Usually, however, this final office of the food service was the responsibility of the *Carver*, or less frequently the *Panter;* whichever, the sauce applied to the dish was the last ceremony at table before eating.

Three types of sauces, available ready-made in London's and Paris's food markets, were golden saffron sauce, the spice mixed with wine; green parsley, and red *saunders* sauces. In addition to these products of the wine shops and spiceries, recipes enumerate the ingredients for

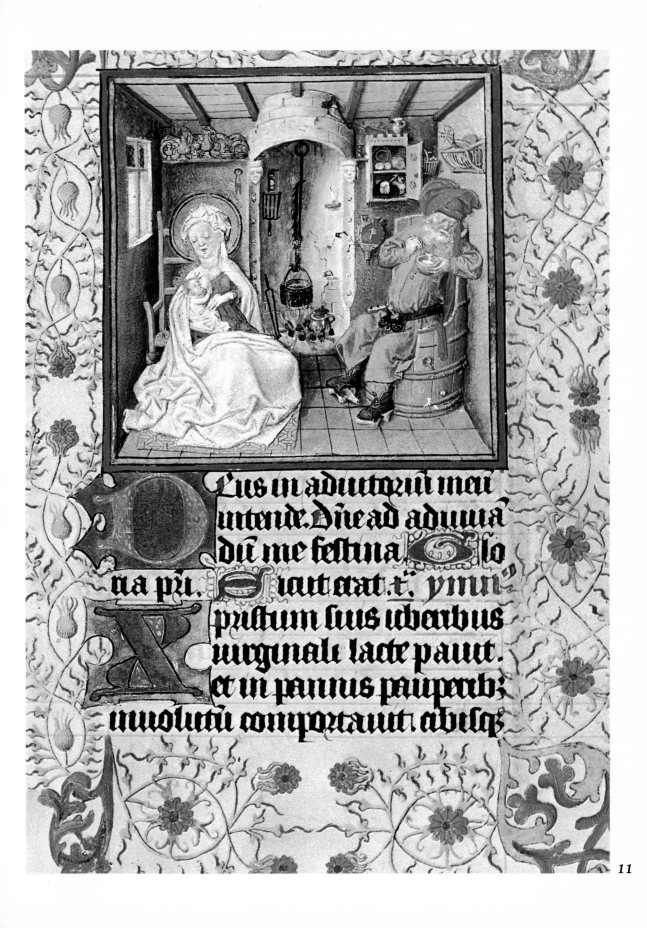

Eus in adiutoriu meu
intende. Dne ad adiuuia
dū me festina. Glo
ria pri. Siait erat. r̄. ymn
priftum sius vberibus
virginali lacte pauit.
et in pānis paupereb;
inuolutū cōportauit. abisq̃

12

II: Fig. 16 *The same peacocks bred to ornament gardens and moats later became food for feasters. Their exquisite feathers as well as their "regal" bearing were preserved from meadow to table by the careful flaying, preserving of skin and feathers with cumin and spices, and refeathering roasted peacocks after their bones were strutted in positions so as to make them "look alive."* (From the Tacuinum Sanitatis, *15th century, Italian. The New York Public Library, Spencer Collection, Ms. 65, f.86v)*

II: Fig. 16

superb spice and herb blends with *verjuice,* vinegar, or wine, as well as with grains such as wheat or rice. From the simplest tempering of cinnamon with red wine as sauce for minced lamprey, to the more elaborate *sauce galentyne* for fowl—consisting of bread, cinnamon, ginger, sugar, claret wine, and vinegar, mixed thick "as gruel"—these medieval seasonings reaffirm qualities of medieval food demonstrable in the cooking techniques: contrast and complementarity in taste, texture, color, and shape. The final triad of sauces appearing most frequently in the courtly cookeries are: *green sauce,* or *sauce vert* (more complex than the commercially prepared green parsley sauce), *frumenty,* and mustard.

Green sauce, for fresh fish as well as other dishes, was a fragrant combination of numerous herbs, breadcrumbs, vinegar, pepper, and ginger; or some other unity between herbs and piquant wine. *Frumenty* was made from wheat boiled in water or milk with spices and herbs; of porridge consistency, it was required for service of various fish, pork, venison, and even beaver tail. But the most versatile of all sauces was mustard—*good mustard alway accordeth welle*[30]—for all manner of dishes, meats, fishes, fruits, creams, vegetables, and puddings.

Thus sauced, the gorgeous kitchen creations cut, carved, and placed on the diner's trencher at last were ready for eating. The ceremonies of service now complete, the lord and guests indulged their own customs of elaborate finger etiquette. Each member of the banquet party was served only those foods appropriate to social station; what a guest ate and how he ate affirmed his place in the mannered passionate enterprise that was medieval court life.

29. See Lynn Thorndike, "A Medieval Sauce-Book," *Speculum* 9 (1934), 183–90.

30. Russell's *Boke,* l. 853; see note 7, above.

Pl. 12 *A cook lifts from the boiling caldron lamb meat of the freshly killed animal. The large round-bottomed pot is held by a ratchyncroke. The boiled meat is then conveyed in a platter to a waiting diner. The cook is none other than Samuel.* (Old Testament, *13th century, French. New York, The Pierpont Morgan Library, M638, f.20r)*

göttlich kunst des ordens
Und bruoder lienhart von
florentz obroster prior prediger
ordens mit ij doctores
theolocie die wurdent mit als
her empfangen als d' barfuß

¶ Och maister maist' nicolaus
obrost prior des hailgen grabs
zu jerln

¶ Och komen do zemal gen
Costentz becken die basteten
buochen mit hüner mit fischen
mit ayern vnd wie jetlich
die habn wolt vnd buochent
och rings von brätstilelen
vnd hattend wägelin mit
ainem rad als man gewonlich
mist od' stain in die gärten
vnd vff den gartn füert.
Daruff hattend si gemacht
bachöfelin darjnn sy die basteten vnd ander sölich Ding
bürtzen Die wägelin mit den
öfen die alweg warm waren
füertend sy durch die statt die
sy dann mantend das r zü
verkofen

Dis schgnc Statt hie
nach mält

A Chicken For Chaucer's Kitchen

MEDIEVAL LONDON'S MARKET LAWS AND LARCENIES

HE raw produce—chicken, fish, and pheasant; beans, oats, and lentils; herbs, spices, and honey—transformed so skillfully into elegant medieval dishes oftentimes was homegrown. Monasteries and manors usually had their own grainfields, orchards, kitchen gardens, beehives, pigpens, and poultry yards, as well as their own game parks for hunting fowl and deer. For their fresh fish, for the numerous *fyssche* versus *flessche* days of the calendar,[1] those far from coast and river kept alive fish in special ponds called *vivaria* or *stews*. Bakehouses and pastry kitchens as well as brewing houses and vinting chambers were part of the wealthiest secular and ecclesiastical dwellings. Yet even the most self-sufficient houses needed to purchase raw materials for the more elaborate recipes. For the variety of choice as well as for the ostentation of rare or imported food, servants of the monied householders patronized town markets.

Food markets served the social classes lower than the wealthiest with particular urgency: the small landholder and the town dweller bought more food than he raised, so that the quality of his eating was closely congruent with

III: Fig. 1 *An itinerant pastry cook produces conical loaves from his portable oven on a street corner in the town of Constance in southern Germany. His* regrater *sells from a cloth-covered round table to the customers lined up for her wares, two of whom look longingly at the large pretzels drying on the post nearby. (From Ulrich von Richenthal's* Constanzer Consilium, *1450–70, German. The New York Public Library, Spencer Collection, Ms. 32, p. 56)*

1. Requirements for two or three meatless days per week led to ingenious "variations" upon favorite meat dishes. See the RECIPES, *Vegetables and Vegetarian Variations,* as well as Chapter V.

III

III: Fig. 2 *One baker's-man rolls dough on a molding-board after weighing it in a balance scale; another conveys eight breads on a long-handled paddle, a* pele, *into a wood-burning oven; a chopping block and hatchet yield ready fuel. A third worker, at left, inserts covered baking vessels into an open furnace. The woman through the window is patron or baker or* regrater, *the retailer who sells baked goods. (From the* Kalendrier des Bergères, *Pierre le Rouge, 1499, French. Paris, Bibliothèque Nationale, Imprimés réservés V, f.1266)*

2. For City ordinances relating to food and regulation of food trades, see BIBLIOGRAPHY classification *Archive Aids,* especially *Liber de Antiquis Legibus* (London, 1846). An excellent introduction to these laws is H. T. Riley, *Memorials of London and London Life* (London, 1868).

3. All legal references are derived from the original thirteenth- through sixteenth-century documents. The original legislation and records of litigation mentioned in this chapter are listed in the BIBLIOGRAPHY, the documents classified according to type: e.g., *Wine, Fish, Bread,* and similar culinary rules.

4. In order to prevent these margins from bristling with Latin, Norman French, and Middle English references, a selection amongst the total documents appears in the BIBLIOGRAPHY, *Manuscripts* ordered by subject, date, source, and language.

the status of the food markets. From the staples of diet through the costliest confections, from raw grains through fully prepared "convenience foods," medieval London's markets offered local and imported foodstuffs, their sales carefully governed by victual laws.[2] Rules controlled price, measure, quality, and competition; prohibited unsanitary methods and malicious adulterations; prescribed special places and exact hours for marketing specific products; assigned investigators to ferret out food malefactors, and enforced trials and punishments for food crimes.

Market laws are as detailed as they are numerous.[3] A gallon of best grade Gascon wine was to be sold in 1331 for no more than four pence or the taverner risked the pillory as punishment. Codfish caught west of London Bridge were to be sold only near the Conduit after 10 A.M., while shellfish were not to be sold at shops but peddled through the streets and lanes by itinerant hawkers—only. Red and white wines from France were not to be sold in the same taverns as sweet wines from Crete. Specific weights and measures—with such titles as *tron, ferdkyn, chopyn, quarter,* and *dorser*—bore official seals and insignia guaranteeing their conformance to city or royal measurement standards. These victual laws, and the cases tried in the courts because of their violation, superbly detail medieval London's concern with public health. So many and delightful are the vignettes of the market rules, perfidies, and follies, that an imaginary meander through London's food markets is possible by uniting about eight hundred disparate legislations and court actions.[4] From the bread statutes in the *Liber de Assisa Panis,* from Mayor's Court and Alderman records in the London Guildhall's *Letter Books,* from the *Liber Horn,* the *Liber Custumarum,* and the *Plea and*

Memoranda Rolls,[5] here follows an itinerary through London's markets around the year 1400.

Here Geoffrey Chaucer or his wife Phillipa or their servants might have bought foods from bakers and wine retailers and butchers and cheesemongers. Here they could obtain all ingredients for such a familiar medieval dish as *Farsed Chycken,* a baked bird stuffed with lentils, cherries, cheese, ale, and oats, and garnished with a sauce of *pandemayne* bread crumbs, herbs, and salt mixed with *Romeney* wine. Here could be heard the regional dialects of the upcountrymen, the foreign languages of the German, French, Venetian, Spanish, and other wine and spice merchants; the chants and songs of the strawberry seller or the charcoal maker; and the public crier's proclamation of the food perfidies of the woman punished at the pillory for selling putrid fish or of the baker's man hurried through the streets on a hurdle-sled with his underweight bread loaf tied about his neck. Here were the prodigious odors of the barrels and pipes of spiced wines, the pig and sheep carcasses of the butcheries, the stinking eels sold by a nefarious pie man who, by baking them in pastry, thought to deceive his patrons. Here were the wholesale "foreign" poultry dealers separated by law and space from the local "freemen" chicken vendors. Here were dairymen wedging and weighing fine, aged cheese. Here the costumes of master food guildsmen vied in color and sheen with household liveries of the noble and the proud. Here the women of the food crafts were so numerous as to require a special stock for their misdeeds. And punctuating the din of hucksters' shouts and public cries was the town clock striking or ringing the hours which asserted in the market the City order.

III: Fig. 3 *A baker is punished for a bread crime— such as the selling of underweight or putrid merchandise—by being tied to a* hurdle-sled *and drawn through the town by horses. His faulty loaf is tied around his neck. (From the* Assisa Panis, *21 Edw. I–16 Henry VI, The Guildhall, the Corporation of London, f.1)*

5. For selected English translations of documents in these volumes see the BIBLIOGRAPHY classification *Archive Aids*.

III: Fig. 4 *Beneath the portrait of* St. Philip the Apostle, *patron saint of pastry cooks, is a small baking scene in which dough is weighed in a balance, formed into round loaves on a mold-ingboard,* then placed on a long rectangular-headed *pele before being closed in a stone oven for baking. Completed loaves, slightly browned, are on long trays with pierced handles. (From* The Hours of Catherine of Cleves, *1440, Dutch. New York,* The Pierpont Morgan Library, *M917, p. 226)*

III: Fig. 4

Breads and Baked Goods

For Chaucer to obtain the bread, wine, ale, and salt for *Farsed Chycken,* the bread venders' street might have been the place to visit first. At least four types of bakers had their shops and stalls in Bread Street and the bread market. Bakers sold retail bread of their own baking. Other bread sellers called *regraters* bought wholesale, and then sold to their own customers. *Public Bakers* ran large ovens to which patrons brought their dough for final cooking. Pie bakers or their regraters sold filled pastries, ready-to-eat pies of fruit, meat, fish, or poultry. While some bake shops served combined purposes, specific rules controlled the activities of each.

Prices were scrupulously monitored. Specific types of bread could be sold for no more than established prices for specific weights.[6] There were numerous variations upon the distinctions between light or white bread, and dark or brown bread. Amongst the most popular were *maslin* or *mixtilio,* a mixture of wheat and rye flours. *Wastelbread* was not only the delight of the delicate dogs belonging to Chaucer's Prioress[7] but of

6. See Sir William Ashley, *The Bread of Our Forefathers: An Inquiry in Economic History* (Oxford, 1928); and H. E. Jacob, *Six Thousand Years of Bread* (New York, 1944).

7. The *Prologue* to the *Canterbury Tales* ll. 146–7.

people favoring a consistency as flaky as the modern French *croissant;* medieval *French bread* was supposed to approximate the native English *wastel.* Three other bread types were finer-grained whites: *simnel* or *artocopi; mancherin* or *manchet;* and *pandemayne,* variously described as "Lord's bread" or "noble bread" or "daily bread." It may have had stamped upon it some insignia of Christ, as in "hot cross buns." These last three were forbidden to be baked during Lent, when only another triad of coarser darker breads was permitted. From unbolted meal came *tourte;* a rough brown bread was called *bis* or *trete;* and common "white" was made from an unrefined meal.

Special fragrant breads were made with parsley, rosemary, basil, and other herbs, the loaves variously shaped and colored. Either made to order or otherwise not subject to the usual price regulations, these were infrequently part of the common retail bread trade. Used and favored for trenchers, the edible platters, parsley bread was green; saffron bread yellow; and *saunders* (or "Alexanders"), colored with sandalwood, was pink or red.

Shapes of medieval breads generally were variations upon round: higher, wider, braided, twisted, twirled circles of dough, rather than elongated loaf shapes. However, twice-baked breads, such as pretzels—which legend suggests were accidentally overbaked in a monastic kitchen and given to pious young scholars to represent in their food their arms crossed in prayer—were more intricately designed and sculptured.

But whatever the type or the shape, all commercially sold breads had to be stamped with the official seal of the baker. This signature implied conformance with the official *assize,* the accepted measurement and price established and enforced by the City of London, and assured quality to the buyer. Bread seals permitted redress if the goods were fraudulent. The rotten or underweight loaf could be traced to its maker. In fact, not only regular breads but also *horsebreads,* oaten and bean cakes for horses, had to be stamped with the baker's mark to assure weight and value. Thus when Juliana, baker, was caught with loaves deficient according to the halfpenny assize, her underweight loaves forfeited to the city were dispatched to feed prisoners in Newgate in 1298; nine bakers in 1310 were accused of overcharging and underweighing; their defense, that their produce was weighed cold and therefore unfairly, led to an only pecuniary punishment, namely, three halfpenny loaves were to be sold for a penny as warning against their future tricks. The usual punishments for conviction of bread fraud were the *pillory* and the *hurdle.* With an underweight loaf hung round his neck, along with the iron piece he inserted in one loaf to make a cartload of deficient loaves weigh better, a baker's man shared the pillory with another who baked breads with good dough outside surrounding foul dough within. Other bakers of bread of bad quality or deficient weight were drawn through the streets tied to a sledlike vehicle called the *hurdle;* a baker thrice hurdled was forced to forswear trade in London forever.

A particularly ingenious petty larceny was practiced by certain bakers using an otherwise innocent and venerable implement called a *molding-borde* or molding board. Every bakehouse had some flat surface of appropriate height upon which loaves could be molded, perhaps also kneaded, before baking. Private kitchens must have met the same requirement similarly; just such a molding board is listed in an inven-

8. For fascinating background to such perfidies, see J. Storck and W. D. Teague, *Flour for Man's Bread: A History of Milling* (St. Paul, 1952); and L. A. Moritz, *Grain Mills and Flour in Classical Antiquity* (Oxford, 1958).

9. See Sylvia Thrupp, *The Merchant Class of Medieval London* (Ann Arbor, 1962), 92f.

10. Fine twelfth-century "take-out" or "fast-food shops" are described by William Fitz Stephen in his "Description of London," in F. M. Stenton, *Norman London* (London, 1934). See also Salzman, *English Industries,* 321; and *London Letter Book L,* 312.

11. See the RECIPES. *Meat,* for "garbage" delights.

Pl. 13 *Barley is cut by sickles while field workers carrying two-pronged mowing forks look on. Bound by cording or selfsame barley stalks, the grain is stacked high in a tower of alternating sheaves while the reapers eat a meal of bread, cut by square-ended knives, dipped in a bowl atop a handled pitcher. (Old Testament, 13th century, French. New York, The Pierpont Morgan Library, M638, f.17v)*

(Overleaf)
Pl. 14 *In this rustic threshing-floor scene two white-shirted peasants work beneath a thatched roof within a wattle enclosure. One beats the grain with a long-handled flail while the other winnows in an oval basket. Stacked sheaves are piled behind each worker. (From the Rohan Hours, 15th century, French. Paris, Bibliothèque Nationale, Ms. Latin 9471, f.9v)*

tory of a merchant's kitchen, dated 1391. However, nine public London bakers built a clever improvement upon the usual simple table by fitting it with a hole, disguised so as not to be evident from the top, covered by a wicket—"such as in a mousetrap," says the manuscript. When the customer's dough was placed on this spot for molding into shape, a servant hidden beneath the molding board opened the hole and scraped out dough from the mass above. The patron then had baked a bread containing less weight than he had brought and bargained for; and the baker sold new breads made with the pilfered dough. After seven men and two women, professional bakers all, were caught not only with their tempered boards but with filched dough still in troughs, molding boards were banned.

Though bread weight and price were publicly advertised, clever entrepreneurs often tried to charge what the rich traffic would bear. Thus it was necessary for a proclamation to be issued when "Peers, Lords, and Commons" summoned to Parliament in 1371 were harbored in the city. The innkeepers and hostelers were limited in the profit they could make from selling bread to their guests or for their horses, and were required not to sell any bread except that bought from the market bakers and stamped with their marks—on pain of double the usual punishment. Several years earlier, a rich goldsmith's servant, desiring to buy wheat of a certain quality, with examples of grain in his hand, reported a vender who insisted that such wheat was available at 21 pence a bushel while "that same day at the same hour" it sold for but 18. Similarly, the "Duke of Tassyle" (probably a member of the entourage of Anne of Bohemia, wife to Richard II) complained in court that a grain seller extorted an inflated price from him for oats.[8]

Still another bread crime drove up the price of the finished product by withholding the raw materials from the market.[9] *Affeering* by bakers and cornmongers (corn meant any grain such as wheat or rye) was an offense punishable by pillory or jail; it was the creation of an artificial scarcity of grain by withholding it from the public, thereby causing a greater demand and higher than normal selling price. The baker John atte Wode, for example, having whispered deceitful and cunning offers to a wheat merchant, drew him into the Church of Friars Minor and there bought from him two *quarters* of wheat (1 quarter = 8 bushels) at $2\frac{1}{2}$ pence per bushel above the common price. Then selling this at an inflated price, John increased the cost of grain by affeering, first withholding, then demanding higher than proper fee.

As strict as were the ordinances against affeering of bread's raw materials, so were regulations for fully prepared, ready-to-eat, "convenience" pastries.[10] Prices were set for meat and poultry pies, some of individual size for the afternoon snack, others family size for the whole meal. Going rate in 1378 for "best roast capon in pasty" was 8 pence, "hen in pasty" 5 pence. Pie bakers were reminded that beef pasty at half-penny was to be as good in quality, though smaller, as the penny pie. Some commercially available pies were so large as to contain whole geese. Such were baked by the *Pastelers* or Piebakers. An interesting ordinance of their guild, dedicated to avoiding inappropriate or misrepresented foods, prohibited piemen from buying giblets or "garbage" from cooks of Bread Street or kitchens of great lords and then baking them in pastry;[11] it also forbade baking beef in pastry and selling it as venison pie.

13

Cy vient le serpent qui deçoit
Eve et adam par le fruit q̃ dieu
leur avoit donne

Aoust a xxxi iour
Et la lune xxx
viij c   Saint piere

14

15

These regulations and court cases certainly ought not imply that medieval bakers were particularly larcenous or their customers especially litigious. Quite the contrary: since bread and baked goods were indeed "convenience" foods, probably more often bought than home-baked, the City of London established just legislation to protect the citizen as well as the profit of the craftsman. The multiplicities of bread types, their staple qualities, and their near-universal acceptance by all classes, ages, and attitudes—even the most ascetic condemners of wine or meat left bread undamned—made bread a subject of celebration by medieval gastronomes but also abuse by venal entrepreneurs. In fact, in the minutiae of ordinances, the bread assizes are equaled by few other victual's rules. Only trade in wines and in fish seem to have been anywhere near so carefully governed.

The power of the various bakers' guilds may be reason beyond bread's ubiquity to explain the medieval city's concern.[12] So too may be accidental though preferential salvation of records: similarly complete rules for poulterers or cheese makers may have been lost through the centuries. Yet another source for civic interest in bread probably was the Church itself, which devoted effort to dietary laws in its definition of piety. Special seasons such as Lent required "penance" bread; specific saints' days, such as St. Agatha's, were celebrated with symbolic loaves; and the liturgy and ecclesiastical laws mandated sacramental breads prepared according to special recipes and stamped with traditional insignia. In all, the sophistication of the civic control of bread production and sale gives clues to the orderly qualities of London's food markets.[13] Ordinances against victualing malpractices demonstrate the city's allegiance to codes of public health as well as to ideals of commercial propriety.

Wines

From Bread Street Chaucer might walk to The Vintry to obtain first the wine and then the ale for saucing and stuffing his chicken. As with bread, so with wine: numerous varieties were available subject to strict regulations of price, quality, and measure.[14] But unlike the baking craft, the London wine industry demonstrated not only concern with foreign fashions but dependence upon imported goods.[15] Wines from France, Portugal, Spain, Italy, Sicily, Germany, and elsewhere were transported in huge *tuns* by boat. Wineships were met by appointed officials, their liquid cargos assayed after "resting" three days, then sealed with official and visible marks, and their wholesale and retail prices established first for the best wine for a gallon, then with prices descending along with the quality. "A cry for the standard," a proclamation of the quality of a wine for a specific year, was to be observed; but vintage 1311, for example, though expensive, according to King Edward II was apparently not worth the cry. Red wine versus white, sweet versus dry, mixed versus straight, adulterated versus sound—all such were circumscribed by regulations enforced by *Searchers of Wines* as well as by specially appointed boards of investigators composed of London Vintners and Bordeaux merchants. Through the fifteenth century almost all the best vineyards of Gascony, including Bordeaux and the Bordelais, were "English" until the Hundred Years War finally affirmed the southwest of France as "French."

12. See Sylvia Thrupp, *A Short History of the Worshipful Company of Bakers of London* (London, 1933); H. S. Bennett's *Life on the English Manor* (Cambridge, 1937), 135f.

13. See H. C. Coote, *Ordinances of Some Secular Guilds of London 1354–1396* (London, 1871); H. Pirenne, *Medieval Cities: Their Origins and the Revival of Trade* (Princeton, 1948).

14. W. Younger's *Gods, Men, and Wine* (London, 1966), especially 337–80. See also Edward Hyams, *The Grape Vine in England,* and his *Dionysus: A Social History of the Wine Vine* (London, 1965).

15. See Margery K. James, *Studies in the Medieval Wine Trade* (Oxford, 1971); André Simon, *A History of the Wine Trade in England* (London, n.d.); and H. Pirenne, "Un grand commerce d'exportation au moyen-âge: les vins de France," *Annales d'histoire économique et sociale* 5 (1933), 225.

(Preceding Page)
Pl. 15 *In a large bakehouse, two bakers convey loaves from a long molding-board to the decorated brick oven. Hanging on hooks on the wall, or on a wall-shelf, are five bread-baskets. (From a Book of Hours, 15th century, French. Oxford, Bodleian Library, Ms. Canon Liturg. 99, f.16)*

Pl. 16 *From the trellised grapevines in the background, a woman and a man pick grapes. The grapes are carried in a fluted basket to a large vat in which a man is treading the vintage which later is poured into a wooden cask through a funnel. A two-handled measure is in the foreground. (From the Rohan Hours, 15th century, French. Paris, Bibliothèque Nationale, Ms. Latin 9471, f.14v)*

16. For discussions of the medieval types, their tastes, and their sources, see H. W. Allen, *A History of Wine* (London, 1961); Alexis Lichine, *Encyclopedia of Wines and Spirits* (London and New York, 1967); L. W. Morrison, *Wines and Spirits* (Harmondsworth, 1957); and compare Henderson, *History of Ancient and Modern Wines* (London, 1824); and H. F. Lutz, *Viticulture and Brewing in the Ancient Orient* (Leipzig and New York, 1922). See also R. Surflet, *Maison Rustique or the Country Farme*, ed. Markham, 1616.

17. For the practices and social lore of British drinking establishments see H. A. Monckton, *A History of the English Public House* (London, 1970).

18. See Alice Beardwood, *Alien Merchants in England, 1355–77* (Cambridge, 1931); E. M. Carus-Wilson, *Medieval Merchant Adventurers* (London, 1967); and compare A. P. Newton, *Travel and Travellers of the Middle Ages* (London, 1930).

At least fifty-six types of "French" wines were available in medieval London, thirty varieties of Italian, Spanish, and Canarian.[16] A red Tuscan wine, Vernaccia, called in London *Vernage,* was to be sold for no more than two shillings a gallon in 1350; for sixteen pence, however, one could purchase: a sweet, Greek *Wine of Crete; Malveisin,* probably a malmsey, from Crete or Morea; *Wine of the River;* as well as the aromatic spiced wines *Piemente* and *Clare,* piment and claret. Beyond these wines mentioned frequently in chronicles and cookeries, others include: *Vernagelle, Cute, Raspay, Muscadelle, Tyre, Osvey, Caprik, Campolet, Whippet, Pyngmedo, Hydromel, Metheglin, Sack, Rhine Wine, Theologicum* (cleric-made), and *Torrentyne of Ebrew. Romeney,* a malmsey, was one of the most popular fifteenth-century wines. Chaucer would have purchased it not only for *Farsed Chycken* but as a table wine. It was sold only from an "upright measure" sealed with the Alderman's sign; the buyer had the right to inspect the measuring vessel as well as the *tun* from which the wine was drawn.

Such pricing and rules for patron investigation—in any London tavern selling wine, one member of a drinking party had the right to check the *tuns* or pipes of wine in the cellar and to examine the wine measures—were not always taken gently by the Taverners. A particularly restrictive act which attempted to control the multitude of foreign wines made prison the penalty if a gallon of the best Gascon wine was sold for more than four pence; or a gallon of Rhenish for more than eight pence; or if the wine-cellar doors were not open to the inquiring public. Tavern keepers revolted and effectively shut all taverns in The Vintry and Chepe.[17] Their protest succeeded in only the mildest liberalization of those rules. Forty years later the base price had risen only slightly and the Vintners' regulations for the Taverners read: any corrupt wine would be condemned and none but sound wines sold; no new wine laid in cellars was to be sold until old wine was purchased or removed; no Rhenish or other wines was to be sold except by "sealed" measure; wine-cellar doors were to be open without hindrance of bars, cloths, or obstacles; when the first fleet arrived "from Gascoigne," merchant vintners were to price the perishable cargo. And no white wine of Gascoigne, of La Rochelle, of Spain or any other country was to be laid where Rhenish wine was for sale.

This last prohibition against selling certain wines in the same tavern with others often occurs in the medieval records. A special dispensation by King Edward III allowed two Genoese tavern owners in London to violate the usual rules forbidding red and white wines in the same house as sweet wines such as those of Crete, "for it is known that mixing one with the other is dangerous." Francesco and Panino of Genoa were allowed to keep those wines, after swearing to maintain separate cellars for them, apparently to protect London's foreign image, lest alien merchants refuse to come to England with their wine and merchandise.[18]

Whether "danger" from mixing pertains to public health or to politics is hard to determine. Various food laws display inherited prejudices elsewhere recorded in medieval medical treatises based on writings of Galen, Dioscorides, and Avicenna, relating to the humoral-balance theory of disease. However, mixing wines was prohibited (and allowed only by special dispensation) not only for theoretical concern with public health—wines might be mixed only if their original components

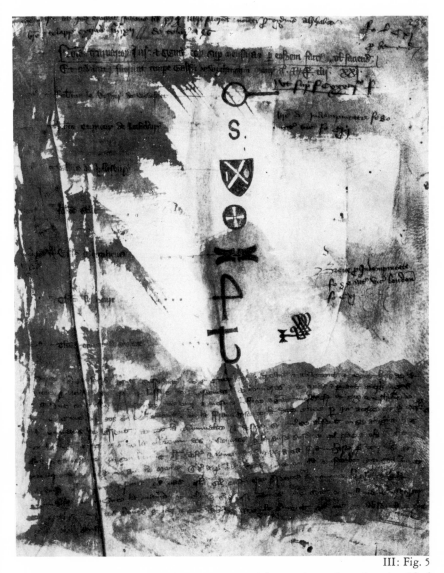

III: Fig. 5 *The* Guild of the Turners *attempted to check frauds and perfidies among its members by promulgating rules for good professional conduct, enforced by civil authority. The maker's marks required by law in an ordinance of 1347* (Letter Book F, *cxxxiv*), *associates fabricators and insignia so that any poorly wrought barrels and measures, or vessels made from inappropriately "recycled" woods, or deceitful weight and measure practices could be easily traced to the culprits.* (From Letter Book F, *14th century, English. The Guildhall, the Corporation of London, last page*)

III: Fig. 5

"grew together," one Bordeaux grape with another—but for justified worry over intentional adulteration. While many wines turned bad by natural causes, and upon investigation were condemned, poured into waste channels in the streets, or dumped in the Thames, others were maliciously mixed, adulterated, and counterfeited.[19] Pure wine mixed with spoiled yielded a corrupt drink unfit for consumption. Such trick was punishable by forcing the recreant to drink his own brew, to bear the remainder poured over his head, and to endure the pillory. But let the taster beware of such as the adulterator of wine who made *Romeney* out of "old and feeble Spanish wine" by adding gum and resin to approximate *Romeney*'s smell and taste; he would have got the third quality, color, perfect by adding powder of bays but he was caught beforehand. Modern wine scandals demonstrating contempt for the patrons' wine palates have their medieval prototypes. Relatively high-priced *Romeney* was a favorite and thus useful to the unscrupulous; a proclamation against adulterating wines was issued in 1419, because wines of Spain, la Rochelle, and miscellaneous remnants of sodden and

19. See Fredrick Accum, *A Treatise on Adulterations of Food and Country Poisons* (London, 1820); and F. Filby, *A History of Food Adulteration and Analysis* (London, 1934). See also Hudson, *Leet Jurisdiction in Norwich*, Selden Society (London, 1891), 13 for cooks and pastry makers selling "old" warmed-over pies; and Tancock, *Notes and Queries.* Series 8, III, 366.

III: Fig. 6 *An ale wife, still holding her fraudulent tankard or measure, is carried by a demon and devoured by a Hell Mouth for betraying the citizens' trust. This vigorous depiction is taken from a* misericord, *the carved underseat of a prayer stall (against which the tired penitents might rest their bottoms during long services; thus the name, from the Latin word for mercy). (From a drawing of a wooden* misericord, *14th century. Ludlow Church, England)*

reboiled wines were reprocessed with additives such as resin, pitch, code, and other dreadful and dangerous substances, and sold as *Romeney*.

Not only wine was regulated in price and quality, but so were vinegars and sauces sold by the wine merchants. These fermented and mixed liquids, subject to similar scrutiny as the wines, were stock additions to common recipes which called for a green parsley sauce, or yellow saffron or red sandalwood sauce—all purchasable ready for pantry or table in London's Vintry.

Mead was a popular English wine, variously in and out of fashion because of its Anglo-Saxon heritage. So too for other honey wines such as *Metheglin* and *Bragget*. When French and "foreign" foods and drinks were ostentatiously cultivated, as were French literature and costume, the fragrant honey mead, though made, sold, and drunk, was adjudged rustic and ignoble. But each chauvinistic English cycle restored the drink of the Anglo-Saxons, with its lore traceable back through *Beowulf's* meadhall,[20] to its rightful place in London. Its use in medicine, however, was consistent despite its intermittent falls from courtly or city fashion. It may be possible to trace medieval English food habits as parallel to the fashions in medieval literature: the Northwest Midland manors and towns which, contemporary with Chaucer's London, created the "alliterative revival" of Anglo-Saxon poetic techniques and themes (such as in *Sir Gawain and the Green Knight*) may also have exulted in Anglo-Saxon food and wines.

While the emphasis in London's victualing laws was upon imported wines, there were also local English wines made from various fruits, vegetables, herbs, and grasses. The circumstances for sale and for fraud

20. Ed. Fr. Klaeber (Boston, 1950).

approximate those for other forms of brew, beers, and ales. Chaucer, remaining in The Vintry, would have walked now from the wine-merchant's shop to the alemonger who, like as not, was a woman, an *alewife*.

Beers and Ales

In 1418 beer was price-listed as cheaper than ale, suggesting that it was thought to be inferior in quality to ale as in earlier, and, indeed, later generations. Writing on drink and its relationship to health, Andrew Boorde called ale, made from barley malt, water, and yeast, a "natural drink," while beer, made of malt, hops, and water, he considered a maker of fat men and killer of those troubled with colic or the stone.[21] Distinctions are made in manuscripts among brewers, keepers of brewhouses, and malt makers, but the various regulations for the arts of brewery converge sufficiently to allow unified consideration of both drinks under the rubric *ale*.[22]

Hucksters or hawkers or regraters sold ale, as did taverners and brewers themselves as well as their families. Local water from wells, rivers, or streams was used in ale-making less frequently than waters piped into London via the municipal system of conduits. Fourteenth-century brewers and taverners many times were forbidden to use Conduit water because they wasted it, thereby depriving local people of their water source. Ale makers caught fetching water forfeited their giant water vessels and tubs, the *tankards* and *tynes*.[23] The insatiable brewers forfeited their temporarily successful arrangement with the water keepers of London by which they rented the large upper pipes and fountain of the Conduit for ale-making; they depleted the small lower pipes reserved for the community by drawing Conduit water indiscriminately, which led to their censure and punishment.

In addition to the various medieval manuals describing ale-making, much of the method can be deduced from inventories of breweries. One such contained lead vessels, a lead cistern, a lead taptrough, mashvat, *rarynfat, tun* and *halftun, yelfat*, brewing tubs called *kemelynes*, handmills, an *alegiste*, and a *clensingbecche*. Ale was kept before sale in large wood *tuns* or *aletonnes* or smaller *halftuns* or *cumelins*.

The brew was measured out at the time of sale by gallon or quart or pint or variations thereupon by special wooden vessels fabricated by *turners*. These measures were required to conform to an *assize* and were stamped with the maker's mark. By accident or by fraudulent design, fourteenth-century turners' elaborate nests and shapes of ale measures did not prove true to established legal capacities; certain "quart" measures were elegant in configuration but held far less than a quart of liquid. Turners were forbidden in 1310 to make measures in shapes of boxes or cups, and especially enjoined against such "false" measures as the one-pint *chopyn* or the half-pint *gylle;* they were required to keep turning out the gallon, the two-quart *potell,* and the single-*quart* containers. Wood for these measures was to be sound and dry. Capacity conformed to the *standard* of the Alderman in whose ward the measure was to be used. Each measure mark of each maker was registered in the London Guildhall; they are there today.

Turners were ·not the only ones occasionally using measures other than par. Hucksters tried to sell ale beyond the price and *assize* to wealthy out-of-towners coming to Parliament; or they thickened and

21. Boorde's *A Dyetary of Helthe*. 256.

22. For charming anecdotes and references to both brews, see J. Bickerdyke, *The Curiosities of Ale and Beer* (London, 1965).

23. For illustration of these, see Chapter IV, Fig. 2.

raised the bottoms of quart measures with pitch; or continued to sell by *chopyn* in spite of its banning. Women seemed particularly prone to these alehouse antics, and spent numerous days on the *thewe*, the women's pillory. An alemonger, Alice, not only sold ale from an unsealed inadequate *quart* but covered the measure's one-and-a-half-inch false bottom with rosemary. Six of her *quarts* did not equal one regular gallon assayed. While she was upon the *thewe,* one-half of her false measure cut down the middle was hung round her neck, the other half preserved in the Guildhall.

The ale buyer and brewer had yet another potential deceiver to watch: the *cooper* who made the tubs called *cuves, aletonnes, tynes, vates, cumelins,* barrels, and buckets. Against three specific types of malice, patrons required guard. If vessels were made of unsound wood sawn in midgrain, and full of sap, they warped and split. Furthermore, they ceased conforming to the King's standards of measurement, placing the brew seller (as well as the cooper) in jeopardy. If the vessels were made of recycled wood of old barrels that had contained soap or oil or dyes, then the liquor or ale newly stored therein would taint and spoil.

Another notable ale malefaction was the taverner's payoff to City officials—or their imposters—in order to avoid seizure of stock. A servant of an investigator from the mayor's office went about The Vintry with a writing tablet in his hand, pretending he was empowered to seize ale from hucksters whose names he listed thereon for some imagined offense. In their fear of losing their ale in punishment, the sellers bribed him to allow them to keep their own brew. Another man preyed upon shopkeepers' recognitions that while doubtlessly splendid to be purveyor of victuals to royalty, it was even nicer to be paid for the privilege. Thomas Stokes, posing as an ale-fetcher to King Richard II, went to numerous brewhouses, including one called "John at the Cock on the Hoop," there marking ale barrels with an *arwehede.* This royal arrowhead insignia so scared the taverner that he immediately bought himself off from the honor of being King's provider. The guilt of Thomas the false ale-taker was proclaimed at the pillory.

Salt

Walking on through the great market of *Chepe,* Chaucer would find salt for cooking sold in various grades, colors, textures, and weights. Salt contributed more to the city's food and health than any other element except water; not only a staple spice, salt was a major preservative.[24] For meat and especially for fish, salt allowed wholesome, dependable storage throughout the winter months during which fresh slaughtering and commercial fishing were difficult either because of climate or law. Salt mined, or reduced from brine springs, or boiled off from seawater, made fortunes for towns or people capitalizing on their nearness to fresh-food sources such as the fisheries of the Baltic or North Sea.[25] Lübeck, for example, became a major Hanseatic town because Baltic herring, which fed much of Europe obliged to *fysschedays,* could be salted there and in Sweden within twenty-four hours after the catch, thus easing transport, reducing spoilage, and avoiding loss. Salzburg, in Austria, sainted the Rupert who introduced the salt industry which gave the town its name and wealth. England's best, finest-grade salt came from Lincolnshire,[26] from the great "saltwicks"—Northwich, Middle-

24. See J. Nenquin, *Salt, a Study in Economic Prehistory* (Brugge, 1961); and compare B. Gomez Miedes, *Alographia* (Ursel, 1605).

25. See A. R. Bridbury, *England and the Salt Trade in the Later Middle Ages* (Oxford, 1955); compare F. Hirth, "Notes on the Early Salt Monopoly in China," *Journal of the China Branch of the Royal Asiatic Society* 22 (1887); M. M. Postan, "The Trade of Medieval Europe: the North," *The Cambridge Economic History,* vol. 2 (Cambridge, 1952).

26. See O. G. Tomkeieff, *Life in Norman England* (New York and London, 1966), 66f.

III: Fig. 7

wich, Nantwich—while largest quantities came from Brittany's Bourgneuf Bay, making the impure but copious "bay salt." Both local and imported salt could be purchased retail in London's markets.

Salt sellers, like bakers, taverners, and brewers, had their own market neighborhood established first by custom and ratified, later, by law. Market streets such as the wine sellers' Vintry or the bakers' Bread Street kept competitive makers and merchants in such proximity that venders were encouraged to reasonable honesty and consumers were protected against certain fraudulent practices. Naturally, merchants who obeyed market regulations did not get into the court dockets; this chapter's emphasis upon the malpractitioners demonstrates not the chaos of the medieval food market but its organization, its ideals, its scrutiny of action, its protection of buyer, seller, and citizenry. To consider the way these rules might have affected the getting of the chicken into Chaucer's kitchen (with asides for meat and fish) as well as the lentils, cherries, and cheese, it is worthwhile examining the two universals otherwise neglected in analyses of food costs and laws: market time and market space.

Interesting spatial configurations of London's markets were complemented by even more surprising chronologies.

Markets and Place

London's food markets had several guises but always one guiding order—certain foods were to be sold in assigned places only, and violators of these rules of space lost their produce or their freedom. Sometimes markets were streets or lanes with enclosed shops with windows or shutters opening to the street. *Sollars* were the bayed, windowed extensions out from the building line which not only allowed natural light into the work area but also augmented display space. Other markets consisted of either permanent or temporary stalls set up adjacent to or in front of shops. Benches and stationary carts further added to opportunities to display produce. Yet other food *fairs* were entirely *nonce markets,* set up on special days and removed betweentimes. Most medieval English food markets seem to have been combinations amongst all three types. The street of the butchers, St. Nicholas Fleshshambles—a *shambles* meant a slaughterhouse—often was so obstructed with benches and tables displaying meats that pedestrians and horses could not move through the traffic congestion. During market time, the shops, stalls, and benches all were utilized; benches and tables were stored at night, lean-to stalls shuttered or removed, and after market, shops simply closed.

Markets were called *cheaps,* from the Anglo-Saxon word *ceap,* meaning "to buy." London's main market was *The Chepe,* with separate areas designated by custom as Eastchepe and Westchepe. Evening markets were conducted by candlelight, though the city government prohibited *evechepynges* in Soper Lane in 1297 because of the prevalence of thieves, rowdies, and cutpurses. Yet it had become customary to hold two markets on Feast Days in Westchepe and Cornhulle, one always extending beyond dark. Because larceny by night was easier than by daylight, *evechepynges* apparently attracted not only hucksters of food but hawkers of stolen goods, and harlots. Evening markets therefore were to close between two bells, one rung one hour before sunset, the second, one half-hour after; all buyers and sellers were to be out at the second ringing.

Whatever the market type, stalls and sellers were allowed by official ordinance to stand only in certain spots or, indeed, forbidden to stand at all. Imported lampreys from Nantes were sold at St. Margaret's Place in Bridge Street for four days after their arrival. Thames fish could be sold at the Conduit beneath the wall of St. Margaret's and beneath the wall of St. Mary Magdalen in Old Fish Street only. Later, even more stringent demarcation was ordained: Thames fish caught west of London Bridge were to be sold in Chepe near the Conduit—only; while fish taken east of the bridge were hawked in Cornhulle. However, *birlesters,* retailers of oysters, mussels, and saltfish, could not stand in any street or lane or shop but were required to move about from street to lane. Itinerant hawkers, the shell and saltfish peddlers risked confiscation of their wares if they sold from stationary positions.

Interesting political reasons caused these assertions of separate place for various types of catch, though the specific selling spots themselves became "traditional" earlier than the records date. A medieval surveyor's determination of the boundaries of Old Fish Street, for example, incor-

Pl. 17 *Herring fishermen packed their catch in salt or brine; herring merchants repacked the salt fish for shipping to various parts of Europe or for sale in local markets. Often prosperous and politically powerful guildsmen, numerous mayors of medieval London belonged to the fraternity of Fishmongers. (From the* Album of the Prague New Town Herring Market, 1619. Archives of the City of Prague, Czechoslovakia)

(Overleaf)
Pl. 18 *Not only in open markets but also in closed shops various foodstuffs were sold to the waiting public by merchants who were bound by law to carefully weigh and appraise all commodities for quality. Here a cheese merchant sells wedges of an aged cheese to a short-robed man handing him coins. The small measuring beam, with a sliding weight visible on a horizontal arm, is adjacent to the sharp knife with which the cheese was cut. (From the* Tacuinum Sanitatis, *15th century, Italian. The New York Public Library, Spencer Collection, Ms. 65, f.72v)*

17

18

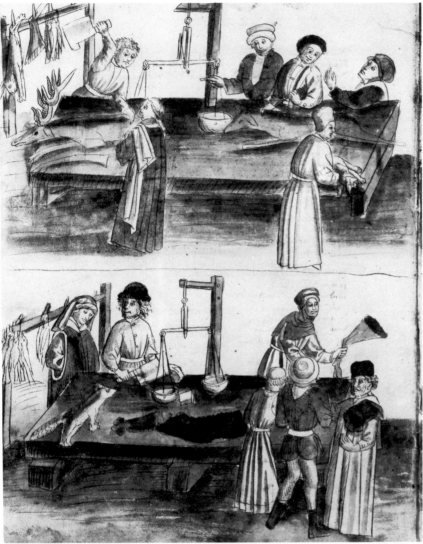

III: Fig. 8 *In this meat market, butchers offer for sale
such viands as stags, hares,
beavers, badgers, otters, partridges, cattle, pigs, and
sheep. Carcasses or parts
thereof are displayed on
spiked racks and weighed on
balance scales. Italian doctors, German peasants, and
clergymen gather round the
stalls discussing and bargain-
ing over their purchases.
(From Ulrich von Richen-
thal's* Constanzer Consilium,
*1450–70, German. The New
York Public Library, Spencer Collection, Ms. 32, pp.
48–49)*

III: Fig. 8

porates phrases such as "fish were sold here from the earliest times," or
from "time out of mind," or from "earliest remembrances." Convenience,
proximity to the waters, wharves, or portage lanes from which produce
was brought must have determined the original markets. But fierce competition between the *city sellers* and *foreigners* enforced jealous inde-
pendence of those sites.

Freemen of the City of London, enfranchised to sell goods and to pay
special taxes to the City in return, generally sold foodstuffs retail. *Foreigners* sold wholesale; *foreign* referred not only to other countries, such
as Spain's wine merchants or Italy's spicers, but to other counties in
England, thus to people not "free" of or to the City of London. Fishmongers were unusually vociferous in claiming their market rights and
sites, and far outheralded butchers' or haymongers' complaints against
foreigners who came by cart or by water and who deserved to be prohibited from retailing since they "paid no aid" nor contributed to the fortunes of the City.[27] The free fishmongers also out-Heroded the municipal officials by proclaiming injunctions against *vitaillers foreins of fish.*

27. See Salzman, *English Industries;* and R. S. Lopez, *The
Commercial Revolution of the
Middle Ages* (Englewood
Cliffs, 1971); coats of arms
and insignia of guilds appear
in J. Bromley, *The Armorial
Bearings of the Guilds of London* (London, 1961).

GRACE CHVRCHE MARKET

III: Fig. 9

To protect foreigners from unfair hindrance by the freemen, the London government insisted that all legal "foreign" venders were to be allowed their rights to sell; any who interfered with them would be jailed.

Poultry selling by foreign wholesalers and freemen retailers demonstrated dramatically the restrictions upon market place.[28] All foreign poulterers were required to stand "at the Carfukes" at Ledenhall. But those foreigners entering the city at "Neugate and Aldrichesgate" had to sell "on The Pavement" in front of the Friars Minor "near the Fountain." Freemen poulterers, forbidden to stand at Ledenhall, could sell wares only along the wall west of the Church of St. Michael on Cornhill, or stand near the Church of St. Nicholas *Flesshammeles*. And no freeman or his wife could purchase fowl from foreign (wholesale) poulterers before the hour of *prime* had rung. Thus the neck of the chicken which reached Chaucer's kitchen might have been wrung by the hands of a foreign poulterer at Ledenhall before dawn; the poet or his servant could have selected the bird in the hours before 6 A.M. However, if predawn marketing was not their habit, they would have had to patronize the freemen poulterers after morning had rung.

Herrings from Scone or Heligoland or the Sound between Sweden and Zealand in Denmark; cooking oil from Lisbon and Seville; talgar cheese from Wales: these are several amongst the diverse foods imported to medieval London and sold in special market places for alien merchants. Occasionally foreigner and freeman conjoined. *Gardeners* who sold *siliquas,* vegetables, beans, peas, lentils, and cherries and other fruits, had "from time of old" sold their produce at the side of the gate of St. Paul's churchyard. But four constituencies of folk found their

28. See P. E. Jones, *The Worshipful Company of Poulterers* (London, 1939). Henry of Huntingdon, an English chronicler, gives fascinating details of regional specialties and jealousies arising from Hereford's hegemony in herds, Winchester's in wine, Worcester's in "corn," "and for fishes," Canterbury. See J. Hampson, *The English at Table* (London, 1944), 13f.

clamor a nuisance. Complaints were made on behalf of priests saying mass, laymen praying, pedestrians and horseback riders in the street, and owners of neighboring houses. Henceforth all garden produce was to be sold from the space between the south gate of the churchyard and the garden wall of Friar Preachers at Baynard's Castle—nowhere else. Here Chaucer's household would have obtained the necessary lentils and cherries for *Farsed Chycken* to accompany the bird, bread, wine, and ale already bought; cheese and oats are the only ingredients which remain.

Markets and Time

The ringing of the hour of *prime* opened the wholesale market at Ledenhall so that cooks and regraters could buy chickens and geese. This reference to the first daylight hour of the eight *canonical hours* into which the twenty-four-hour day was separated is one of an astounding number of time rules within the food ordinances. The eight "hours" —*matins, lauds, prime, terce, sext, nones, vespers,* and *compline*—were rung on church or civic bells not only to call the faithful to prayer but to regulate work of the day. Suddenly in 1379, the same food references that had depended upon the bell now were governed by the clock. Amidst hundreds, here are a random few market times.[29] Markets at Cornhulle were to take place only between matins and nones in 1310; anything sold after the hour of nones risked forfeiture. In the market at Les Stokkes there was to be no cutting of meat after nones had rung at St. Paul's, and all meat was to be sold by vespers—for it was against the City custom to sell meat by candlelight. Foreign haymongers had to sell by the hour of nones or forfeit their hay. No cook or regrater could buy poultry at Ledenhall's stalls before prime was rung at St. Paul's; between matins and prime the wholesaler could sell to "reputable men" for their own households, but not to retailers. Futhermore, there were to be no more *evechepynges* at Cornhulle after the vespers bell was rung at the *Tun.* Foreign cheesemongers in 1377, whose cheese and butter were brought by cart and horse, had to sell all their wares at Ledenhall before nones had rung; they were forbidden to store any unsold dairy produce after nones' ringing; and no huckster could buy cheese from the foreigners before the hour of prime, or imprisonment was punishment for disobedience.

This Cheesemongers' ordinance of 1377 is followed by a municipal ordinance of 1379: no poulterer, cook, piebaker, or regrater shall go out from the city to meet foodmongers coming to it or purchase anything for resale in markets before *ten o'clock shall have struck.* Later that same year, while fish could be bought for private households, no Thames fish at specific markets could be purchased for resale before eleven o'clock. And again in 1383: no citizen might purchase any manner of fish for resale until *ten of the clokke be smyte.*

By 1412 the specific hours of the clock are mentioned for the victualers who were to keep their shops closed on two June holidays: no vintner, taverner, brewer, piebaker, or huckster would keep open after "ten of the clock" nor would sell wine, ale, fish, or flesh, boiled, roasted, or baked before "six of the clock" the next morning. Bells rang hours as they had before the prevalence of clocks, which themselves chimed as well as struck. Audible here, however, is the echo of one unappreciated, pervasive market sound: the measurers of time, the bells and clocks

III: Fig. 9 *Food merchants from various areas of England were allowed to sell their produce only in specific places and at prescribed times. At one such, vendors from London, Middlesex, Essex. Kent, and Sorre (Surrey) sit in sequence; the Londoners apparently sell vegetables, Middlesex, boar's head, and Essex sellers are butchers. Wine is in a horse-drawn cart, while other produce is conveyed via dorsers and a basket worn on a woman's head. (From Hugh Alley's* Caveatt for the City of London, *1598, English. Washington, D.C., The Folger Shakespeare Library)*

29. See a partial list in the BIBLIOGRAPHY, classification *Manuscripts,* "Time." The usual scholarly notion is that the Renaissance "discovered" time. A corrective to such nonsense is J. T. Fraser's pair of important studies: *The Voices of Time* (New York, 1966) and *Of Time, Passion and Knowledge* (New York, 1974).

III: Fig. 10

demarking time for selling chickens, time for regrating cheese, time for closing shop. These loud, clear time calls could not be ignored, or forfeited produce or prison restored accuracy to a market merchant's hearing.

Regulation of food services by time is another dimension of the sophistication of medieval London's markets, the City's civil order, and the medieval perception of time.[30] These unprepossessing documents of time embedded within the food laws suggest that the differences between medieval and modern ideas of time are dependent not so much upon the machinery for measuring time as upon the technology for making good use of that time. Candlelight was not sufficient for working pewter tableware[31] (sight for pewter is not "so profitable or so certain by night as by day") nor for filleting meat. Probably not until high-candle-power gas or electricity itself could the use of time change; light denied, there could be little night labor.

Weights and Measures

All of Chaucer's ingredients but the oats now obtained, he or his servant might make one more stop at the *ostler*, and then scurry back to the kitchen. However, all the commodities purchased had been carefully weighed and measured before or at time of sale. Formidable numbers of market documents directly associate food and cost as well as food and quality with measurements.[32] *Assizes* for weights of solids and capacity for liquids were codified early on. In fact, these laws as well as cases of their violations are the most numerous of all medieval culinary documents. Medieval systems of weights and measures were astonishingly accurate, effective, and standardized, sometimes to local but most often to city and royal templates of size, capacity, and weight.

While there are references to some nebulous, subjective judgments of quality in food pricing, such is usual only for the fully cooked "convenience" foods. For example, a Cooks' ordinance of 1378 prices best roast curlew at 6½ pence; best roast partridge, 3½ pence; best roast heron, 18 pence; best roast bittern, 20 pence; three roast pigeons, 2½ pence. All of these were "ready-to-eat," "take-out" foods. However, most other victuals were sold by more objective measure. Not surprisingly, estimates of size for establishing sale price proved as faulty as judgments of quality. "Foreign" eels (probably Dutch) earlier had been sold by size, the largest called *stobelele;* the middling, *shastele;* and the smallest, *pympernele;* but defrauding hucksters had renamed the grades and charged prime price for middling size and medium price for least eels. Henceforth, eels were sold only by weight.

Establishing prices by standards of measure was equally important for fixing duties on imports.[33] Pricing and taxing were the two major market concerns with weights and measures. The devices, numerous and ingenious, and the services associated with measurement—there were special *assayers* and *keepers* of the weighing beams—present an intriguing vocabulary best ordered by the types of food measured. Sometimes separating dry measure from liquid is awkward: coopers' *barrels* had specific capacity, for example, not only for wine but eels; however, the liquid-dry distinction permits reasonable foray into a multitude of technical terms and ideas of measurement.

Most dry goods were measured by one of two variations upon the same technique of balance: the *Small Beam* or *balance* weighed finer,

III: Fig. 10 *Fish were sold live or freshly killed or filleted or salted, according to the customer's preference. Special knives were used by fishmongers, who sold their fish by weight or size or quality according to local laws. Balance scales adjusted to the civil assize were checked regularly by inspectors appointed either by town authority or the fish-sellers' guilds. (From Ulrich von Richenthal's* Constanzer Consilium, *1450–70, German. The New York Public Library, Spencer Collection, Ms. 32, p. 51)*

30. For comparisons see R. S. Lopez, *The Three Ages of the Italian Renaissance* (Charlottesville, 1970).

31. See F. W. Robins, *The Story of the Lamp and the Candle* (London, 1939); as well as studies on pewter fabrication and decoration: H. H. Cotterell, *Pewter Down the Ages* (London, 1932); M. Bell, *Old Pewter* (London, 1905); J. Bedford, *Pewter* (New York, 1966); and A. de Navarro, *Causeries on English Pewter* (New York, 1911).

32. See B. Kisch, *Scales and Weights* (New Haven, 1965).

33. See H. A. Miskimin, *The Economy of Early Renaissance Europe* (Englewood Cliffs, 1969).

lighter goods by pounds, while the *Great Beam* or *tron* measured grosser, coarser goods, usually by hundredweight. Basically, the *Beams* were balance scales in which goods to be weighed were placed in a vessel or pan on one side of a calibrated upright, and specially assayed weights counterbalanced in a pan on the other. The weights themselves generally were metal, oftentimes nested for convenience, and stamped with official insignia of the town in which they were made or used. These weights conformed to a local or national standard; and most such standards were registered in merchants' concordances for international trade. A measure in London had its known equivalent in Cordova, Nuremberg, or Paris.

Another measurer of heavy goods was the *steelyard,* particularly useful for such as meat weighing. Rather than an equal-armed balance, this steelyard consisted of hooks on chains dependent from arms of unequal length moving on a fulcrum, and with a sliding counterweight. The *tron* sometimes was a measure of the steelyard type.

The Small Beam was either "granted" or "let" for a specific period or, indeed, for the life of the grantee. The Keeper of the Beam, for a fee, weighed for all buyers and sellers who requested it the wares appertaining to his type of measure—or *her* type, for the grant of the Small Beam often went to a woman. The King had requested of London's mayor that Jacobina la Lumbard hold it; but apologetically, the Mayor revealed he had already awarded it to a man, for life. Later, the Beam belonging to the Chamber of the City was rented for ten pounds yearly, payable quarterly. In addition to weighing goods, the Beam Keeper also served as an official calibrator for personal or commercial beams. All weighing devices in the same locality thus conformed to the standard of the official Beam, in turn measured against a more "universal" weight which in England was called the *King's Weight.* Imported goods were forbidden to be sold by *subtile* or light weight, but only by that of "our Lord the King." Most large houses owned sets of weights and measures for their pantries and storehouses. A series of these, "a beam with scales," "four pairs of balances," and "one brass auncer" (a very small balance) are listed in a fourteenth-century household inventory.

Since the unit of measure for the Small Beam was the pound or its subdivisions, goods weighed on the Small Beam themselves were called *avoirs du poys,* our modern avoirdupois, and included fine wares sold or taxed by the pound. Spice weighing exemplifies the difficulty in assigning by type all goods to one or the other of the two Beams. Generally the Small Beam was associated with silk and "diverse spices." However, spicery in medieval England meant not only spices for cooking or medicine or preservation, but also coloring agents and other commercial stuffs. Furthermore, larger quantities of spices were sold according to special weights in which one hundredweight equaled 112 pounds, one pound equaled 15 ounces, except for powdered or confected spices which had yet another weight, 12 ounces to the pound!

Among special weights for products associated with food was the goldsmith's weight, by which much tableware as well as kitchen gear was appraised.[34] Weight was expressed in pounds, shilling, and pence; in 1371 three dozen silver porridge bowls called *esqueles* or *esquielles*—with a specific liquid capacity of one-half quart—weighed "by the goldsmith's weight" 49 pounds, 12 shillings, 7 pence for raw material plus 6

34. See A. O. Curle, "Domestic Candlesticks from the Fourteenth to the Eighteenth Century," *Proceedings of the Society of Antiquaries of Scotland* 11 (1925–26); and M. and C. Quennell, *A History of Everyday Things in England* 1066–1179.

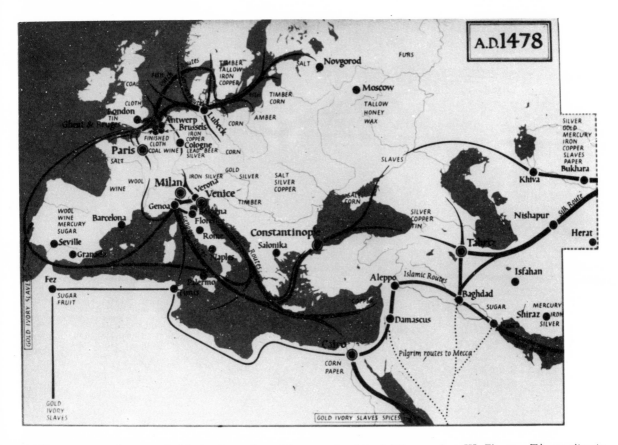

The map image contains the following labels:

A.D.1478

Novgorod · FURS · SALT

Moscow · TALLOW HONEY WAX

TIMBER TALLOW IRON COPPER

TIMBER CORN

AMBER

CORN

SLAVES

London · TIN · CLOTH

Ghent & Bruges

Antwerp · Brussels · FINISHED CLOTH · COAL WINE

Cologne · IRON COPPER · LEAD SILVER BEER

Paris · SALT

Lübeck

GOLD SILVER

IRON SILVER · SILVER

SALT SILVER COPPER

SILVER GOLD MERCURY IRON COPPER SLAVES PAPER · Bukhara

Khiva

WOOL WINE

Milan · Verona · Venice

Genoa · Bologna · Florence · Rome

TIMBER

WOOL WINE MERCURY SUGAR · Barcelona

Seville · Granada

Naples

Salonika

Constantinople

SILVER COPPER TIN

Nishapur · SILK ROUTE

Herat

Tabriz

Isfahan

Fez · SUGAR FRUIT

Palermo · Tunis

COPPER

Aleppo · Islamic Routes

Baghdad · SUGAR

Shiraz · MERCURY IRON SILVER

Damascus

Cairo · CORN PAPER

Pilgrim routes to Mecca

GOLD IVORY SLAVES

GOLD IVORY SLAVES

GOLD IVORY SLAVES SPICES

shillings tax and cost of fabrication, thus 70 pounds, 19 shillings, 4 pence, total.

While certain cruder goods such as hay were sold by shipload or cart-load by "foreign" wholesalers, there were smaller configurations which had more accurate weightings than their names imply. Hay for domestic animals was sold by half-load or *quarter,* as well as by *boteles,* which were small bundles, and *fesses,* trusses larger than *boteles.* While seemingly general rather than specific quantities, in numerous court cases hay sellers are accused of overcharging and underweighting. More significantly, other goods, such as charcoal for cooking, were sold by *the quarter* which had a very specific quantification. Some charcoal venders were sentenced to the pillory when their *quarters* did not pass the expected assay of eight bushels per *quarter,* theirs being deficient by one or two bushels each. One document lists six separate cases of underweight *quarters,* while another demonstrates a magistrate's compassion for an aged though perfidious charcoalmonger whose eight *quarters* were each one bushel short; his sentence to the pillory was reduced to the time necessary to burn his empty coal sacks beneath him. A *quarter* of charcoal sold in 1405 for not more than ten pence.

In addition to bushels as a measure of capacity, there was also the *peck.* Both were required to be stamped with the Seal of the City or the Seal of the Alderman. *Dorsers,* special baskets for goods loaded on pack horses, and carrying cargo of such fish as conger, plaice, and gurnard, had an exact capacity equivalent to one bushel of oats.

Such dry measures exemplify but do not complete the extraordinary diversity of medieval measures sealed to standard by law. A merchant

III: Fig. 11 *The startling international food-trade routes are suggested by this map of Europe in 1478. Sugar from Seville, beer from Cologne, and honey from Russia are amongst the commodities which were imported to medieval city markets and there regulated by stiff laws for their taxing, quality, and sale. (From the map by John Woodcock in Colin McEvedy's* Penguin Atlas of Medieval History, *Harmondsworth, 1961)*

III: Fig. 12

dealing in several localities or in international markets either had to commit to memory a formidable set of names and numbers or carry a manual of standard weights. Extant merchants' manuals give concordances for weights and measures, town to town and nation to nation.[35] In medieval England, for both wet and dry measurements, most local standards ultimately conformed to the King's.

Especially for the medieval wine and ale trades, a huge variety of liquid measures evolved through the years. A Coopers' ordinance of 1413 defines a *barrel* as consisting of 30 gallons, a *ferdkyn* as 7½ gallons. A *kilderkyn* seems to have held the capacity of some portion of a barrel, probably one-half. Such multigalloned vessels held not only liquids such as wines and ales, and such other more viscous substances as oil, soap, and woad, but also eels. A venal fishmonger had constructed for himself 260 barrels and ferdkyns for eel-selling which, after their confiscation and assay by the King's Standard, proved wanting several gallons each. *Tankards* for fetching brewwater had the capacity of three gallons, and *tynes* were gigantic tubs but documents differ in ascribing exact measure. *Tuns*, in which wine or ale were stored and then sold from, measured, for the *tun mascill*, 252 gallons.

Wines and ales were sold in officially marked measuring vessels ranging down from the *gallon* through the two-quart *potell*, the *quart*, to the often-banned but not abandoned pint *chopyn*, and the half-pint *gylle*. Butter was measured by liquid, not solid, standard, suggesting it probably was sold in liquid or semifluid form, measured by the half-quart *esquielle*. *Cuves* (tubs used in brewery), *buckets*, *butts* (Richard III drowned his relative in a butt of Malmsey), *kemelynes* and *cumelins*

35. For examples of commercial treatises and ledgers, see the superb catalogue to the exhibition *The Secular Spirit*, The Cloisters of The Metropolitan Museum of Art, New York, 1975, especially 118–30 and 144–53.

III: Fig. 13

III: Fig. 14 *Butchers' scales which weighed heavy carcasses and sides of meat generally were steelyard scales. Sometimes produce was hung on the hook at the end of strong chains, and a weight slid along the calibrated post. (Iron-and-brass scale, 15th–16th century, Spanish. New York, The Metropolitan Museum of Art, Harris Brisbane Dick Fund, 1957)*

(both brewing tubs and coolers), *costret, cag, cade*—these casks also had their capacities established by custom and confirmed by law.

Medieval London's weights and measures suggest a mercantile sophistication comparable to such highly organized and elegant Mediterranean markets as Venice and Florence.[36] While English spice documents, for example, were not quite so astonishing as Italian import bills listing 288 different spices,[37] nevertheless London's food markets displayed estimable variety of domestic and imported products, scrupulous standards for their measuring, and just regulations avoiding their abuse. Confirming impressions of medieval London from such other sources as Chaucer's literature, the market archives preserve the discrepancies between civic ideal and human foible. Codes for proper market behavior were founded upon theoretical hope for ethical order tempered by practical expectation of temptations and tendencies toward fraud. The delightful vagrancies of Chaucer's Miller, Cook, and Pardoner are not dissimilar to those of the Pepperers and Spicers of Soperlane who tended to dub up, dress up for deception their poor stuff to sell as choice, and who moistened their saffron, ginger, and cloves to increase their weight and price.

One final aspect of London's food laws and larcenies is notable: the punishments for victualing crimes. As example to potential deceivers, tradesmen on the pillory or hucksters on the *thewe* had burned beneath themselves the objects of dishonesty: the rotten meat, putrid pigeons, or falsely measured charcoal sacks. Or the malefactor wore a necklace of the underweight bread or fraudulent alemeasure while the town crier proclaimed the punishment. Repeat offenders were threatened with suspension from trade. More serious food crimes were punishable by prison. Intentional violations of market times and market spaces resulted in forfeit of produce. Such confiscated goods benefited the town; underweight bread loaves fed Newgate prisoners, and wine casks emptied of unsound vintage paid the public crier.

This concern for fitting punishment to perfidy is more than humorous justice in, for example, forcing the adulterator of wines to drink his foul brew. After investigation of the "facts" of an accusation, or after trial, punishment was immediate and related directly to some aspect of public health. Politics of the xenophobic fishmongers notwithstanding, the purpose served by the rigid rules for market places and ringing of market hours, as well as for the sealing of weights and measures, was public order. Furthermore, food rules demonstrated the medieval English passion to protect the physical environment. Butchers were granted by the City—in return for a boar's head at Christmas—a special property of land near the Fleet River so that blood from their slaughtering would not pollute the channels of the streets. Salomon Salomon's twelve *barrels* and one *kilderkyn* of stinking, putrefying eels, nosed out by a vigilant inspector, were carted far outside the town and buried deeply so as not to infect the air with horrid stench. Here once again, the City's attitude toward its citizens and the environment which supports them is demonstrated by its foods and their markets.

36. See Archibald Lewis, *Naval Power and Trade in the Mediterranean A.D. 500–1100* (Princeton, 1951); compare F. Braudel, *Capitalism and Material Life 1400–1800,* trans. M. Kochan (New York, 1974).

37. See R. S. Lopez, *Medieval Trade in the Mediterranean World* (London, 1955); for the maps detailing the trade routes of such imports, see Colin McEvedy, *The Penguin Atlas of Ancient History* (Harmondsworth, 1967), as well as his *The Penguin Atlas of Medieval History* (Harmondsworth, 1961); compare H. H. Kimble, *Geography in the Middle Ages* (London, 1935). A startling introduction to personalities and tribulations of merchantmen is the selection of eighty astonishing letters from the Cairo *Geniza* translated by S. D. Goitein in his *Letters of Medieval Jewish Traders* (Princeton, 1973).

Fountain, River, Privy, Pot

MEDIEVAL LONDON'S POLLUTED WATERS

IN the midst of the main London food market of Chepe was a meeting place for foodcraftsmen, a selling site for certain commodities, and an ingredient source for others: the water fountain and pipes of the Great Conduit of Chepe. Here cooks and bakers drew water for their boiling pots and dough troughs, taverners and brewers fetched water for making ale and malt. Fishermen and fishmongers washed their freshly caught Thames fish and desalted their salt-preserved imported fish from the North Sea and the Baltic. Butchers and poulterers washed their meats of blood and viscera, readying for sale. And citizens carted Conduit water to their kitchens for cooking and drinking.

The Conduit system was complex, having not only the main fountains and pipes but subsidiary branches within the markets of Eastchepe and Westchepe as well as Conduit extensions serving households, neighborhood wards, and larger sections of the City. London's piped water system had its own keepers, keys, and customers; special problems of waste, neglect, cupidity, and pollution; and selfish abuses of public water property infrequently balanced by altruistic citizenship.

IV: Fig. 1 *Wines and foods tasted by the process called* credence *were then served to the nobility of State or Church. Wine is carried in by servants under guard in a gigantic multigallon tankard. Unable to enter the precincts of the cardinals at the Council of Constance, the servants deposit the victuals at the gate behind which a group of bishops attest to the provisions' purity and safety by tasting. They drink from* artichoke glasses. *(From Ulrich von Richenthal's* Constanzer Conzilium, *1450–70, German. New York Public Library, Spencer Collection, Ms. 32, p. 227)*

IV

1. See Dorothy Hartley, *Water in England* (London, 1964); F. W. Robins, *The Story of Water Supply* (New York, 1946); and H. R. Vallentine, *Water in the Service of Man* (Harmondsworth, 1967).

2. For intriguing examinations of "historical refuse" see E. L. Sabine, "Latrines and Cesspools of Medieval London," *Speculum* 9 (1934), 303–21; D. Hartley and M. Elliot, *The Life and Work of the People of England* (New York, 1929); C. Singer *et al*, *A History of Technology*, vol. 2 (New York and London, 1956), 680–94; and Sir Walter Besant, *Medieval London, Historical and Social* (London, 1906).

3. On scavengers and scavenging, see Lynn Thorndike, "Sanitation, Baths, and Street Cleaning in the Middle Ages and Renaissance," *Speculum* 3 (1928), 192–203; E. L. Sabine, "City Cleaning in Medieval London," *Speculum* 12 (1937), 19–43; G. Salusbury, *Street Life in Medieval England* (Oxford, 1948); and R. Mitchell and M. Leys, *A History of London Life* (New York, 1958), chapt. 2.

London's Conduit water was diverted via surface and underground aqueducts from rivers, streams, and brooks.[1] These water courses themselves were important resources for catching fish and making beer, cleaning fowl and fish, and milling grains. For transporting food produce and merchants to and from the City, as well as for power source for mills and mechanical devices, London's rivers and smaller waters were essential to the city's victualers. Householders also drew water for their kitchens directly from river bank and brookside. Clearly, such multiple uses of these naturally flowing waters, as well as of their artificial channelings in the Conduit system, made success against water fouling vital.

However, London's water sources were also the City's waste disposals.[2] Kitchen garbage, excrement from privies and chamber pots, offal from slaughterhouses, detritus from cookshops and taverns, domestic animals' excreta, confiscated, putrefied, and contraband foods and wines all were dumped into London's waters. Thus no consideration of water "intake" is complete that ignores "output" of the human body or of the body politic.

Since no single element was as indispensable as water to medieval London's food and health, stinking, reeking waters were a cause for concern, agitation, and legislation to citizens, municipal officials, and the King himself. Water waste and water pollution then as now resulted from inadvertent stupidity of individuals or institutions, as well as from felonious use of public resources for private greed. Against water malpractices, effective laws controlled water usage, exacted fees for foodcraftsmen's water privileges, prescribed financing of services and improvements, and defined responsibilities for cleansing waterways.[3] Enforced by punitive tax, property forfeits, and imprisonment for malefactors, the civil rules document an unsavory aspect of medieval cookery, yet an admirable struggle to prevent abuse of the three most significant water sources beyond wells: the Conduit, the river, and the brook.

THE CONDUIT

The "Great Conduit" brought water into the center of London so that, as a 1345 ordinance stated, the rich and middling might obtain water for preparing food, and the poor might drink. Municipally appointed Keepers of the Conduit were required to prevent water waste, collect fees from users, and check, cleanse, repair, maintain, and protect the whole system. Among their greatest troubles were the perfidies of the brewers, taverners, and malt makers, and other food and drink craftsmen whose inordinate use and wastage of water caused shortages for those the Conduit originally was built to serve.

Water Waste

The Conduit Keeper in 1310 pledged under oath to keep brewers and fishmongers from wasting water; nor would the keeper himself sell water. Later, Conduit officials assessed brewers, cooks, and fishmongers for money to be used for Conduit repairs and maintenance. By 1357, so blatant had wastage become that householders from the Conduit neighborhood complained in court against brewers and their giant water-carrying tubs, the *tynes*. As sanction, any brewer caught filling a tyne lost his vessel to the Conduit Keeper. This punishment failed as deterrent. Eight years later, in 1345, a water shortage was blamed on the brewers and taverners. Thereafter they were forbidden to make ale or malt with Conduit water. Violators of that rule lost their multigallon tankards and tynes, paid fines, and risked jail; forty pence was penalty for first offense; the water receptacles plus money for second and third; for a fourth misdeed, they went to prison. Length of sentence was at the mayor's discretion. In 1415, brewers rented the fountains and the large upper pipes of the Conduit; however, they also infringed upon the small lower pipes reserved for common folk. An ordinance forbidding this imposed a six-shilling, eight-pence fine for each offense.

Water Protection

Account Books of Conduit Keepers detail the care and the special problems of so important a water source.[4] The keepers recorded the monies collected for use of the Conduit from specific householders and foodcraftsmen, publicly listing the dues-defaulting wretches; the books enumerate illegal vessels confiscated and then redeemed by cash pledge. Salary lists for Conduit personnel are particularly intriguing. Wages per day were augmented by stipends for drink, or with the refreshing wines or ales themselves; from this drink allocation, called the "noon quench" or *nuncheon,* may come the modern word "luncheon." Not only did employees repair and extend the waterpipes, maintain and improve all facilities and fountains, but they were charged with investigating the Conduit when it was thought to be poisoned, *esclandre de poyson.* This last marks a major vulnerability of the public water system.[5] References are frequent to real or imagined poisonings and the grand, superstitious methods to overcome them—Chaucer's greedy Pardoner, after all, peddled pigs' bones as saints' relics capable of curing poisoned waters.[6]

Conduit Improvements

Private enterprise and municipal initiative cooperated in remedying water distresses, as well as in increasing water services.[7] A group of Fleet Street citizens, for instance, no longer willing to abide their houses and cellars flooded and their goods ruined when Conduit pipes and watermains broke, built at their own cost an *aventum,* a protective vent for the overflow of the public aqueduct. They promised to restore all pipes to their original position if their new expediency any way violated the Conduit's or the city's welfare. Another year, wealthy Londoners, recognizing the utility for their own kitchens of a subsidiary conduit, personally funded its building, giving surety against infringement upon the main pipes. Here public-water projects were sponsored and paid by private individuals—no doubt for their personal gain as much as for their patriotism—with provision for restitution to the municipality in case of damage to the public good.

THE RIVER

While London's many streams ultimately served the city as water supply as well as sewer, several of them became "lost rivers"[8] because of natural changes or because of medieval engineering interventions. Thames, Fleet, and Tyburn[9] were three of the fifteen waterways which suffered depredations by silt and sediments, human carelessness pollut-

4. See the BIBLIOGRAPHY classification, *Water.* See also Lynn White, Jr., *Medieval Technology and Social Change* (Oxford, 1962); Frederick Tout, *Medieval Town Planning* (Manchester, 1948); J. Van Veen, *Dredge, Drain, Reclaim* (The Hague, 1962); S. J. Fockema Andreae, "Embanking and Drainage Authorities in the Netherlands," *Speculum* 27 (1952), 158–67; and C. H. Talbot, *Medicine in Medieval England* (London, 1967).

5. The relationship between water and health is discussed in numerous investigations of the medieval plagues, particularly P. Ziegler, *The Black Death* (New York, 1969); Charles Mullett, *The Bubonic Plague and England* (Lexington, 1956); Frank Wilson, *The Plague in Shakespeare's London* (London, 1963); compare also Anna Campbell, *The Black Death and Men of Learning* (New York, 1931).

6. The Pardoner's *Prologue* to his *Tale,* ll. 350–65, and the *Prologue* to the *Canterbury Tales,* l. 700.

7. Compare Baron A. de Calonne, *La vie municipale au XVme siècle dans le nord de la France* (Paris, 1880).

8. See N. J. Barton, *Lost Rivers of London* (London, 1962).

9. See Roger Griffiths, *A Description of the River Thames* (London, 1758); J. Ashton, *The Fleet: Its River, Prison, and Marriages* (London, 1939); E. De Mare, *London's Riverside* (London, n.d.); and E. Howe, *A Short Guide to the Fleet River* (London, n.d.).

10. See L. Salzman, *English Life in the Middle Ages* (New York, 1960), 276f.; Christopher Lloyd, *The British Seaman, 1200–1860* (London, 1968); and *Flanders in the Fifteenth Century* (Detroit, 1960); and consult the BIBLIOGRAPHY classification *Fish* for numerous original medieval documents.

11. See the BIBLIOGRAPHY classification *Nets* for samples of twelfth- through sixteenth-century sources.

Pl. 19 *Probably drawn around 1153 for the engineer who completed the plan for the water-inflow and sewage system of Canterbury cathedral, this remarkable scheme describes the paths of the water brought from outside the cathedral walls (after passage through a conduit house, lead pipes, and five settling tanks). For drinking, washing, irrigating gardens (the* herbarium), *cooling wine in the* cellarium, *circulating in the fishpond (the* piscina), *and flushing the latrines of the* necessarium, *the elaborate system utilized piped water augmented by rainwater. Kept in octofoil reservoirs, this "artificial" system had a back-up series of natural wells (e.g., the* puteus *in the* cloister). (From the Canterbury Psalter or Psalter of Eadwine, 12th century, English. Cambridge, Trinity College Library, Ms. R71.1, f. 284b, 285)*

ing clean waters, and artificial wallings, diversions, dammings, and burials beneath urban construction. Both the favorable and the destructive changes in London's water resources directly affected the food trades which caused some of these changes. Problems of pollution as well as examples of benevolent water stewardship connected the state of the rivers with the interests of catchers and sellers and buyers of fish, butchers, abbots and abbesses of important monasteries, and King Edward III.

Fisheries

The most frequent of all medieval river documents pertain to fishing. Since fresh fish were so important to menus of all classes of London's citizens, fishing and sale of fish were among the city's most significant industries.

Ordinances determined fishing seasons for specific varieties of fish.[10] Laws specified places for fishing and emphasized minutely the types of nets, their sizes and meshes, and when, where, and how they were to be used. So clever were the violations of the laws, and so angry the complaints against fish destruction, that the hundreds of legislative injunctions and case records would make a praiseworthy study entitled "Conservation of Medieval Fish." Illegal fishing nets not of the assize fixed by the Guildhall were publicly burned in the marketplace; their users fined, pilloried, or jailed. Nets with minuscule meshes indiscriminately caught all fish, causing "kills" of specific fish otherwise protected, depletion of fry and hatchlings, interference with important food sources—and a floating, smelly skim of dead fish on London's waters.

Fishermen were apprehended for using such "false" nets as the *kyddle, tromekeresnet, pursnet, draynet, stakenet, forestat, stalker, coanet* (or *codnet*), *smeltnet, hebbyngnettes, treinkes,* or *weirs*.[11] Masters of the Guild of Fishmongers, consortia of fishermen, the Conservator or the Keeper of the Thames, and the Surveyor of Nets investigated complaints, testified against violators of the river, and enforced ordinances against water and fish abuse.

Almost all fish in almost all seasons were to be caught with nets having two-inch meshes. However, for very small fishes, or the particularly delectable fry of others, nets of narrower mesh were necessary and permitted in season. Worthy fishermen testified in 1386 before London's mayor and aldermen that "since time out of mind" nets of one-inch mesh had been used for smelts and *gojons* for fishing beginning on February 2nd, fifteen days before Candlemas, and ending on March 25th, the feast of Our Lady in Lent, and this was just and proper since the tiny fish slipped through the spaces of nets with larger mesh and could not be caught. However, since *smeltnets* of the one-inch assize were illegally used during times other than permitted, causing wanton destruction of fish large and small, any fisherman desiring to use such nets was required to store them throughout the year at the Guildhall, with visiting privileges for checking and repairing them, redeeming them only at the smelt season.

A fourteenth-century shortage of seasonable fish in the Thames was caused by clerical greed exploiting certain fishes' natural habits. Fish that swam into coves on the land owned by the abbot of Stratford and the abbess of Berkyng would be forced by ebb tide farther inland to water-filled ditches; the two dignitaries were accused in court as

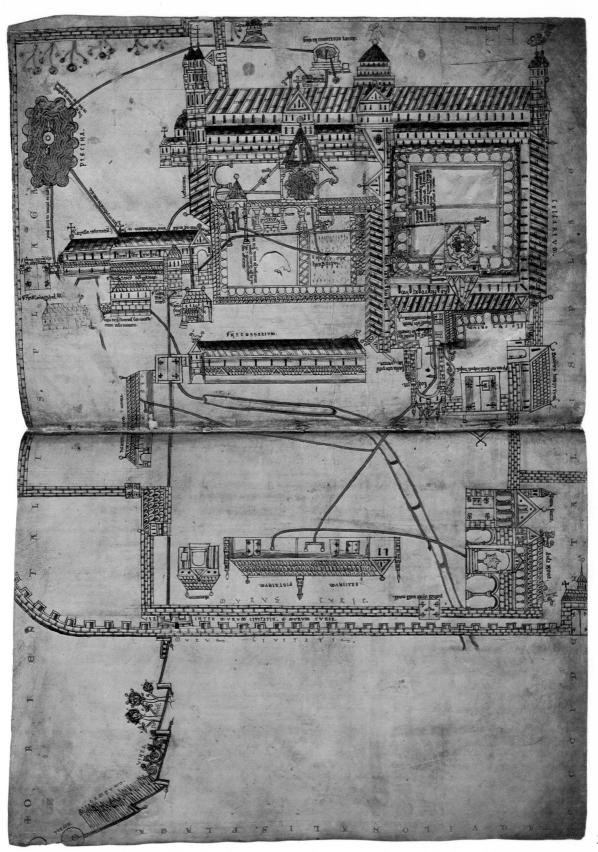

19

20

"destroyers of fish" for renting out these ditches to people who, using *weirs* and other *engyns,* would catch all fish great and small.

12. See E. L. Sabine, "Butchering in Medieval London," *Speculum* 8 (1933), 335f.

Butcheries

On *fyssche days* fishmongers stood at a market place called *Les Stokkes,* while in that same place butchers sold their wares on *flessche days.*[12] Animals were brought live to the markets and there slaughtered in the *fleshshambles*—or were, until King Edward III insisted otherwise. The King was infuriated with London officials because of dangerous malpractices of butchers and beast slaughterers who dumped blood, offal, and entrails directly into the Thames. On June 8th, and again on August 8th of 1369, he required that slaughtering of beasts take place outside the City, and that the *Bochersbrigge,* from which unsalable or putrefied animal innards were dumped into the river, be pulled down.

London's leaders dragged their feet; Edward's injunctions against the bloody butchers' fouling the air and waterways increased in irritated expressions both from personal pique at being ignored and civil urgency. Well into the last years of his long reign (1327 to 1377), the King inveighed against defilement of his river, especially by people in the food trades. In 1372, rushes, garbage, dirt, and harmful matter from the city and environs of London were still daily flung into the Thames so that the watercourse was narrowed enough to impede shipping. Odorous mud in England's rivers oozed past King Edward into later centuries bearing such Swiftian trophies as sweepings from butchers' stalls, dung, guts, blood, drowned puppies, stinking sprats, all drenched in mud, dead cats, and turnip tops tumbling down the sluggish flood.

Water Access

Clever entrepreneurs abused the river in other ways than by fouling it. Amusing documents testify to ingenuity of illegal private uses of river property, to the nuisance and loss of the citizenry. Though buildings and walled estates were built at the water's edge, and their inhabitants drew water and fished therefrom, common people had free access to the Thames through various "gates" and stairs. The "Great Gate of the Templars," for example, always had been open to the public for fetching water, for trade, and for use of a communal toilet. The Prior of St. John of Jerusalem, however, one year began refusing passage through his gate, antagonizing the citizenry; moreover, he steadfastly refused to maintain the public latrine.

Others controlled wharves and stairs to the river for personal advantage, not by public assignment. They impeded Londoners' access to the Thames for drawing cooking water, washing, or relieving themselves, and charged for use of river property. Egregious petty extortions are recorded such as that of the Master of St. Katherine's opposite the Tower of London, who collected payment for passage to the river—a halfpenny for a jar of water—or illegally confiscated property in its stead: a silver covercle, twelve blocks of stone, a scoop, a bottle from a woman washing in the river, a towel from another—even one penny each from every poor beggar coming to public celebrations of St. Katherine's feast night. Acts of mean-minded knavery, such nuisance fees from a numerous populace could be parlayed into decent income. Only finite shorelines curbed the sly and their water rascalities.

Pl. 20 *Outside the monastery walls of the* Grande Chartreuse, *three monks (or lay brothers,* donates) *fish with net and line on an upper pond; another rows his boat in the lower. Waters are divided by a watergate with a mechanism for raising and lowering water levels, like canal locks. Since the Cistercian order forbade eating flesh except for occasional fish, the fishermen probably are preparing for a feastday. (From the* Belles Heures *of Jean, Duke of Berry, f.97v; 15th century, French. New York, The Metropolitan Museum of Art, The Cloisters Collection)*

IV: Fig. 2 *London's Thames River banks accommodated commercial activity with multiple docks, wharves, loading platforms, and stairs. Inland, right, is a major market cross,* Cheapcrosse; *forward, the* Stilliarde *or steelyard, warehouses, and offices of the wealthy Hanse merchants. Produce ships carrying eels, herrings, wines, and spices unloaded at such commercial ladings as* Three Cranes. *Bells and clocks of St. Paul's Church regulated market hours for selling imported and domestic produce. (From a View of the City of London, J. C. Visscher, 1616. London Topographical Society)*

13. See the BIBLIOGRAPHY classification *Water.*

The River as Sewer

Noisome river filth was complained about constantly.[13] In 1345, London's mayor judged the Thames at the *portus,* or dock, of "Douegate" as so dreadfully polluted that water fetchers and carters could no longer draw from it to serve the community with drinking and cooking water. The remedy: dock and waters henceforth were to be cleansed by a specially appointed group of five carters paid by taxes collected from dock users. Either group which defaulted, cleaners or payers, was to be punished by imprisonment.

Earlier, in 1290, a Carmelite monastery on the Fleet River petitioned King Edward I because accumulated filth caused unbearable stench, interfering with divine service and causing deaths among resident monks. Along the Thames, the Friar Preachers, the Bishop of Sarum, and assorted suffering neighbors pleaded for protection against illegal dumping in the rivers, prohibited by a royal proclamation of 1309 commanding that house garbage be carried to the Thames, thence out of the city by *dongebotes,* or householders would be fined and charged cartage expenses. However, royal and municipal complaints as well as pollution alarms were sporadic until the mid-fourteenth century; suddenly there was an efflorescence of laments and legislation against water pollution.

A Year of Great Stink

Thirteen fifty-seven may have been a Year of Great Stink. In its more definitive form, "The Year of the Great Stink," that title was bestowed on the nearly uninhabitable London by Victorian critics and parliamentarians during a nineteenth-century pollution emergency of the Thames which forced construction of underground sewage disposal.[14] Five hundred years earlier, stench imperiled London. Excited proclamations by King Edward III depicted both Thames and Fleet rivers as smelling so horribly that dumping of garbage and detritus was strictly forbidden. Another royal edict reminded the mayor and sheriffs of London that in the city's honorable past, waters had been clean and the health of the city praised. But now along the Thames, King Edward found *laystowes* (laystalls or defecation depots), various accumulated filth, and abysmal stench arising therefrom, endangering citizens dwelling within the city and others traveling the river. As precaution against peril and for preservation of London's honor, the King commanded cleansing of filth forthwith.

Yet another document dated 1357 detailed methods for waste disposal and river redemption. No one was permitted to throw household rubbish, earth, gravel, or dung from dwellings or stables into the rivers. All waste was to be carted outside the city by the *rakyers,* the street-cleaning rakers, to *dongebotes* (dungboats), and thereon transported away without anything being dumped into the Thames. The purposes: to save the river; to preserve usage of the quays; to avoid increasing the destructive filthiness of the water and its banks. Anyone violating this proclamation faced prison and such other stern punishment as civil authority decided.

These 1357 documents among other pollution complaints of the same year may represent fortuitous convergence, not olfactory crisis. While evidence is not yet complete, it seems likely that social, political, and natural circumstances coalesced in the warm summer of 1357, causing eutrophication of the already burdened river. In so hot a season, Ben Jonson later asked, how dared nostrils attempt smelling a river "when every clerke eates artichokes and peason, laxative lettus, and such windie meate?"

Monastic Water Systems

Castle compounds and monastic communities were the aquatic microcosms of the city. The pleasures and perils of London's waters were experienced in small within the precincts of Canterbury or of Fountains Abbey.[15] The Yorkshire Cistercian house called Fountains Abbey utilized the river Skell as well as the nearby streams for an elaborate water system of millponds, fishponds, garden and orchard irrigations, drinking fountains, running washing-water supplies, and sewage disposals. There was even running water for the *misericord,* the chamber close by the infirmary to which dying monks were taken for a ritual bathing of their bodies before burial. Canterbury's twelfth-century water plan ingeniously channeled the river Stour for the needs of the church and the kitchen. With special conduits and disposal channels for all major buildings, with natural flushings of the cookhouse and the necessary houses, with superb garden fountains and holy-water fonts—such sophisticated water systems suffered problems of polluted-water inflow and polluting outflow similar to those of London.

THE BROOK AND THE FOSSE

Distinctions among river, brook, and *fosse* might rankle a modern hydrologist but they adhere to the nomenclature of the medieval water

14. Carlton Chapman's delightful article, "The Year of the Great Stink," *The Pharos* (1973), traces medieval through modern sewage plans and plants.

15. See F. H. Crossley, *The English Abbey* (New York, 1936); A. H. Gardner, *Outline of English Architecture* (London, 1945); Sir Niklaus Pevsner, *The Buildings of England* (London, 1951); and the informative pamphlets published by Fountain's Abbey, Ripon, England. Compare Whitney Stoddard, *Monastery and Cathedral in France* (Middletown, 1966).

16. See A. S. Foord, *Springs, Streams, and Spas of London* (London, 1920); F. W. Reader, "On Pile Structures in the Wallbrook," *Journal of the Archaeological Society* 60 (1903), 137–204; C. R. Smith, "Observations on Roman Remains Recently Found in London," *Archaeologia* 29 (1842); R. Bruce-Mitford, *Recent Archaeological Excavations in Britain* (London, 1952). Particularly fascinating background material is found in the extraordinary Monte Cassino Codex, *De Aquis,* attributed to Petrus Diaconus, c. 1168–1170; see Clemens Herschel, *Frontinus and the Water Supply of the City of Rome* (Boston, 1899), and the revision and translation by Charles Bennett, *Frontinus* (London, 1925).

17. See Lawrence Wright, *Clean and Decent: The Fascinating History of the Bathroom and Water Closet* (New York, 1960); Elizabeth Donno, on Sir John Harrington's water closet, *A New Discourse on a Stale Subject called the Metamorphosis of Ajax* (New York, 1962); and Reginald Reynolds, *Cleanliness and Godliness* (Garden City, 1946) with fine illustrations of "garderobes" and similar latrines.

record keeper. *Brook* here refers to a natural watercourse, narrower and shorter than a river. A *fosse* was a man-made channel, ditch, or moat or an enlarging, deepening, and walling of a small natural watercourse. Both brook and *fosse* provided water for culinary purposes. The important Walbrook (or Wall Brook) exemplifies the special problems of the medieval small waterway,[16] the methods for overcoming its pollution, and the intelligent utilization of rentals and fees to preserve its cleanliness.

The Walbrook waterway ultimately reached the Thames but first passed Finsbury Moor and meandered through those sections of London listed in a 1383 document as the Wards of Colemanstret, Bradstret, Chepe, Walbrok, Vintry, and Douegate—which included in the fourteenth century both private houses and commercial premises. Certain foulings of the brook were identical to those of the river; and the more polluted the brook, the more defiling its effect upon the river.

Household Debris

Cleaning the brook was accomplished in various ways: one Latin document dated 1288 demanded that dung and filth be removed from the watercourse by reinstalling "rakes" upon every tenement from the Moor to the Thames.[17] Such rakes or grates stopped dropped kitchen debris and fecal matter before they could fall into the waters below. Detritus then was collected and carted out of town.

A Brewer's Stewardship

More direct control over Walbrook's cleansing was achieved by leasing the Moor as well as the custody of the watercourse. A brewer named Thomas atte Ram was allowed use of the Moor and the water required for his ale-making, rent-free for seven years. In return he properly cared for the Moor, cleansed and cleared the whole watercourse. For his efforts, he collected twelve pence yearly for each latrine built by others on the borders of the waterway, and kept anything valuable he or his servants found in scavenging through the junk. Thus the brewer derived free use of water necessary to his craft, free access to public property, plus "income" via latrine funds and collectibles; the City achieved protection and conservation of both land and watercourse.

Public and private need here were profitably balanced. However, Thomas the Brewer's seven-year charge was over in 1381. Whether he or the municipality decided to part their ways or serendipity or death interfered, the records do not tell. Two years after his tenure, the watercourse once again was stopped up by dung and mud. Aldermen of the six wards through which the watercourse ran determined who owned houses or stables from which filth fell, reported violators' names, numbers, and types of pollution offenses. City officials thus reassumed responsibility for pollution control as well as latrine-privilege fees. Private and public enterprises thereafter alternated, with Moor lands sometimes cultivated as vegetable gardens and sometimes vacant. By 1415, the neglected Moor and Walbrook waters, carrying with them the flow from a public toilet, frequently flooded cellars, houses, and lanes, causing intolerable conditions. A municipal scheme eliminated the offending latrine, crisscrossed the Moor with gardens—let at proper rents—and built a new public convenience within the walls of the City upon the *fosse* of Walbrook.

The Walbrook waterway *outside* the City walls of London was called brook, and that part *within* the walls, *fosse*. Inside the City walls, the watercourse banks were artificially piled and walled. Garbage flowing in from without the walls was intercepted by a watergate called a *scluys* (sluice) or *speye* and carted away. City dwellers around the marches of the *fosse* shored its banks and propped up its walls so that no breaking or sinking walls impeded the water's flow to the Thames. That fifteenth-century sluice for catching rubbish was the public equivalent of the private householders' "rakes" which in 1288 caught kitchen debris. Who funded *fosse* cleaning? Generally the City itself paid. An interesting source for municipal money was legacy bestowed in return for masses for the soul. One hundred pounds sterling were bequeathed by Thomas Legge for cleansing the *fosses* of the City so that Guildhall chaplains in their masses and prayers might remember the souls of Thomas, Alice, Margery, and Simon Legge and commend them unto God.

Pollution Abatement

Against water depredations and pollution by food tradesmen, various schemes were proposed beyond forcing butchers and fishmongers to ply the messy preparations of their produce outside the city markets. Since victualing guilds were politically powerful, they often objected to interferences in their customary or convenient practices. London's mayor Thomas Fauconer promised in 1415 personally to pay for restoring the original water system if the commonality found unacceptable his project for alleviating pollution caused by household debris, blood from butcheries, and wash-water of fishmongers. This offer of sureties was comparable to those of the citizens' repairs and extensions of the public Conduit. Such Conduit and river documents assert the medieval recognition of the dangers of water pollution to citizen, City, and country. Noxious exhalations from fouled water, aesthetic nuisances of water littered with dead fish, and political follies condoning venality of a few to the detriment of public health—such abuses were overcome by elaborate techniques for apprehending and punishing offenders, and damage was reduced by laudable water-reclamation efforts.

Clean waters were crucial to livelihoods in the food trades. Polluted water mixed with flour made putrid bread; *weir*-killed salmon hatchlings prevented adequate supplies of fish on fast days. Since the hand which stirred the brew-vat also opened the Conduit's pipe, the food-craftsmen themselves—the cooks, bakers, taverners, brewers, fishmongers, and butchers—joined with municipal officials, citizens, and King to assure an equipoise among culinary needs, self-interest of industry, and the City's welfare.

Sex, Smut, Sin, And Spirit

MEDIEVAL FOOD AND CHARACTER

FOOD allusion and culinary actions described character and personality in medieval art and literature. People *were* what they ate: what, how, how much, when, and that, beyond subsistence, they ate and drank at all. Food references demonstrated social class, intellectual and emotional states and, most importantly, spiritual condition. Humor, pathos, and social commentary were expressed in exercises of table and gullet. Complementing these relationships between food and character were medieval convergences between food and social class, food and sex, food and scatology, food and sorcery, and food and sin.

Characterization by Food Habit

In the vast repertoire of medieval gastronomic allusions, one of the finest sources is Chaucer's *Canterbury Tales*. Its several hundred food references range from brief mentions to elaborate descriptions of feasts, triumphs, and nuptials, noble suppers, drinking parties, and humble cottage repasts, penance meals, wild-fruit pickings, and precoital imbibings of aphrodisiacs. To the descriptions of each pilgrim's social rank, costume, and profession, Chaucer adds their food

V: Fig. 1 *Eating nude in the baths, indoor or outdoor, was a popular medieval erotic sport. Devotees of Venus, this disporting pair is regaled by food, drink, and music. (From* Le Grant Kalendrier et Compost des Bergiers, *end of 15th century, Nicolas le Rouge, Troyes)*

V

1. Such instruction books have a venerable heritage traceable as far into antiquity as Isocrates' *Ad Nicoclem*, 374 B.C. Generally referred to as *miroirs de princes,* they served not only the noble but those who cared to emulate their habits. Excellent analyses of the genre are L. K. Born's *Erasmus, The Education of a Christian Prince* (New York, 1936) and his "The Perfect Prince: A Study in Thirteenth and Fourteenth Century Ideals," *Speculum* 3 (1928), 470–504; see also W. Berges, *Die Fürstenspiegel des hoben und späteren Mittelalters* (Stuttgart, 1938). My own *Education of the Hero* considers the qualities and traditions of these etiquette books (pp. 138–96).

2. The *Prologue* to the *Canterbury Tales* ll. 139–40.

3. Line 200.

4. Line 626.

habits. For both the ecclesiastical and secular figures, gastronomy demonstrates social standing and personal sensibility. Several characters belong to victualing trades; some eat with the same frugal or ostentatious habits with which they practice their crafts; others gorge or souse their way to Canterbury.

Food portraits of the Nun, Monk, and Summoner intimate medieval clerical customs and hypocrisies. Few descriptions of medieval table manners and elaborate ceremony for finger-eating excel the Prioress's etiquette; her manners are corroborated by medieval courtesy manuals and instruction books for the nobility.[1] In charge of an abbey of nuns, and a social climber eager to imitate courtly habits, *to countrefete cheere of court*[2] (delicately and dexterously she lifts food to her lips; fastidiously she avoids crumbs or grease in her wine cup), she displays the digital finesse required by that courtly custom which disdained forks as acceptable implements. The wealthy, hard-riding hunter of a Monk loves a fat swan best of any roast. His round, well-stocked body testifying to his fine eating (*a lord ful fat and in good poynt*),[3] his speech is larded with food analogy: for him monastic rule is "worthless as a plucked chicken"; worry about a monk out of a cloister is "not worth an oyster." The Summoner, who hails sinners to ecclesiastical court, demonstrates his venality and intimates his venereal disease by his food choices. For a quart of wine he allows a rascal to keep his mistress for a year. His sense of taste diminished by tertiary syphilis (*saucefleem he was . . . hoot . . . and lecherous as a sparwe*),[4] he eats only the odoriferous and the pungent—garlic, onions, leeks—and drinks especially strong wine, red as blood.

Just as food references make exuberant portraits of human foible and fallibility in the medieval church, so they vivify characterizations of secular figures. Though not born to the court—but nobly landed and lardered—the Franklin enjoys lordly breakfasts of a sop of bread in wine; his magnificent *table dormant* is so well set with fine wines and daintily crafted foods that in his house it seems to snow food and drink.

> His breed, his ale, was alweys after oon;
> A bettre envyned man was nowher noon.
> Withoute bake mete was nevere his hous
> Of fissh and flessh, and that so plentevous,
> It snewed in his hous of mete and drynke,
> Of alle deyntees that men koude thynke.
> After the sondry sesons of the yeer,
> So chaunged he his mete and his soper.
> Ful many a fat partrich hadde he in muwe,
> And many a breem and many a luce in stuwe.
> Wo was his cook but if his sauce were
> Poynaunt and sharp, and redy al his geere.
> His table dormant in his halle alway
> Stood redy covered al the longe day.[5]

5. Lines 341–54.

Gourmand, epicure, and gracious host, in his display of table splendor food substitutes for pedigree. Chaucer's Physician, on the other hand, practices the dietary measure and restraint he counsels his patients: *of his diete mesurable was he./ For it was of no superfluitee,/ But of greet norissyng and digestible.*[6]

6. Lines 437–8.

The pilgrimage's professional Cook, though filthy and scabrous, knows techniques for roasting, baking, broiling, boiling, and otherwise preparing chickens, *mortreux* (stews), and pies; he admirably creates the familiar white culinary treat *blankmanger*.[7] However, his running, pustulous *mormal* sore is insignia of the blind folly of the nouveaux riches Guildsmen who employed him for semblance of nobility. Lastly, the Host to the pilgrims voyaging to Canterbury swears oaths on wine and ale, welcomes the sundry folk to supper, serves them fine food and strong wine, and suggests the very ruse for telling the Tales: free supper at his inn as prize for that story which best instructs and best delights.[8] Thus the tavern more than the shrine of St. Thomas of Canterbury is architectural frame for all the later Tales.

7. Lines 379–87.

8. Lines 796–9.

Food and Social Class

Chaucer describes kitchens to give gastronomic distinction to the moral qualities of the social classes. In well-provisioned, well-served noble houses, feasts demonstrate wealth and political might. Middle-class "messes" ape the noble banquets and substitute for refined manners crude gobbling and guzzling. In contrast to both is the simple decorum of the rural table. A banquet in the *Squire's Tale* details the setting, splendor of costume, music, and service along with the actual menus and the "apparelling" of food, shocking the guests into wonderment—strange and wonderful foods, stews, roast swans and herons, and foreign dainties followed by fine wines and spices elegantly served by stewards, ushers, and squires. Through the day and night, lords and ladies drink and enjoy marvels of culinary art for which cooks labor and noblemen pay dearly: that elegant artifice of food which turns "substance into accident."[9] A contradistinction is the farm dinner, dignified by such simple fare as the aging dairywoman's (whose barnyard was home to the spectacular rooster Chaunticleer). The poor widow eats "slender" meals with no piquant sauces or dainty morsels; temperate of diet, she drinks no wines red or white but lays her table white and black: milk, brown bread, a rind of bacon, an egg or two.[10] Such necessary temperance and enforced moderation avoids the "pride of table" that corrupts the rich.

9. *The Pardoner's Tale*. ll. 538–39.

10. *The Nun's Priest's Tale*, ll. 2833–46.

"Outrageous luxury" was deemed destructive to morality and to social order. Exotic, imported foodstuffs diminished domestic commerce and upset international balances of payments. Luxury also was accused of interfering in the individual soul's relationship to God. Against culinary extravagance in all levels of medieval English society, sumptuary laws were passed, particularly during Edward III's reign in the fourteenth century. These statutes of diet (and apparel) regulated numbers of courses per meal, number of dishes within courses, varieties of victuals, even types and costs of their sauces.[11] What was permissible for one social station was forbidden the class below; the Church stratified eating habits similarly within ecclesiastical ranks. Since the rich were "much inconvenienced" by extravagance, and the lesser folk who attempted to imitate them were "greatly impoverished" thereby—while other "equally deplorable evils attacked their souls as well as their bodies"—moderation was legislated in startling lists of forbidden fruits.

11. See F. E. Baldwin, *Sumptuary Legislation and Personal Regulation in England* (Baltimore, 1926).

Food service also was stratified by class. Social class dictated precedence in the dining hall. Not only what was eaten by which class, but who sat with whom at which table, and in what social order guests were

V: Fig. 2

served, was scrupulously controlled by the noble household's Marshall or Chief Usher of the Hall. Russell's *Boke of Nurture* enumerates the five social classes and their careful groupings at table.[12] Equivalent classes could eat the same foods together; some could sit two by two, others four by four; still others were not to see the food served their equals or superiors. The First Class: pope, emperor, king, cardinal, prince, archbishop, and duke, were of such dignity as to dine alone. Second Class, bishop, marquis, viscount, and earl, might sit together if on friendly terms personally: *yf they be lovyngely*. The mayor of London, a baron, a mitered abbot, the chief justices, and the speaker of Parliament—members of a Third Estate—could sit at an equivalent level, two or three "at a mess." Fourth Class equaled the knight's rank: a cathedral prior, a knight-bachelor, a dean, the Master of the Rolls, the mayor of Calais, a doctor of divinity, a prothonotary. Fifth and last, the Squire's degree, including doctors of law, ex-mayors of London, preachers, masters of arts, city bailiffs, rich merchants, gentlemen and gentlewomen—*alle these may sit at a table of good squyeris*. Even the social embarrassments of the well-born poor man and the marriages out of class were provided for in table regulations. For lords of royal blood though poor in goods versus rich low-born men the rule was: blood eats better than money; *the substaunce of lyvelode is not so digne/as is blode royalle,/ Therefore blode royalle opteyneth the sovereynte in chambur and in halle*. When a lady royally born married a lowly knight, or a poor lady married a lord of noble blood, the lady of royal station kept her state as before her marriage; and the lady of low blood took with her husband his high seat at table.

While classes of clergymen were accommodated in noble dining halls according to their parity with secular ranks, monastic houses generally tended to level class distinctions with food rules. Strict fast and frugality as prescribed in the *Rule of St. Benedict* discouraged many forms of hieratic eating.[13] However, an abbess or an abbot, privileged to eat alone and served special dishes, might invite members of the house to share feasts. Abbots also allocated to brethren those extra portions of food and wine honoring particular benefactors or saints' days called *pittances*.[14] Abuses of these mild social distinctions in food service included undisciplined clerics imitating secular food entertainments with their social seatings (along with their feast-day hilarity, scurrilous songs, and burlesques). Bishop Eudes visiting the nuns' abbey of Monvilliers in 1260 forbade eating in the refectory in little groups or cliques, and insisted that all take seats haphazardly and eat the same food.[15] Benedictine monks demanding special dishes served to them in their cells, "apparelled" delicacies rather than simple rations, habitual additions of the special pittances, and elegant table gear causes Pope Gregory IX to issue statutes to reform their food practices. Their ration was to consist of one dish and one cup, not including pittances. No one was to cause anything more delicate in food or drink to be prepared for him or served beyond usual fare. Silver or gold cups or those banded or based by precious metals were forbidden in the refectory as were knives embellished with gold or silver.

These ecclesiastical and secular attempts to regulate appetite by restricting its expression probably were no more enforceable than more modern prohibitions on drink and food. Medieval English sumptuary

V: Fig. 2 *Feasting in this remarkable bathing chamber is a communal activity. The long banquet board is placed athwart rims of individual bathing vessels in each of which a couple sits, nude save for hats and jewels. Some touching bodies over or beneath the boards, one couple in the back needs no aphrodisiac food or stimulation, while another at left has proceeded from bath to bed. (From the* Master of the Housebook, *late 15th century, German)*

12. Rank and precedence are discussed, in ll. 1003–1172, according to all states of birth and dignity likely to grace a banquet hall; but if ever a servitor is in doubt, he must ask his lord's advice: "resorte euer to youre sovereyne."

13. *Regula Commentata*, in *Patrologia Latina* 66:322; *The Rule of St. Benedict*, trans. Ruth Dean and M. Dominica Legge (Oxford, 1964).

14. Provided in the Norman English monasteries by a special officer called the *Pittancer*, a *pittance*—there might be three or four per meal—was shared by a pair of monks, just as courtly diners often shared a dish. See O. G. Tomkeieff, *Life in Norman England*, 95f.

15. Trans. Sydney Brown, *The Register of Eudes of Rouen*. ed. Jeremiah F. O'Sullivan (New York, 1964), especially 436.

Nequando rapiat ut leo animam
meam: dum non est qui redimat neque

V: Fig. 3   *Fecal, light-green
eggs are defecated into a
gold toilet bowl, gathered
up, and conveyed to a waiting woman. Similar charm-
ingly grotesque scenes in
which men and animals in-
vert natural functions—cows
milk womens' breasts, for
example—grace the margi-
nalia of devotional books.
(From a* Book of Hours,
*early 14th century, Flemish.
Cambridge University, Trinity College Library, MS B
11.22, f.73)*

V: Fig. 4   *The Hell Mouth
is vivid representation of the
fiery ovens of the nether
world. The central illumination has three concentric hell
mouths whose lips are
opened by devils and whose
sides are surmounted by
boiling caldrons into which
bodies are tossed. (From* The
Hours of Catherine of Cleves,
*1440, Dutch. New York,
The Pierpont Morgan Li-
brary, M917, f.168v)*

laws, obeyed or ignored, were not repealed until Queen Victoria's era. Legislation and literature confirm the medieval identification of social class by food.

Food and Sex

Other indulgences are allied with appetite. Chaucer associates food and sex via medieval aphrodisiac lore. An importunate lover attempting to attract the sexual attentions of a lady sends her fine mead, spiced ale, piment, and wafers piping hot. An eager old lover, before entering bed with his new young wife, strews the house with spices and drinks *hippocras* and claret and vermage of hot herbs "to increase his courage"—potions recommended for stimulating sexual qualities by the medieval sex manual *De Coitu*.[16] So too the joyously sexy Wife of Bath suggests strong wine for stimulating the two appetites of taste and sexual sensation: a lecherous mouth, she says, has a lecherous tail. When Chaucer describes the lustful Summoner as "hot and lecherous as a sparrow" he alludes not only to the English bird's reputed sexual incontinence but also to the medieval belief that eating cooked sparrow or sparrow eggs stimulated lust. As an early natural historian stated it: *All sparrowes flesshe is euyl/and their egges also. The flesshe is very hote, and moueth to the operacion of lechery.*[17]

Fruits such as pomegranate and pear were eaten as aphrodisiacs.[18] Chaucer plays upon multiple sexual implications of the pear tree in the *Merchant's Tale*. Young, voluptuous Lady May—married to wealthy, loathly, jealous, scrawny-loined, old January—while walking with her aged, blind husband in their garden, insists on picking pears from their green pear tree lest she die if she cannot eat what she desires. By clever ruse, however, more than one variety of succulent pear hangs in that tree; May's young lover waits in the branches for an arboreal orgy. Up she climbs for her fruit, cuckolding old man January in the pear tree. But no surprise; that ardent old fool thought best in food analogy: he was a mature fish, a full-grown pike, no mere pikerel; she was tender veal. He thought women over thirty were beanstraw and animal forage. But his toothsome wife desired stronger wines than his in bed, or tree.

Outdoor medieval feasts with dalliance in or under the arbors sometimes united eating with nude bathing. The more spectacular culinary water pleasures, however, were indoor diversions. Naked lovers dined *in* the baths, tasting erotic aquatic delights. The eternal opposites of water and fire, superbly juxtaposed in the *aqua ardens* of succulent wines, lubricated the voluptuaries' passage from bath to bed.

Many wines and foods were construed as having the quality of promoting sexual desire. St. Thomas Aquinas noted in the *Summa Theologica*: "Gluttony and lust are concerned with pleasure of touch in matters of food and sex."[19] Since "concupiscence is desire of the delectable," abstinence from certain foods was required to counteract sexual urges as well as to decrease seminal flow. Accordingly,

the Church forbade those who fast to partake of those foods which both afford most pleasure to the palate, and besides are a very great incentive to lust. Such are the flesh of animals that take their rest on the earth, and of those that breathe the air and its products, such as milk from those that walk on the earth, and eggs from birds. For,

16. See C. Maillant, *Les aphrodisiaques* (Paris, 1967).

17. John Russell's *Boke*, l. 706, note 104.

18. K. A. Bleeth, "The Image of Paradise in the Merchant's Tale," in *The Learned and the Lewd*, ed. L. D. Benson (Cambridge, 1974), 45–60, as well as the delightful article by Raymond Sokolov, "The Drinking Man's Pear," *Natural History* 85 (1976), 86–90.

19. Part II, second part, question 15, article 3, "Sins Against Understanding" (London, 1916), vol. 9, 189; see Joseph Rickaby, *Aquinas Ethicus: The Moral Teachings of St. Thomas* (London, 1896).

20. Question 147, article 8, "Fasting," vol. 13, 71.

since such animals are more like man in body, they afford greater pleasures as food, and greater nourishment to the human body, so that from their consumption there results a greater surplus available for seminal matter, which when abundant becomes a great incentive to lust.[20]

Touch thus was important to the sensuality of medieval food; this "feel" of food is a sense denied the modern gourmet who interposes the metallic implements of cutlery between textured foods and willing mouth.

Food and Smut

Scatological associations with food are as frequent as the sexual. Chaucer's rude, crude, lewd *Summoner's Tale* introduces a mendicant friar begging food for himself and his brethren from wealthy parishioners. At the home of an aged, ill man whose young wife he had found friendly before, the friar, hypocritically unctuous, begs for a bushel of wheat, or round of cheese or bacon or beef. Invited for dinner, he requests capon's liver and soft bread, condemning constantly the evils of gluttony and haranguing against table sins. Finally, he angers the bedridden old man into giving him marvelously just desserts. Old John's promise of a gift of great wealth requires the friar to swear to share it equally with his brethren. Implying a worthy gift of food, the old man invites the friar to put his hand in the bed where the treasure is hid. Down across the buttocks goes the friar's hand feeling for the wondrous gift when all of a sudden old John lets fly a prodigious fart. How could one carve for twelve brothers this fundamental honorarium?

V: Fig. 6

V: Fig. 7

Dashing to yet another feast, the friar tells this tale at table, revealing his promise to divide his gift. A young meat-carving squire, skilled in the art of service, invents an ingenious method for parting farting. Were there no food references and no gastronomic expectation, Chaucer's humor would be less outrageous and the ultimate conclusion less exquisitely revolting.

Unnatural and Supernatural Food

Oral as well as anal analogy intensified medieval expressions of both good and evil. Evil portrayed in sculpture, painting, manuscript illumination, and literature emanates from or enters into mouths or anuses of demons, or the mouth of Hell. Grotesqueries in marginalia of prayer books abound with part-human part-bestial creatures spurting foul scintillations from their buttocks or jaws.[21] One of the most frequent medieval locations for the torments of the damned is the Hell Mouth.

Just as evil is expressed in alimentary allusion, so good is associated with divine eating. God sups with the righteous, and miraculously feeds the devoted. Transubstantiation in the Christian sacrament allows the consuming of Godliness.[22] The altar—*mensa domini*, the Lord's table —is table for God's feast.

These medieval gastronomic passions of course had a venerable tradition in classical, Biblical, and popular lore. A noble heritage of food reference existed in epic, lyric, and "kitchen humor" of classical Greek and Latin literature.[23] An astounding number of classical heroes and heroines determined their fates by eating special, sacred, or forbidden foods. Three among those important in medieval texts include Saturn, who, to prevent his children from castrating and killing him as they were destined, ate them. Medea had an unnatural culinary interest in her children she served to Jason. Young Achilles' food both prefigured and caused his later prowess;[24] he garnered strength and courage from eating the entrails of lions and the bowels of she-wolves.

Even more compelling to medieval Christians than the classical were the Old Testament food miracles and food symbols. Since Christian Biblical interpreters attempted to find in Hebrew scripture predictions, prefigurations, precursors, and typologies for New Testament events, every Jewish feast, each grape and crumb, was food for exegesis. Christian moralists reinterpreted food scenes from *Genesis* through *Song of Solomon,* in adventures of David, Samson, Job, Judith, Esther, and Ruth. Manna falling to feed the faithful in the desert, Moses smiting the Horeb rocks for water, elaborate burnt offerings of seared flesh and fried bread, ritual Passover feasts, and complex prohibitions and prescriptions for "kosher" fish, flesh, and fowl in the Book of Leviticus: Hebrew tradition associating food practices with spiritual tests inspired later Judaic food rites.

While medieval Jewish food habits merit their own volume—the symbolic braided Sabbath bread *challeh* is medieval in origin; the philosopher–rabbi–physician Miamonides gave his own recipe for the ritual Passover food *charoseth*; for the harvest feast of Sukkoth, *fluden*, a layered pastry with symbolic fruits, derives from twelfth-century Judeo-German cooking records[25]—Old Testament food tradition is important in medieval Christian "moralized Bibles." Expounding the letter of the Word, and celebrating the vivid, visual details of tradition, rather than

V: Fig. 7 *Manna from heaven was gathered and eaten, just as the salt waters made sweet, and sweet waters from the rock in Horeb were drunk from mazers, buckets, and flagons by Hebrews watching Moses. (From the Old Testament, 13th century, French. New York, The Pierpont Morgan Library, M638, f.9v)*

21. See E. Mâle, *L'Art réligieux de la fin du moyen-âge* (Paris, 1922); and Lillian Randall, *Images in the Margins of Gothic Manuscripts* (Berkeley, 1966), especially *obscaena*, cx, cxi, cxii, cxiii, for amusing nude defecating hybrid beings.

22. Ethnological, psychological, Biblical, pseudoepigraphal, and exegetical backgrounds to the idea are discussed by F. R. Tennant, *The Sources and Doctrines of the Fall and Original Sin* (New York, 1968).

23. See Ernst Curtius, *European Literature in the Latin Middle Ages,* trans. Willard Trask (New York, 1953), "Jest and Earnest in Medieval Literature," 431–6.

24. See D. S. Robertson's "The Food of Achilles," *Classical Review* 59 (1940), 177f.

25. A good introduction to ancient, medieval, and Renaissance traditions is the *Encyclopaedia Judaica* (Jerusalem, Israel), index, s.v. *Food*; also I. Abrahams, *Jewish Life in the Middle Ages* (1896; New York, 1969).

113

26. An example is the extraordinary *Rohan Hours* from the Bibliothèque Nationale, Ms Latin 9471, published in facsimile by George Braziller (New York, 1973).

27. Facsimile, marginal paintings 102–103 (original folios 221v–222).

28. In addition to the lugubrious tales in the old *Catholic Encyclopedia,* the best source is Jacobus de Voragine, *Legenda Aurea,* trans. G. Ryan and H. Ripperger, *The Golden Legend* (New York, 1941).

29. See Aanti Aarne, *Types of the Folk Tale,* trans. Stith Thompson (Helsinki, 1961).

30. See Louise Loomis, "Nationality at the Council of Constance," in S. Thrupp, *Change in Medieval Society* (New York, 1964), 279–96.

31. The sixteenth-century woodcut by Jasper Isaac is reproduced in Emile Grillot de Givry, *Illustrated Anthology of Sorcery, Magic, and Alchemy* (orig. 1929; New York, 1973), Fig. 33.

32. On the psychiatric implications of saltlessness and sexuality, see Ernest Jones, "The Symbolic Significance of Salt," in his *Essays in Applied Psycho-Analysis* (New York, 1964), 22–109.

epistemology, these Bibles have food scenes almost as frequently as armed battles.[26] "Moralized" explanations of the Hebraic prohibitions against Jews eating such "unclean" birds as the heron and hoopoe became counsels against gluttony and impoliteness at table, and against bishops' nepotism and simony. *Le heron senefie le glouton qui tout boit et riens ne donne a sa compaignie. La hupe qui fait son nyt en sa merde senefie les mauvais evesques qui donnent leurs benefices a leurs nepveux et a garssons qui riens ne scevent.*[27] Such suggest that medieval habit of mind which transformed food notions of the Old dispensation into teaching devices for the New.

In the New Testament itself St. John the Evangelist *ate* the book of Prophecy before preaching the Apocalypse: bitter in his stomach, the words were sweet upon his tongue. Christ's culinary miracles regaled not only the guests at the Wedding of Cana, but the multitudes requiring loaves and fishes. The Last Supper became one of the most popular subjects in medieval art.

Holy Food had its counterpoise in the unnatural foodstuffs of medieval martyrdoms, satire, and witchcraft. Early Christian saints were tempted or tortured with food, or performed food miracles, or themselves were minced, boiled, broiled, roasted, or served as foods in their martyrdoms.[28] The folklore theme of destroying enemies by consuming them[29] (the giant in "Jack and the Beanstalk" wants to grind Jack's bones to eat as bread; the wicked ogre in "Puss in Boots" shifts his shape to a mouse and is gobbled by the cat) was important in medieval satire. Virulent anti-papal attitudes were expressed in portraits of wine-making by pounding the juice in a vinting vat from a cardinal mash. A fifteenth-century recipe for curing the digestive troubles of St. Peter required clergymen marinated in Rhine water: take 24 cardinals, 100 archbishops and prelates, the same number from each nation, and as many curials as you can get. Immerse in Rhine water and keep submerged there for three days. It will be good for St. Peter's stomach and for the cure of all his diseases.[30]

Witches' sabbath feasts, caldron cookery for brewing up storms and magic illusions are remarkable inversions and perversions of courtly and of sacred ceremony. Depictions of witches' kitchens detail rare raw ingredients (chopped children, for instance), elaborate cooking and distilling techniques, prescribed embellishing procedures, and complex rituals for eating and drinking. The *Abomination des sorciers,*[31] for example, illustrates the "cookbooks" from which satanic recipes were concocted, the open hearth with pots ready to cook bizarre animal and human ingredients, the caldron of prophecy in which fantastic, symbolic animals are prepared for boiling, the hanging cupboard containing "ready-mixer" philter and potion pots, and the strainer or sieve used in divination. Just as were lordly feasts, sorcerers' and witches' banquets were reported in numerous sources as opulent, well-served, delicately cooked extravaganzas with golden cloths, jeweled drinking vessels, and attentive servitors. However, the inversion of the ideals of courtly cookery was this witch banquet consisting of no other meats than carrion, and the flesh of hanged men, unbaptized children, and unclean strange animals, all cooked to be savorless and served without salt.[32]

Natural or unnatural, divine or profane, this medieval foodlore of popular, Biblical, and classical origins presented food "forbidden," or

V: Fig. 8 *Saint and queen, Elizabeth of Hungary smuggled scraps from her own table to feed the poor while her jealous, niggardly husband the King tried to grab the bowl from her. By miracle the food became roses. (From a hand-colored woodcut, 1470s, South German. New York, The Metropolitan Museum of Art, Harris Brisbane Dick Fund, 1930)*

V: Fig. 8

V: Fig. 9 *A Clerical Mash makes fine vinting for devils who pound fruits in the vat until they are crushed to an acceptable demonic brew. The nude pope with his triple crown lies nearby. (From an Anti-papist broadside, late 16th century, Germany. The Dover Pictorial Archive:* Devils, Demons, Death, and Damnation, *No. 231)*

33. The basic review is M. Bloomfield, *The Seven Deadly Sins* (Michigan, 1952); and see references in note 36, below.

34. *The Pardoner's Tale.*

35. Consult the *Patrologia Latina* for the original texts.

"magic," rituals of eating, and "unnatural" transformations of food into something other than what it seemed; food was proof of supernatural power (as in the sweet waters of Horeb or the wedding wine at Cana); in ritual offerings (as the Hebraic sacrifices). Food was a praise or propitiation; foods of sympathetic magic (as Achilles' offal and the witches' carrion dinners) transferred to mortal beings qualities heroic, divine, or devilish. In all instances, the eating was allied to a spiritual condition, and the food an insignia of the state of the soul.

Food and Spirit

So pervasive was this medieval unity between food and spirituality that eating habits determined a human being's association with a pantheon of virtues and vices. *Gula*, gluttony, that seducing sin which had corrupted the world, had a medieval definition both fascinating and unsettling. Just as Adam ate his way out of Paradise, so man eats his way into sin. Surprisingly, the dire and deadly sin to which writers such as Chaucer and a host of theologians ascribed Adam's loss of Eden was

V: Fig. 10 *Foods in sorcery create witches' stews with unnatural raw ingredients and magical cooking methods. Malevolent kitchen productions, these dishes are the unholy Sabbath feast fare. ("The Witches' Sabbath," an engraving by Hans Baldung Grien, 1510, Germany. New York, The Metropolitan Museum of Art, Gift of Felix M. Warburg and his family, 1941)*

not pride but gluttony.[33] While the nobleman cultivated tastes and appetites as proof of education, political power, and economic supremacy, the Christian moralists saw in elaborate foods and eating ceremonials a way the devil acquired disciples.

While Adam fasted in Paradise, all was perfect; when he ate the forbidden apple, God cast him out to woe and pain. Gluttony, then, the source of man's complaint and all subsequent maladies, was the sin which tempted him daily, easiest to commit, hardest to shrive. Alas for him who made his "throat a privy because of cursed superfluity!"[34] Food into stomach, and maw into food for worms; God ultimately destroys both, as Chaucer quoted St. Paul. Argued by Thomas Aquinas, Augustine, Paul, and Gregory in his *Moralia*; reviewed in Peraldus's *Tractatus*, Pennaforte's *Summa Casuum*, and numerous other exegetical texts,[35] this question of gluttony's primacy—the first sin, the cardinal, the deadliest—permeated theoretical expositions of theologians as well as popular medieval pulpit preachings and visual arts.[36] While others of the Seven Deadly Sins sometimes led the way to Hell, gluttony was the

36. See A. Katzenellenbogen, *Allegories of the Virtues and Vices in Medieval Art* (London, 1939); F. Saxl, "A Spiritual Encyclopedia of the Later Middle Ages," *Journal of the Warburg and Courtauld Institutes* 5 (1942); Samuel C. Chew, "Spenser's Pageant of the Seven Deadly Sins," *Studies in Art and Literature for Belle Da Costa Greene*, ed. Dorothy Miner (Princeton, 1954), 37–54; and D. T. B. Wood, "Tapestries of the Seven Deadly Sins," *Burlington Magazine* 20 (1912), 210–22, 277–87.

V: Fig. 11

V: Fig. 11 *The root or fruit of evil was the apple Adam and Eve shared in the Garden of Eden. This Paradise scene depicts the process by which the evil Serpent (or Lilith) enticed Adam and Eve to eat their way out of bliss into sin. (From a woodcut in a Bible, Vérard, c. 1501, Paris. New York, The Metropolitan Museum of Art, The Elisha Whittelsey Fund, 1951)*

V: Fig. 12 *The insidious idea to eat the apple came to Eve from the Serpent, whose tortuous female form here is winged. (From a woodcut, probably by Erhard Reuwich,* Der Spiegel der Menschen Behaltniss, *c. 1481, German. New York, The Metropolitan Museum of Art, Harris Brisbane Dick Fund, 1931)*

V: Fig. 13 *Gluttons are punished in Hell by being forced to eat repulsive, slimy creatures and other revolting foods. (From* Le Grant Kalendrier et Compost des Bergiers, *Nicolas le Rouge, Troyes, 1496)*

V: Fig. 13

37. The "literary" effects of gluttony both as human vice and artistic device are discussed in G. F. Jones, "The Function of Food in Medieval German Literature," *Speculum* 35 (1960), 78–86; J. Horrell, "Chaucer's Symbolic Plowman," *Speculum* 14 (1939), 82f; A. C. Cawley, "The 'Grotesque' Feast in the *Prima Pastorum*," *Speculum* 30 (1955).

most simplistic explanation for sin in this world and man's temptation to it. Conversely, it was the most complex: the sacramental act of eating the body and blood of Christ had its perfect parallel, its special urgency, and its graphic vividness, as an undoing, by eating, of an evil deed caused by eating. As Adam ate his way to sin, so man might eat his way to salvation.

Chaucer's Parson, following St. Thomas Aquinas, described gluttony as the unmeasurable appetite to eat or to drink, or else inordinate covetousness of food or drink. He who gives in to gluttony is incapable of withstanding other sins.[37] He is in the service of all vices; for gluttony is the devil's hoard wherein he rests and hides. Gluttony has many definitions. The first is drunkenness, that horrible sepulcher of man's reason. Second is that confusion of spirit caused by drunkenness which bereaves man of the discretion of his wit. Gluttony's third mode occurs "when man devours his food and has no rightful manner of eating." Fourth is that too great abundance of food which causes distempering of the humors of the body and illness. Forgetfulness is fifth, caused by excess eating and drinking.

Other levels of gluttony delineated by the Parson took inspiration from Gregory the Great. To eat before the time to eat; to obtain too delicate and dainty foods and drinks; to take too much, beyond measure; to fashion food with *curiositee* or preciosity, with too great intention to "apparel" or decorate it; and to eat too greedily. These five fingers of the devil's hand lure folk to damnation.

Such insistence upon gluttony as Original Sin had amazing implications. All human beings had to admit and to expiate their guilt because

ICI EST ENFERS ELIANGELS KI ENFERME LES PORTES:

21

cx illa de scõ iohē baÿ.   cauit me dominus no
                                   mine meo et posuit os
                                   meũ ut gladiũ acutũ
ms meꝰ no   sub tegumento manuꝰ

22

23

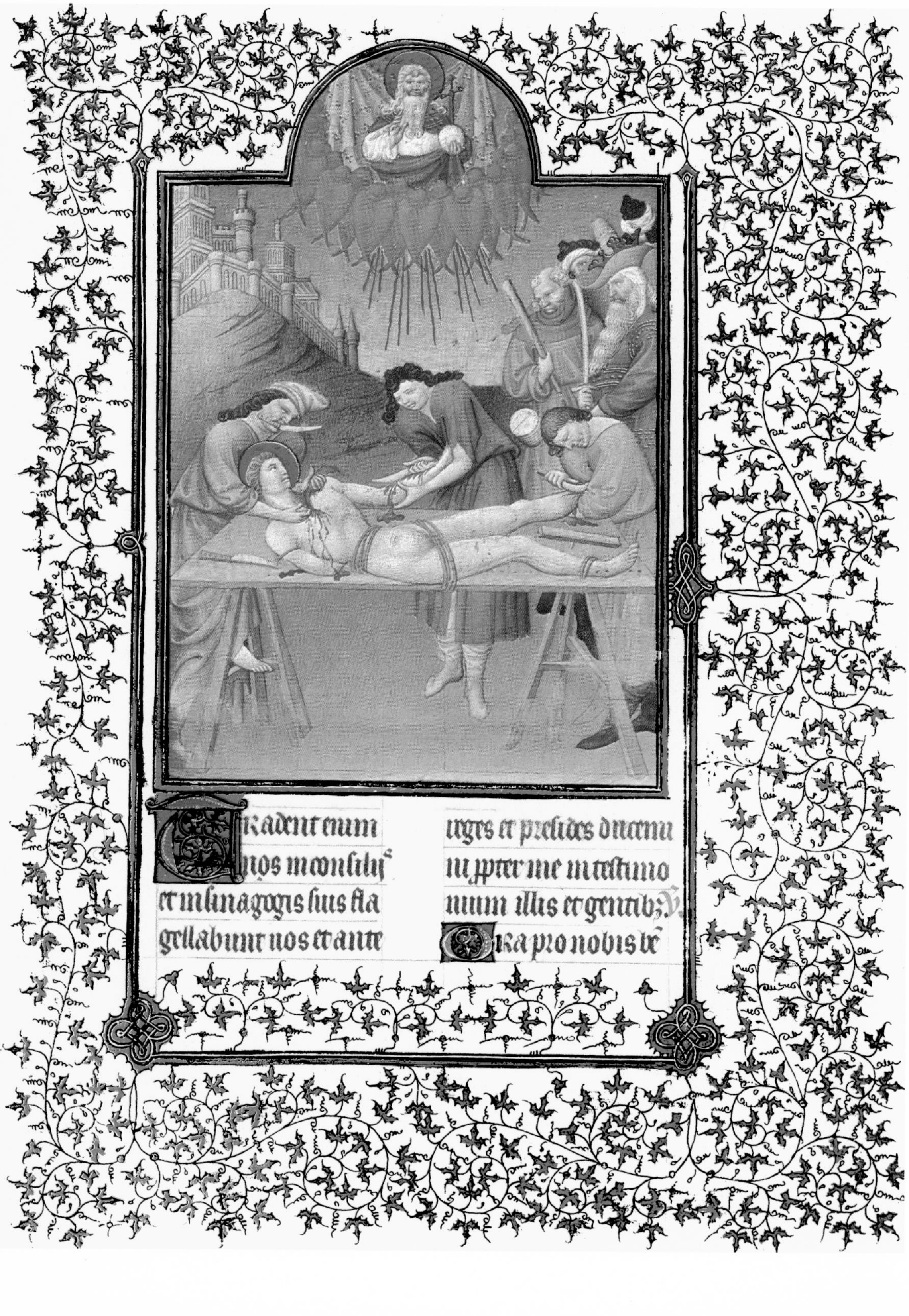
Tradent enim
vos in consiliis
et in sinagogis suis fla
gellabunt vos et ante
reges et presides ducemi
ni propter me in testimo
nium illis et gentibus
Ora pro nobis be

V: Fig. 15 *A winged triple-mouthed devil devours three sinners; two are eaten up to their chests, another bitten in half. Animaloid demons stir hot caldrons. In one hellhole, three men, one wearing a bishop's mitre, and a woman are immersed in flaming fluids, arms bound to their sides, gazing at the round table's foods and utensils. (From a woodcut in Antonio Bettini's* Monte Sancto di Dio, *Florence, 1491. New York, The Metropolitan Museum of Art, Harris Brisbane Dick Fund, 1925)*

(Preceding Page)

Pl. 23 *An angel helps St. John the Evangelist to* eat *the Book of Revelations in the* Apocalypse. *(From the* Apocalypse, *f.16v; 14th century, Norman. New York, The Metropolitan Museum of Art, The Cloisters Collection)*

Pl. 24 *Saints in their martyrdoms sometimes were slaughtered as food animals. Here Saint Bartholomew is flayed on a butchering table, the chief butcher working at the head with knife between teeth while steadying the board with his foot. The others skin and disjoint the body with carcass knives; a hone keeps the cutting edge keen. (From the* Belles Heures *of Jean, Duke of Berry, f.161r; 15th century, French. New York, The Metropolitan Museum of Art, The Cloisters Collection)*

the definition of sin was so comprehensive. Trivial food peccadillos endangered salvation. If eating between meals or poor table manners constituted sin then no Canterbury pilgrim nor few among ourselves would escape guilt. This same sin which caused the Fall, the Flood, and the destruction of Sodom had numerous forms and guises insinuating itself into man's soul at his dining table.

How might a human being who must eat to live avoid gluttony? Chaucer's Parson sagely quoted St. Augustine's recommendation for "abstinence" not as total deprivation but as holding the mean in all things. Sufficiency: no seeking rich foods or drinks, no "outrageous apparelling" of food; measure, restraining by reason the appetite for eating; and soberness, limiting drinking. "Sparingness" was the watchword—only enough, nothing too much. Even sitting positions at table defined

Itaspatrum Eñ is ghenoemt dat vader boeck Inhou
den de die Historien ende legenden der hetligher vade
ren die haer leuen in strenger penitencie ouerghebracht
hebben Ende met veel schone exempelen Ende miracu
len Dat welc is seer oerbaerlic ghelesen voer alle kerstē
menschen gheestelic ende waerlic Ouergeset in gueder
ōstandelreduptscher sprake eñ is āderwerf gecorrigeert

state of the spirit. The holy avoided sitting long and languorously at mealtime, sometimes standing in order to eat at less leisure. While feasible for monastic orders or for penances, such restraint, such "abstinence," was infrequent at medieval courtly tables.[38]

Literary and philosophic inveighings against gluttony show notable disdain against "apparelling" food. Apparelling meant decorating to create an appearance or an illusion—a pretense of something other than what was. Such excessive adornment of food was called "pride of the table." Primarily the vice of the rich, table pride was expressed in contrivances of baked foods and "dish meats" and foods burning with wild fire (flambé) and painted and "castled with paper." Courtly cooks, "straining to turn substance into accident" by transforming elemental foods into sculpture, achieved art but, by creating "appearances," deceived, sinned, and led others into sin. By pandering to their patrons' insatiable desires for "newfangledness," cooks aroused "newer appetites," seducing men into other vices by their delicious devices. These are the very delicacies lauded by the medieval banquet manuals recommending food painting, food sculpture, and illusion foods. Here condemned are the pastry and aspic designs, marzipan armorial quarterings, meat dishes such as the *Yrchoun* and *Cockentrice,* and the "musician pies" which presented live instrumentalists in pastry. Such wonders exciting the eye as well as the palate expressed too much wealth, too great magnificence, and a too worldly pride.

These strictures against adorned food and the ceremony of eating, these condemnations of table pride, and these assertions of gluttony's quintessence are just as true to the medieval world order as are the exaltations of fine foods in the romances, cookery tomes, household accounts, and health manuals. Medieval food and ceremony could be most artful expression of God's plenty or most degrading, dangerous temptation toward damnation. These contrary views were consistent with the preachings of Chaucer's Parson: food potentially was expression of a human being's most corrupt or most holy nature.

V: Fig. 16 *In this allegorical feast,* The Author *dines with* Understanding *at a round table set outdoors before a trellis. Sitting on tripod turned stools, the men drink from small glass tumblers and eat finger foods from an oval serving bowl. (From a woodcut in Olivier de la Marche,* Le Chevalier délibéré, *1486, Gouda, Holland. In St. Jerome's* Vitas Patrum, *Leiden, 1511. New York, The Metropolitan Museum of Art, Harris Brisbane Dick Fund, 1933)*

38. Practical and psychological implications of such guilt and its avoidance are implied in T. S. R. Boase, *Death in the Middle Ages* (New York, 1972); Kathi Meyer-Baer, *Music of the Spheres and the Dance of Death* (Princeton, 1970); Walter J. Ong, "From Allegory to Diagram in the Renaissance Mind: A Study in the Significance of the Allegorical Tableau," *Journal of Aesthetics and Art Criticism* 17 (1959), 423–40. Compare G. Vann and P. Meaghter, *The Temptations of Christ* (New York, 1959).

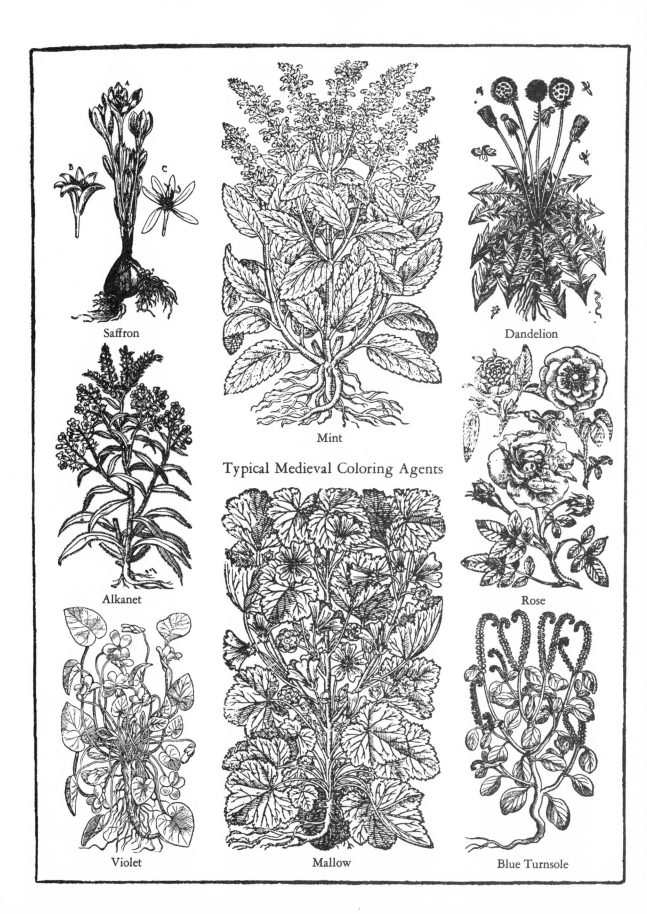

Saffron

Mint

Dandelion

Typical Medieval Coloring Agents

Alkanet

Rose

Violet

Mallow

Blue Turnsole

Medieval Feasts For The Modern Table

A PRACTICAL PRELUDE TO THE RECIPES

SUMPTUOUS, elegant medieval feasts today require more ingenuity than cash. The raw ingredients for the foods and the decorations are not difficult to obtain, but occasionally are found in unexpected places. Esthetic courage paired with polite insistence and tenacious good humor will convince reluctant butchers or dry-goods venders that indeed you mean to buy what you request.

While a neighborhood supermarket manager might meet the request for St. John's Bread with astonished incomprehension ("Why not ask at a church?" said one), any large "health-food" store gladly will sell this common carob, used by those desiring to avoid chocolate. While few glassware departments will provide twenty-four "chalices," a local "Five and Ten" or variety store will stock chalice-shaped, glass "flower planters" making delightful, inexpensive drinking vessels.

The least familiar spices and herbs, such as galingale or cubebs, are relatively easily accessible, even in small suburbs and towns, in natural-food or gourmet shops—when not in the surprisingly varied commercial spice racks of local markets. "Ethnic" food stores (Hungarian, Jewish, Arabic, Chinese, Italian, and Greek) carry many foods which graced the medieval cook's kitchen. For the meats, cheeses, fruits, and vegetables for feasts, the shopper needs to risk only a little time and a lot of amusement (requests for such exotica as deer pizzle or cow udder will cause comment); but most other raw foods, delicious and unremarkable, are obtainable easily in local shops. Fabulous medieval feasts in the modern setting thus initiate inventories of the resources of one's town as well as the resourcefulness of oneself. Suggestions follow for assembling materials with ease and pleasure in order to create the ambiance of the medieval banquet hall, its table, and feast accoutrements, after the preparations in a modern house according to techniques of the medieval kitchen and wine cellar. Modern versions of medieval menus celebrate the startling variousness of medieval food.

The Modern Medieval Banquet Hall

Even the coldest, starkest modern room can be transformed into a festive medieval banquet hall by judicious use of textured fabrics and multiple candles. Walls ought to sport a few "tapestries," obtainable "ready-made" by hanging geometrically designed and well-woven bedspreads. Such design names as "Cordova" or "Mediterranean" or "Renaissance" suggest the appropriate style (one American manufacturer once sold bedspreads patterned after the Cloisters' Unicorn Tapestries). Large, exuberantly crafted felt banners also serve splendidly for wall-hangings, embellished with armorial patterns copied from available medieval texts, or with fanciful coats of arms. For the *baldaquin* behind the *settle* of honor at the *high table,* velvet or velour fabric is useful, decorated with gold braiding in an heraldic design. Numerous candles in candelabrums and sconces on tables, walls, and furnishings such as credenzas or servers give a soft, "authentic" ambient light.

The Table

Since medieval tables were round, oval, "T" shaped, "U" shaped, square, or rectangular, any shape of large table will serve for a banquet. However, the most frequently depicted medieval feast tables are long rectangles, arranged in "the hall" in inverted "U" shape, the *high table* for the most honored placed perpendicularly to long tables along the "sides" of the hall, the *sideboards.* For such medieval feast tables, few elements serve better than old doors. Placed athwart two carpenter's saw-horses, a large door makes a sturdy, long banquet board. A door placed on top of a conventional dining table of convenient shape also extends length, and seating capacity. (If no excess doors are unhinged easily, scavenge in second-hand furniture shops or building demolitions or old houses in process of redecoration for eight-foot high, solid-core doors.) Or fabricate a table top, using stout boards well braced and bolted from beneath, balanced across saw-horses, or a pair of small tables at either end of the boards, propping it securely, avoiding "sway" in the middle.

Cover the table with long white cloths, made of simple muslin fabric or bed sheets. For a particularly lavish high table, spread an old, clean, richly patterned Oriental rug on the table; over it, in a long, longitudinal "stripe" down the middle, place a white linen strip or folded sheet or table scarf, one to two feet wide, upon which breads and foods will be set.

126

For seating, long wooden benches, picnic-table type, or stools, serve admirably. A congenial source for stools is a college or school dump from which chairs with broken slats or backs are gotten for the asking, the backs quickly sawed off, the few rough surfaces sanded and stained; "medieval" stools result. Old discarded church pews also make serviceable, sometimes elegant *banquettes,* the long, backed benches from which the very word for the banquet is derived.

The Table Setting and Accoutrements

Six basic elements ought to decorate the feast table: "the salt," drinking vessels, knives, spoons, trenchers or platters, and large napkins.

The salt, reaffirming social rank—the honored sitting "above the salt," while lesser feasters "below"—ought to be an elaborate object with some open crevices for accommodating salt. Exuberant in shape, it need not be costly. The prosaic easily can be transformed into an imaginative, medieval-style *nef*: a toy or model boat, with decks or poops fillable with salt, requires only painting and gilding before seeming "medieval." Or sculptured glass or porcelain bric-a-brac make a striking "salt"; amusingly shaped vases, rimmed platters, planters, candle holders, tools, or toys can be ingeniously reconstituted by gold paint. Similarly, salvage from second-hand shops or antique stores could create the *table fountain* for wine or cider if there are sufficient spaces for fluids and their ladling.

Goblets and tankards of medieval style are not always found in dinnerware departments. A chalice-shaped, white-glass, footed flower planter makes a pleasantly inexpensive, commodious, two-cup-capacity mead vessel. However, crystal stemware also was used at the medieval table, so the modern, unadorned or faceted, large wine or water-glass size—your best, or sale merchandise—is adequate for medieval quaffing. Metal or wooden tankards usually are available where bar accessories are sold; while pewter and silver are costly, alloys and "aged aluminum" make buying in quantity painless. Even medieval-style *artichoke glasses* appear in variety stores in poorer neighborhoods, the best locales for gaudy glass. Inexpensive, heavy, pressed glass, clear, amber, green, or blue, deeply "faceted" or "thumbprinted," they are worthy substitutes for museum treasures.

Since fingers are the major food implements at a medieval feast, one spoon at each setting is all that is required for service of soups and sauces. However, if you do not follow the medieval modality of requesting each guest to bring his own knife, then provide one sharp knife for each two guests to share.

For holding the foods of the feasts at table, pewter platters or small round wooden trays or simple white porcelain platters are utilitarian. Even more proper and dramatic are bread *trenchers.* Round, fairly flat breads with a good crust, cut horizontally, make excellent trenchers. One bread thus serves two feasters. Medieval green parsley bread is particularly effective background for feast foods. Purchase or prepare breads relatively "flat" as opposed to "puffed" so that trenchers remain stable on the table.

A large napkin tied or pinned around the neck or placed on the lap protects costumes and clothes of those not yet expert in medieval culinary etiquette.

The Serving Board

A serving table or credenza ought to display several important ceremonial and practical objects of the feast: a laver, panter's knives, an alms dish. and spice vessels.

For ceremonial washing of hands before and after the meal, a large pitcher with a bowl beneath, and a long towel ready nearby, ought to be filled with warm water and crushed fragrant herbs such as rosemary, rue, and thyme. Before the beginning of the feast, gently pour the water over the hands of each seated guest, catching the residue in the basin, and offering the towel for drying the fingers.

Breads for eating (not the trenchers) ought to be cut in the banquet hall with sharp *panter's knives*; the *upper crust* ought to be offered to the noble host or guest. Extra "trencher breads," in ready reserve, cut with the panter's "trencher" knife, will replace those which have broken or leaked or been nibbled away.

A large decorative bowl serves well as *alms dish* to collect the uneaten trenchers as alms for the poor, to be distributed at the "castle gate" at the banquet's end.

During the service of the feast several small spice dishes ought to be taken from the serving board to the tables, easily accessible to each feaster. One small dish of mustard, another of brown sugar, and a third of crushed, sweet basil ought to serve every four to six feasters.

Assembling the Rare, Raw Ingredients

Initiate your local butcher or supermarket meat-department manager into the adventure of medieval cookery. With his cooperation, many of the kitchen chores are considerably easier. Convince him that you are neither mad nor perverted though you request marrow bones, suckling pigs, quail, and deer entrails. If intelligent, he will delight in this culinary exercise and correctly predict a happy effect for his business; also he will preserve for sale various animal parts which otherwise he would discard. From the modern cook's viewpoint, the meatman's professional cutting gear (cleavers, axes, and knives, essentially identical to the medieval) substitute for the array of kitchen servants the medieval cook had at command. Let the butcher crack open bones for marrow or instruct in preparing tripe. Often the most hospitable meat merchant in a town is the Kosher butcher, accustomed to preparing custom cuts of most poultry and meat, except pork, for a varied, traditional cuisine with qualities, like the medieval, both western and eastern.

Medieval herbs and spices, available in modern groceries, gourmet shops, health-food and "ethnic" emporia, might be augmented by your own garden's. Such common ornamental herbs as basil, fennel, parsley, rosemary, and mint are far better fresh than dried: more tasty, more aromatic, more beautiful in the cookery. So too for roses, dandelions, and the flowers of medieval desserts.

Wines

Such good medieval and Renaissance wines as malmsey or sack or Vernaccia are not hard to find, but good mead may require ordering. To accustom your wine seller to the pleasant chore, suggest a few imported brands his distributor is likely to handle, such as Honey Mead Bandor from Denmark, or Wawel from Poland; England exports St. Edmund

Hall—Archbishop's Mead from Oxford University, and Merrydown Mead; and New York makes Shapiro's. An ancient wine well known to most cultures of the world, mead is one reason for earliest man's keeping of bees; it is the quintessential medieval drink.

Servitors and Service

A small cadre of costumed servitors will add to the ceremony of the modern medieval feast. Family members and banquet guests or local college or high-school students might delight in the esthetic adventure. Let them meet once or twice before the feast to "rehearse" the movements and services. For the most elaborate presentation, "servants" ought to include:

a *Ewerer,* to pour water from the laver upon the hands of each guest at the beginning and end of the feast;

a *Panter,* to cut the breads which will supplement the trenchers already on the table, and substitute new ones;

a *Butler,* to serve the wines and ciders. (Equip him with a large key and a corkscrew on a chain about the neck);

a *Surveyor,* to coordinate activities of all the other servitors. At the "serving board," he or she will hand the necessary knives or spice dishes to the other serving people;

Carvers and *Sergeants-at-arms,* to bring the resplendent dishes to each table of feasters. If time and space allow, one large bird ought to be carved, at the table, by the *Carver,* someone graceful, unflustered, and reasonably practiced.

Music

Musicians playing trumpets, recorders, bagpipes, cymbals, tambourines, or drums ought to signal each dish within each course, as well as to play interlude music. If live musicians are unavailable, use a record of medieval and Renaissance fanfares and secular songs. Encourage guests to perform songs or dances between courses. A nearby college probably has a *Collegium Musicum* or a medieval recorder consort whose penurious members would play for a modest fee and the joy of performing.

Costumes

Styles depicted in the illustrations in this book easily are emulated with available materials and little sewing. Starting with a choir robe or an academic gown, fine costumes for men can be created with the addition of rope belts with tassles (curtain and drape tiebacks work well) and a few flamboyant chains and amulets around the neck. Indian and other "Eastern" embroidered velvet or cotton shirts, tunics, and caftans worn with tights and low boots make delightful, passable medieval garments.

Similar styles also serve for women. However, a useful source for inexpensive, elegant gowns is a local robe and lingerie collection in which high-waisted lounging robes in velour or velvet require only a fur collar and cuffs (borrowed from an old coat) to imitate the authentic. Augment the costume with "jewels" and necklace chains.

For both men and women velvet or brocade or "fake fur" fabric easily can be translated into an elegant cape—floor-length or waist-high —for excellent effect at little expense or effort.

Hosts, servitors, and guests all ought to be encouraged to re-create by clothing an aspect of the medieval aura and thus delight the more in the cultural context of the medieval foods.

Emboldening the Feasters

By gracious jollying and by example, inspire guests not only to wear costumes of the period, but also to emulate the manners at table, utilizing fingers for most foods. After initial awkwardness and hesitancy, even the most formal and staid guests will share the spirit of the ceremonial motions, and may well claim that food tastes better fingered than forked.

Making Menus for Fabulous Feasts

The menu depends upon the cook's boldness, available time, and, occasionally, ingenious perseverance. From the simplest to the most opulent modern medieval feast, and for the smallest to the grandest gathering, one food rule obtains: it is better to serve small portions of many than to serve large portions of any. Since the medieval courses did not follow our modern appetizer–entree–dessert pattern, the following recipes have been classified in nine categories. By selecting one recipe from each of the nine classes, your guests are assured of at least:

ONE APPETIZER OR APPETIZING APHRODISIAC;

ONE SOUP OR SAUCE OR SPICED WINE;

ONE BREAD OR CAKE;

ONE MEAT;

ONE FISH;

ONE FOWL;

ONE VEGETABLE OR VEGETARIAN VARIATION;

ONE FRUIT OR FLOWER DESSERT; AND

ONE SPECTACLE OR SCULPTURE OR ILLUSION FOOD.

Attempt to balance the menu according to a reasonable judgment of "heavy" versus "light" food, creamed versus simpler, more complex cooking versus dishes easier to prepare. Avoid a succession of dishes with essentially the same spices. Contrast, variety, and surprise ought to be criteria for taste, color, and aroma. Their ordering in the service conveniently might follow the nine classifications.

Modern Re-creations of the Medieval Recipes

All recipes are derived from original medieval manuscripts or early printed sources. Most are fifteenth-century. Occasionally a medieval recipe is said to be "traditional" in the year 1477, thus truly dating back to the twelfth century or earlier. Original cookery documents are listed in the BIBLIOGRAPHY section entitled *Manuscripts*. Although these texts were used in English households, the cuisine is international medieval fare, with Italian, French, and other recipes inspiring the names of such dishes as *Leche Lumbarde* and *Blankmangere*.

Medieval cookbooks for royal and noble kitchens are supplemented as sources by the extraordinary gastronomical suggestions for keeping "hale and hearty" in the health handbooks. *Wes hael!*, "Be well!" the medieval epithet for greeting with good cheer, is also the same word for the festive drink, *wassail*.

All recipes have been tested and tasted in modern kitchens, my own and those of colleagues, students, friends, and professional chefs who have prepared dishes for me and with me in catering medieval feasts at the Institute for Medieval and Renaissance Studies, or the Cloisters, or Columbia University, or various other modern medieval banquet halls across the United States.

Recipe Yield

Since the original recipes give few clues to actual quantities, all spices, herbs, and ingredients are happy approximations of the medieval tastes; modern ingenuity and your personal preference ought to make emendations upon these suggestions. In the following recipes, quantities of ingredients in each recipe should be sufficient to serve:

10 to 12 SMALL PORTIONS
(many separate dishes, served in sequence)
—or—
6 to 8 LARGE PORTIONS
(as if for modern entrees)

Food Paints and Pigments

Since color added luster to medieval foods I suggest in certain recipes that the modern cook augment the natural colors in certain ingredients in order to approximate the visual excitement of the original dishes. While modern commercially available food colors composed of vegetable dyes are useful, the medieval cooks and bakers made their kitchen paints from garden leaves, herbs, and flowers. To imitate that method, experiment with boiling specific leaves or petals in 1 cup of dry white wine. Plain water also serves. To intensify color and diminish fluid, continue boiling slowly until the "paint" is reduced by half. To thicken food paint for *endoring* surfaces, slowly add flour to the coloring liquid, to approximate the consistency of modern poster paint; or mix a pigment with egg yolks. The following are typical medieval coloring agents.

Pigment	*Source*
RED	roses, sandalwood, alkanet
YELLOW	saffron, dandelion
GREEN	mint, parsley, mallow, hazel leaves
BLUE	blue turnsole (heliotrope)
LAVENDER	violets
BROWN AND BLACK	animal blood

Once the feasting hall is prepared, the delectable foods cooked and garnished, the musicians and servitors take their positions, the costumed guests file to their places at the banquet boards, and the sparkling candles, exquisite aromas, and musical fanfares signal the start of a cultural adventure. Delight in the modern re-creation of one of the most significant events of medieval daily existence: the fabulous feast, its cookery and ceremony. *Wassail!*

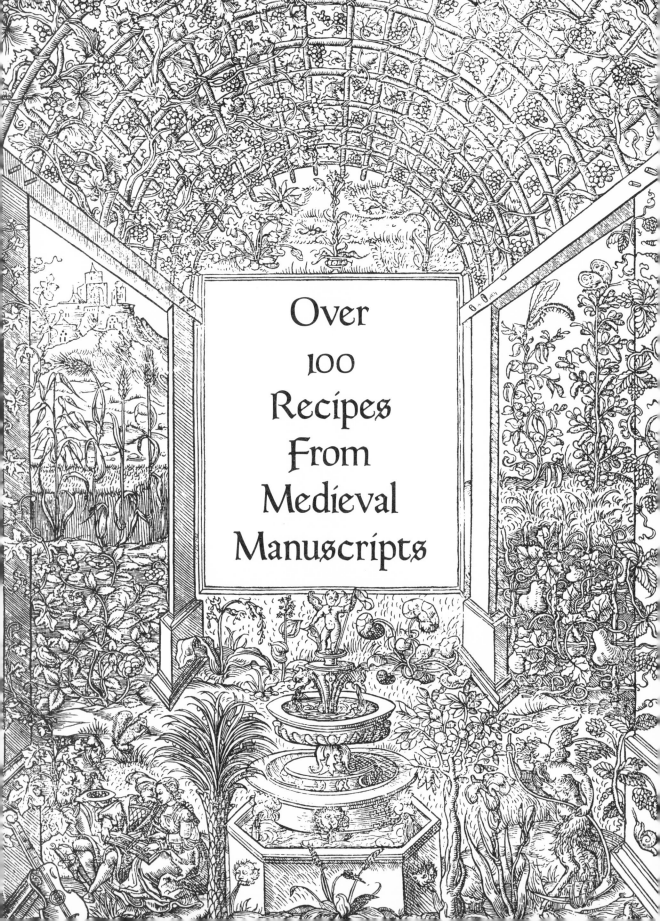

Over
100
Recipes
From
Medieval
Manuscripts

The Recipes

Appetizers, Cheese, and Appetizing Aphrodisiacs

BRIE: Brie Tart
NUTTYE: Spiced Chestnut Cream
JUSSELLE DATE: Dates Stuffed with Eggs and Cheese
LECHE LUMBARDE: A Wined Date Confection
POTROUS: A Spicy Egg in a Coddler
PARSNIP RYALLE: Parsnip Mousse with Almonds and Wine
AMONDYN EYROUN: Almond Omelette
HANONEY: Simple Onion and Parsley Omelette
BRIE CHEESE WITH HONEY AND MUSTARD
TOWRES: Light "Summer" Omelette with Chopped Veal
ARBOLETTYS: A Spiced Cheese Dish
LEEKES: Leeks with Walnuts
ORO: Fried Artichokes
CANEL EYROUN: Figs Stuffed with Cinnamoned Eggs

Soups, Sauces, and Spiced Wines

SORRELYE: Sorrel Soup with Figs and Dates
COBAGES: Cabbage and Almond Soup
ROTA: Barley Fruit Soup
CHARLETTE: Curded Beef Soup
TURNYPES: Creamed Turnip and Parsnip Soup
GALANTINE SAUCE: Spiced Broth for Fish
GOS SAUCE: Wined Cheese Sauce for Goose or Chicken
SAUCE VERTE: Parsley and Pine-nut Sauce for Fowl
CREME SAUCE: Honey Cream Sauce
BRUNE SAUCE: Prune Sauce for Poultry and Cheeses
STRAWBERYE SAUCE FOR BYRDES: Strawberry Cream Sauce for Fowl
SAUCE DE LIMON: Lemon Wine Sauce for Fowl
CORANS SAUCE: Wined Currant Sauce for Meat
SAUCE VERTE: Basil Sauce
VYNE SAUCE: Grape Sauce for Fowl
SAUCE BLANC: White Butter Sauce
MULLED APPLE OR PEAR CIDER
MAUMENYE BASTARDE: A Prodigiously Mulled Wine
WYNE POTAGE: Spiced Wine Broth
SPICY POMEGRANATE DRINK
YPOCRAS: Hippocras: A Spiced Red Wine

Breads and Cakes

PARSLEY BREAD
BURREBREDE: Shortbread
FLOTERES: Salmon and Currant Dumplings
RYSBRED: Rice Pancakes
SOPPES DORRE: Spiced Toast with Almond Sauce

TANSY CAKE WITH PEPPERMINT CREAM
NUTTERBREDE: Nustort or Nutcake for the Jewish Festival of Passover
OREOLES: Elderberry Funnel Cakes
CIRCLETES: Almond-Cardamon Cakes
FOYLES: Layered, Spiced Pancakes

Meats

CUSTARD LUMBARDE: Marrow and Fruit Tart
MAWMENYE: Lentils and Lamb
GALANTINE PIE: Meat and Berries in Pastry
A ROSTE: Beef Roast with Crisps
CANELYNE: Caneline Beef Pie
DILLED VEAL BALLS
NOMBLYS DE ROO (OR VENYSON): "Humble Pie" or Spiced Tripe
VISORYE: Veal Custard Pie

Fish

PORPOISE PUDDING: Oat Stuffed Pike
VYAND DE CYPRIS IN LENT: Almond Fish Stew
LUCE WAFERS: A Delicate Fish Cake
PYKE EN DOUCETTE: Smoked Pike Salad in Pastry
SAUMON ROSTED: Roast Salmon in Onion Wine Sauce
SAUMON PIE: Salmon and Fruit Tart
PLAYCE YSOD: Boiled Plaice with Mustard Sauce
GYNGERE: Gingered Carp
ROSEYE: Fried Loache with Roses and Almonds
LAMPROI: Baked Lamprey

Fowl

MAWMENYE RYALLE: Spiced Capon (or Pork or Partridge) in Nutted Wine Sauce
VYAND DE-CIPRYS RYALLE: Spiced Minced Chicken Relish
BLANKMANGERE: Chicken with Cumin and Cream
NEKKESAN: Swan Neck Pudding (or Capon or Turkey-Neck Pudding)
SMALLE BYRDES: Bird Stuffed with Dates and Mustard
FESAUNT AND GELYE: Baked Pheasant or Chicken with Cold Herbed Jelly
FARSED CHYCKEN: Chicken Stuffed with Lentils, Cherries, and Cheese
FARSED FESAUNT: Pheasant (or Chicken) with Spiced Apples and Oats

HENNE DORRE: Golden Cardamon Chicken
GARBAGE PYE: Giblet Custard Pie

Vegetables and Vegetarian Variations

FRUYTES RYAL RICE: Artichokes with Blueberry Rice
LEMONWHYT: Lemon Rice with Almonds
RAPES: Lentil Crisps
SALLAT: A Medieval Salad
FLORE FRITTOURS: Fried Squash Flowers
AMYNDOUN SEAW: A Vegetable Gruel
ST. JOHN'S RICE: Currant Rice with Carob Cream
CAUDELE ALMAUNDE: A Nut Dish Served as a Vegetable
MARY CABOGES: Cabbage with Marrow
JOUTES: Herbed Beets (or, a splendid, spiced "Borscht")
VEGETARIAN CUSTARD LUMBARDE: Almond and Fruit Tart

Fruit and Flower Desserts

QUYNADE: Quince Sauce
CHARDWARDON: Spiced Pear Sauce
DAMSON: Plum and Currant Tart
FRUYTE FRITTOURS: Parsnip and Apple Fritters
FYGEYE: A Tricolored Fig Confection
BLAK PERYS: Pears with Carob Cream
PERYS COFYNS: Lentil- and Berry-filled Pears
BOLAS: Wild Plum and Stuffed Pear Dessert
TROYCREM: Tri-Cream
FAUN TEMPERE: Gilli-Flower Pudding
VALENCYE: Fried Valencia Oranges

Spectacle, Sculpture, and Illusion Food

HASLET: Mock Entrails
GELYE DE FYSSHE: An Elaborate Jellied Design
COCKENTRICE: A Marvelous Beast
POUMES or POMME DOREE: Golden Apples of Meat
MARCHEPANE: Basic Marzipan for Food Sculpture
APPRAYLERE: The Pitcher That Is Not What It Seems
FOUR AND TWENTY SINGING BLACKBIRD PIE or LIVE FROG AND TURTLE PIE

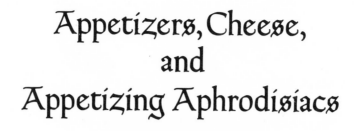

Appetizers, Cheese, and Appetizing Aphrodisiacs

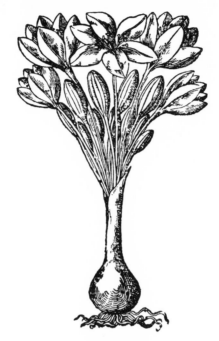

BRIE
BRIE TART

Ingredients

1 8-inch unbaked pastry pie shell or 12 individual unbaked pastry shells, 1-inch diameter

1 pound brie cheese, with rind

6 egg yolks

¼ teaspoon ginger

1 teaspoon brown sugar

⅛ teaspoon saffron

¼ teaspoon salt

1 teaspoon white sugar

½ teaspoon cinnamon

Method

1. Bake pastry shell "blind" to harden for 10 minutes at 425°. Cool. Reset oven to 375°.
2. Remove the rind from chilled cheese and cut the rind into small pieces with moistened knife. Reserve.
3. Beat softened brie cheese, yolks, ginger, brown sugar, saffron, and salt until smooth.
4. Pour into pastry shell.
5. Strew cut rind evenly over the surface of the pie.
6. Combine cinnamon with white sugar and sprinkle around pastry edge.
7. Bake until set and golden brown, about 30 minutes at 375°. If you make individual tarts, bake for 12 minutes or less. Serve warm or cool.

NUTTYE
Spiced Chestnut Cream

Ingredients

1 pound fresh chestnuts

2 cups cold water

1 unblemished lemon, cut in eighths

⅔ cup raisins

½ cup coarsely ground almonds

½ teaspoon ground ginger

1 teaspoon cinnamon

¼ teaspoon ground cloves

2 pints heavy whipping cream

2 Tablespoons sugar

¼ teaspoon salt

Method

1. In 400° oven, roast chestnuts for 10 to 15 minutes. Remove the shells and cut nuts into quarters.
2. In a large enameled pot, mix all ingredients, except for the cream, sugar, and salt, and bring to boil; simmer very slowly for 45 to 55 minutes. Remove the lemon wedges. Drain.
3. Mash the chestnut mixture (coarsely) with a fork. Cool.
4. Whip the cream with the sugar and salt until it peaks.
5. Fold in chestnut mixture, swirl, and serve. Or, spoon a helping of cream onto each dessert platter; scoop out a hollow in the center and fill it with one heaping Tablespoon of spiced chestnuts.

JUSSELLE DATE
Dates Stuffed with Eggs and Cheese

Ingredients

1 pound dates, pits carefully removed

1 cup crumbs of gritty brown bread or date-nut bread

2 Tablespoons dried, sweet basil, crushed

½ teaspoon salt

3 hard-boiled eggs

½ pound cream cheese or ricotta

½ cup beef bouillon

Method

1. Cut dates along one long axis to achieve a "canoe" shape suitable for filling. Place on damp towel to avoid sticky nuisance. Cover with another damp towel.
2. Add basil and salt to crumbs.
3. Mash eggs well.
4. Cream the softened cheese with broth in a large mixing bowl.
5. Add eggs and spiced crumbs to cheese and stir well. Mixture should have "pasty" consistency. If too stiff, soften with a small amount of milk.
6. Place mixture in a pastry tube with serrated nozzle and pipe into each date.

LECHE LUMBARDE
A Wined Date Confection

Ingredients

1 pound dates, pits removed

2 cups sweet wine (port or sherry)

¼ cup brown sugar

3 Tablespoons flour

¾ teaspoon cinnamon

½ teaspoon ginger

4 hard-boiled eggs, mashed or crumbled

2 cups hard brown bread, grated or crumbed

Method

1. Gently boil dates in wine, 10 to 12 minutes.
2. Pour off half of the liquid. (Reserve the wine for later mixing with ricotta cheese as a "sauce" for fish.)
3. Add sugar to the dates and return to low heat for 2 to 4 minutes until mixture is thick and stiff.
4. Remove mixture from pot and place on a bread board or strong "kneading" surface, lightly floured.
5. On the dates evenly sprinkle the ginger, cinnamon, eggs, and one cup of the grated bread.
6. Moisten hands with warm water and knead mixture. Shape into a cylinder or "log."
7. Roll log in remaining bread crumbs to coat evenly.
8. Chill in refrigerator for three hours.
9. With sharp, moistened knife, slice or "leech" the cylinder into rounds, ¼ to ½ inch thick, and serve.

POTROUS
A Spicy Egg in a Coddler

Potrous is an intriguing egg dish originally made in a fireplace shovel hardpacked with salt. Since such are not easily available in the modern kitchen, the common egg coddler (the tightly covered porcelain variety placeable in boiling water is best) makes a utilitarian vessel. For each portion one extra-large egg ought to be united with the spices and cheeses in a "two-egg-capacity" coddler.

Ingredients

1 raw egg per portion

½ teaspoon butter for greasing coddler

1 Tablespoon ricotta cheese

1 Tablespoon honey

½ teaspoon spicy brown mustard

1 sliver spicy cheddar cheese

⅛ teaspoon salt

¼ teaspoon dried sweet basil

½ teaspoon crushed fresh sorrel

Method

1. Break the egg into the well-greased coddler, piercing the yolk.
2. Carefully spoon the ricotta into the center of the egg.

3. Make a cavity in the ricotta and then spoon in the honey.
4. Into a well in the honey, spoon the mustard.
5. Place the cheddar sliver in the middle of the mustard.
6. Sprinkle salt, basil, and sorrel on top. Cover the coddler.
7. Measure enough water into a small pot so as to equal the height of the coddler; bring the water to a rapid boil. Gently place the coddler in the pot and continue boiling for about 7 minutes.
8. Check to determine whether egg has hardened and the concentric egg stuffings have warmed. If egg is still soft, return to pot for another 3 minutes. Serve hot.

PARSNIP RYALLE
Parsnip Mousse with Almonds and Wine

Ingredients

  7 eggs

¼ teaspoon salt

¼ teaspoon cinnamon

  1 teaspoon ground pine nuts

  1 cup brown sugar

½ cup cracker crumbs or whole-wheat toast crumbs

1⅔ cups parsnip, finely cubed, blanched and drained

⅔ cups coarsely ground almonds

  3 Tablespoons white wine

  1 Tablespoon butter for greasing baking dish

Garnish

    fresh fennel

Method

1. Preheat oven to 350°.
2. Separate the egg whites from the yolks in two separate bowls. Beat the egg whites with salt, cinnamon, and pine nuts until they peak.
3. Beat the yolks to a pleasant lemon color. Slowly add the sugar while beating.
4. Add the crumbs and parsnips to the sweetened egg yolk.
5. Fold in the almonds and wine.
6. Fold in the egg whites.
7. Pour the parsnip mixture into a well-greased glass baking pan, or 8 to 9 cup souffle dish. Bake for 55 to 65 minutes until surface is gently browned.
8. Garnish each portion with a sprig of fresh fennel. Serve hot.

AMONDYN EYROUN
ALMOND OMELETTE

Ingredients

1 cup ricotta cheese

8 Tablespoons butter

¾ cup slivered or coarsely ground almonds

⅔ cup oats

4 hard-boiled eggs, chopped

½ cup softened raisins

6 raw eggs

2 Tablespoons honey

½ teaspoon salt

½ teaspoon fennel seed, crushed

2 Tablespoons oil for sautéing

Method

1. Place ricotta in a large bowl.
2. In a large, heavy skillet, melt half of the butter; toast the almonds and oats until golden. Pour off almonds, oats, and butter into the ricotta and mix well. Reserve skillet, and any residual butter therein, for later.
3. Stir chopped hard-boiled eggs and raisins into the ricotta mixture.
4. Beat the raw eggs with honey, salt, and fennel.
5. Stir the sweetened eggs into the cheese.
6. Heat remaining butter with oil in skillet. Pour mixture in to fry until golden, about 5 to 8 minutes on very low heat. Turn the omelette if you prefer the eggs well done. Cut into individual wedges and serve hot.

HANONEY
SIMPLE ONION AND PARSLEY OMELETTE

Ingredients

6 eggs

1 small onion, coarsely chopped

½ cup fresh parsley, minced coarsely

½ teaspoon salt

4 Tablespoons butter for sautéing

Method

1. Draw egg whites and yolks through a strainer.
2. Slowly melt butter in heavy skillet and gently sauté onions and parsley, until onions are golden yellow, not brown.
3. Pour on eggs, mixing them together with onions and parsley, and fry.
4. Flip the omelette, if desired, to crispen both sides; or serve as scrambled eggs. Salt to taste.

BRIE CHEESE WITH HONEY AND MUSTARD

Brie makes a particularly delightful finger food, utilizing its own rind as a "casing." With a sharp knife dipped in warm water, cut the chilled brie into bite-sized wedges or artistic shapes appropriate for finger-picking. Cut each piece horizontally in half, placing cheese rind at the bottom. With a spoon or a cake decorator having a small nozzle, drizzle one small line of honey and one line of sharp mustard on each piece.

Arrange the brie on a prechilled platter and keep refrigerated until immediately before serving; otherwise the honey and mustard tend to melt, inconveniently.

TOWRES

Light "Summer" Omelette with Chopped Veal

The fifteenth-century manuscript suggests this omelette as fine for summer: "for soperys in somere." Depending upon the size of skillet, one "towre" will serve eight to ten feasters; however, small "towres" make splendid, attractive individual dishes within courses of a feast. If one regulates heat carefully, there is a nice contrast in color between the sweet white outside of the omelette and the golden contents.

Ingredients

8 egg yolks	½ teaspoon salt
Beef marrow from 4 bones, minced small	2 Tablespoons butter for sautéing
¼ teaspoon pepper	⅔ cup chopped raw veal
¼ teaspoon mace	8 egg whites
⅛ teaspoon powdered cloves	1 Tablespoon white sugar
⅛ teaspoon saffron	¼ teaspoon salt
1 teaspoon brown sugar	¼ cup butter
	¼ cup oil

Method

1. Make a thick yellow batter by combining egg yolks, marrow, pepper, mace, cloves, saffron, brown sugar, and salt.
2. Sauté chopped veal in butter until nicely browned.
3. Stir in chopped veal to the batter.
4. In another bowl, with a fork gently beat the egg whites with white sugar and salt.
5. Slowly heat butter and oil in heavy large skillet.
6. Carefully pour egg whites into skillet, making a large "pancake." Cook over very low heat.
7. When this holds its shape and browns slightly around the edges, pour the yolk mixture into the exact center of the white.
8. Carefully raise the edges of the "pancake" to fold over the mixture, "closing" it, as the manuscript suggests, into "foure square." Fry until nicely golden brown. If the size of your skillet does not permit a complete folding-over of the edges of the egg white, simply turn the D-shaped edges over the yolk and veal so that the bottom of the omelette is square. Then slowly fry until done. Serve warm.

An interesting variation makes the egg whites into a meringue. For this, follow steps 1 and 2. Preheat oven to 450°. Then vigorously beat the egg whites with a rotary beater, slowly adding sugar and salt, until a stiff froth forms. In a well-greased baking dish, carefully place the whites. Scoop out a shallow depression and evenly spread in it the yolk mixture. Bake in hot oven 4 to 5 minutes until the meringue is nicely browned at its tips.

ARBOLETTYS
A Spiced Cheese Dish

Ingredients

4 eggs

½ teaspoon salt

1 cup milk

3 Tablespoons butter

1 cup ricotta or cottage cheese

1 teaspoon fresh parsley, finely crushed

½ teaspoon ground sage

¾ teaspoon finely grated candied ginger

¼ teaspoon galingale

Garnish

½ teaspoon cinnamon

1 teaspoon sugar

Method

1. Beat the eggs and salt with a fork. Reserve.
2. In a large porcelain pot, gently heat the milk, butter, and cheese, stirring intermittently until the mixture is smooth and slowly simmering. Slowly beat ½ cup hot liquid into eggs.
3. Add eggs to pot and stir; simmer for 2 minutes, stirring while custard thickens. Remove from heat.
4. Unite parsley, sage, ginger, and galingale.
5. Stir these spices into the "arbolettys."
6. Spoon into serving bowl. Sprinkle mixed cinnamon and sugar on top. Serve warm.

LEEKES
Leeks with Walnuts

Leeks were cultivated copiously in medieval Europe as a vegetable both nourishing and stimulating to the "desires of Venus." The aphrodisiac qualities were thought dependent upon the leeks' beneficent effect upon the production of sperm.

Ingredients

10 to 12 fresh leeks

1½ cups beef broth

½ cup white wine

¼ teaspoon salt

1 Tablespoon sugar

1 cup coarsely ground walnuts

1 teaspoon vinegar

½ cup walnuts, cut in quarters

Method

1. Wash, trim, and coarsely chop the leeks.
2. Simmer slowly in broth and wine for 12 minutes, in a covered pot.
3. Add salt, sugar, ground nuts, and vinegar. Simmer another 7 minutes, uncovered.
4. Spoon leeks into individual serving bowls. Garnish each portion with quartered nuts. Serve warm.

ORO
Fried Artichokes

Artichokes and rue were known for exciting appetites for sex as well as for wine. These golden fritters were a common medieval aphrodisiac.

Ingredients

12 small artichokes

1 cup water

½ lemon

2 cups boiling salted water

3 eggs, well beaten

¼ teaspoon salt

⅔ cup flour

½ cup oil for sautéing

Garnish

1 teaspoon crushed, fresh rue
or
¾ teaspoon dried, powdered rue

Method

1. Snip off the ends of the artichoke leaves with a pair of scissors.
2. Cut the artichokes into quarters or eighths, depending upon their size: each piece ought to equal two "bites."
3. Immediately soak the artichokes in water into which the lemon has been squeezed. After ten minutes, drain the vegetables and discard the fluid.
4. Blanch artichoke pieces in salted boiling water for 7 minutes. Drain and dry.
5. Dredge each piece of artichoke in flour.
6. Heat the oil in a heavy skillet.
7. Add the salt to the well-beaten eggs.
8. Dip each artichoke piece in the egg and fry in oil until pleasantly golden. Drain.
9. Strew rue upon each fritter as a garnish. Serve warm, preferably as the last course of a meal.

CANEL EYROUN
Figs Stuffed with Cinnamoned Eggs

Ingredients

12 large fresh figs

4 large hard-boiled eggs

1 Tablespoon cinnamon

¼ teaspoon salt

½ teaspoon crushed fresh basil

⅔ cup flour

½ cup oil for sautéing

Method

1. With a spoon or with fingers, make a "crater" in the side of each fig.
2. Chop the eggs finely.
3. Blend cinnamon, salt, and basil, and add to the eggs.
4. Stuff each fig with the spiced egg mixture.
5. Lightly dredge each stuffed fig in the flour.
6. Sauté in a heavy skillet with hot oil for 4 to 6 minutes, until golden brown. Drain. Serve warm.

Soups, Sauces, and Spiced Wines

SORRELYE
Sorrel Soup with Figs and Dates

Ingredients

- 1 pound fresh young sorrel
- 2 quarts boiling water
- 1 teaspoon salt
- ½ cup dates, pits removed, finely minced

- ⅔ cup figs, stems removed, finely minced
- 2 eggs
- 2 Tablespoons sugar
- 2 turnips cut into thin strips
- ⅔ cup white wine

Method

1. Coarsely chop the washed sorrel, utilizing both the leaves and the tender stems.
2. To the slowly boiling water in large soup pot, add the sorrel, salt, dates, and figs, and simmer for 15 to 20 minutes.
3. Beat the eggs. Add ½ cup of the hot soup and stir well. Add this mixture to the soup pot, stirring constantly. Add sugar and remove from heat.
4. In a small sauce pan, simmer the turnip strips with the wine for 7 minutes, or until the pieces are cooked yet still hold their shape. Pour the wine into the soup, reserving the turnip strips.
5. Serve the soup cool with several strips of turnip as garnish for each portion.

COBAGES
CABBAGE AND ALMOND SOUP

Ingredients

1 head of cabbage, shredded

1 cup coarsely chopped almonds

6 cups beef broth

4 Tablespoons honey

½ teaspoon salt

½ teaspoon dried sweet basil

2 cups fresh peas

Garnish

2 Tablespoons grated candied red anise
(or grated red or black licorice)

Method

1. Slowly simmer all ingredients, except peas and garnish, for 20 minutes.
2. Add peas and simmer for another 10 minutes.
3. After ladling into soup bowls, garnish each portion with candied anise strewn on the surface of the soup.

ROTA
BARLEY FRUIT SOUP

Ingredients

1 cup pearl barley

⅔ cup tart apple slices, cores and stems removed, cut thin

½ cup minced dried apricots

8 cups chicken broth

1 teaspoon ginger powder

½ teaspoon salt

Pinch pepper

1 cup fresh peas

Optional

2 Tablespoons flour

2 Tablespoons butter

Method

1. In a large covered pot gently simmer all ingredients, except the peas, for ¾ hour.
2. Add fresh peas and continue simmering another 15 minutes. Serve hot.
3. If you prefer a thicker soup, melt butter in frying pan over low flame; stir in flour, constantly stirring until frothy. Add this roux to soup, stirring well. Cook 5 minutes longer.

CHARLETTE
CURDED BEEF SOUP

Ingredients

1 quart milk

1 teaspoon salt

⅛ teaspoon saffron

1 cup lean minced beef (or pork)

6 eggs

1 cup ale

2 Tablespoons, or more, butter for sautéing

Method

1. Gently heat milk with salt and saffron, preventing boiling but slowly simmering. A skim will form which can be either removed or simply stirred into the milk.
2. Briefly sauté beef in butter until meat is brown (or sauté pork until every piece is thoroughly cooked through). Drain well on absorbent paper towel.
3. Add meat to the spiced milk and continue simmering ten minutes. Stir occasionally.
4. Beat eggs with ale.
5. Add aled eggs to the pot, constantly stirring, until, as the manuscript advises, it "croddes"—it forms curds, in 2 or 3 minutes.
6. Ladle into individual bowls, assuring each portion of meat, curds, and hot soup stock.

TURNYPES
CREAMED TURNIP AND PARSNIP SOUP

Ingredients

1 cup peeled, fresh turnips, diced

½ cup scraped, fresh parsnips, diced

2½ cups beef broth

½ cup coarsely ground almonds

1 cup heavy cream

3 egg yolks

½ teaspoon salt

Juice of ¼ lemon

Method

1. Gently boil the turnips and parsnips in the broth until the vegetables are soft, about 12 minutes.
2. Stir in the almonds and heat for 3 minutes.
3. Mix the yolks and salt with the cream; add the lemon juice; pour ½ cup hot soup into egg mixture, stirring well. Then slowly pour this mixture into the soup. Stir well.
4. Heat 2 or 3 minutes, stirring, and serve warm.

GALANTINE SAUCE
SPICED BROTH FOR FISH

Ingredients

1 cup crumbled bread crusts

¾ teaspoon galingale powder

¾ teaspoon cinnamon

¼ teaspoon ginger

¼ teaspoon salt

2 cups beef broth

2 Tablespoons wine vinegar

Method

1. Unite spices and salt evenly with crumbs.
2. Slowly simmer spiced crumbs in the broth and vinegar for 7 minutes. Serve with fish or green vegetables.

GOS SAUCE
WINED CHEESE SAUCE FOR A GOOSE OR A CHICKEN

Ingredients

1 cup finely slivered almonds

1 teaspoon butter

1 cup ricotta cheese

½ cup apple butter (or quince butter or preserves)

⅔ cup dark raisins or currants

1 cup red wine

2 Tablespoons honey

Method

1. Generously grease a cookie sheet with butter. Evenly spread almond slivers upon surface and toast in oven at 375° for 5 to 7 minutes, making sure the almonds do not burn. Remove from oven and reserve.
2. In frying pan, gently simmer raisins in wine for 5 minutes. Remove from heat.
3. Add apple or quince butter to ricotta and stir well.
4. Stir in ricotta and toasted almonds to the wined raisins, and heat for 3 minutes.
5. Drizzle honey on top of heated sauce; serve hot with chicken or goose.

SAUCE VERTE
PARSLEY AND PINE-NUT SAUCE FOR FOWL

Ingredients

1 cup fresh parsley	¼ teaspoon salt
½ cup fresh bread crumbs	⅛ teaspoon pepper
¼ cup vinegar	2 cups red wine
2 Tablespoons ground pine nuts	

Method

1. Pound parsley, bread crumbs, and vinegar in a mortar until well blended.
2. Add the pine nuts, salt, and pepper and briefly blend.
3. Pour this parsley mixture and the wine into a saucepan and simmer 7 minutes. Cool and serve.

CREME SAUCE
HONEY CREAM SAUCE

Ingredients

3 Tablespoons honey	¼ teaspoon grated lemon rind
3 large egg yolks	2 cups milk
3 Tablespoons flour	1 Tablespoon fresh butter
⅛ teaspoon salt	

Method

1. Mix honey, yolks, flour, salt, and rind.
2. Heat the milk in a saucepan over a very low flame.
3. Slowly add to the milk the honey, yolk, and flour mixture, beating constantly. Continue slow, intermittent stirring for about 7 minutes, carefully avoiding boiling. Remove from heat.
4. Add the butter; stir and serve warm, with fish or broiled meat.

BRUNE SAUCE
PRUNE SAUCE FOR POULTRY AND CHEESES

Ingredients

24 prunes	⅛ teaspoon powdered ginger
2 cups strong red wine	3 Tablespoons honey
1 cup water	1 Tablespoon vinegar
½ teaspoon powdered cinnamon	2 Tablespoons flour

Method

1. Gently simmer all ingredients, except the flour, in a porcelain pot for 30 minutes.
2. Remove the prunes, extract their pits, and sliver and reserve flesh.
3. Remove ½ cup of the spiced wine syrup and stir the flour into it, blending thoroughly.
4. Stir this thickener into the rest of the sauce.
5. Return the prunes to the pot, stir, and slowly simmer an additional 4 minutes.

STRAWBERYE SAUCE FOR BYRDES
STRAWBERRY CREAM SAUCE FOR FOWL

Ingredients

2 cups fresh strawberries	¼ teaspoon ground cinnamon
2 cups heavy cream	⅛ teaspoon salt
1 cup white wine	2 Tablespoons honey

Method

1. Remove all stems and blemishes from strawberries. Mash 1 cup of strawberries with a fork; or crush them with a mortar and pestle; or briefly blend in a blender. Cut the other cupful of strawberries into quarters or eighths.
2. Slowly heat the cream in a pot, carefully avoiding boiling.
3. Add the wine, cinnamon, salt, honey, and strawberry pulp; stir while heating slowly for 4 minutes.
4. Add the cut strawberries immediately before serving.

SAUCE DE LIMON
LEMON WINE SAUCE FOR FOWL

Ingredients

3 unblemished lemons	½ teaspoon cinnamon
2½ cups white wine	¼ teaspoon salt
4 Tablespoons sugar	

Method

1. Grate the peel from the lemons and reserve.
2. Squeeze the lemons, reserving the juice and pulp but discarding the membranes.
3. Add the peel, pulp, and juice to the wine and simmer the mixture for 4 minutes.
4. Add sugar, cinnamon, and salt; simmer one minute longer. This tart syrup is splendid on chicken, capon, or pheasant.

CORANS SAUCE
WINED CURRANT SAUCE FOR MEAT

Ingredients

2 cups currants

2 cups red wine

1 Tablespoon sugar

⅛ teaspoon ground cloves

⅔ cup beef broth

Method

1. Soak the currants in wine for 3 hours.
2. Combine all other ingredients with the wined currants in a porcelain pot and simmer for 10 minutes. Continue slow simmering to reduce sauce, if you prefer a thicker consistency.
3. Serve warm over lean meat or fowl.

SAUCE VERTE
BASIL SAUCE

Ingredients

⅔ cup fresh basil

¼ teaspoon salt

½ cup dry bread crumbs

¼ cup vinegar

1 cup beef broth

1 cup white wine

1 Tablespoon ground pine nuts

Method

1. Pound the basil with the salt in a mortar until it is pulpy.
2. Soak the bread crumbs in vinegar for 10 minutes.
3. Pour into a sieve and squeeze out excess vinegar.
4. Combine all ingredients in a pot and simmer over a low flame for 3 minutes. Serve cool.

VYNE SAUCE
GRAPE SAUCE FOR FOWL

Ingredients

1 pound black grapes, pits removed

2 cups red wine

1 cup beef broth

7 Tablespoons honey

Dash of pepper

¼ teaspoon salt

4 egg yolks

Method

1. Crush the grapes in a mortar with a pestle.
2. Soak the grape pulp in the red wine for several hours or overnight.
3. In a porcelain pot gently simmer the marinated grapes and wine with the beef broth for 15 minutes.
4. Combine honey, pepper, and salt with the egg yolks. Pour ½ cup hot broth mixture into yolks; stir.
5. Stir the yolk mixture into the simmering broth. Remove from heat. Serve with chicken or duck.

SAUCE BLANC
WHITE BUTTER SAUCE

This fourteenth-century version of the classic "balsamella" sauce probably was introduced to England from Italy where it was recorded as early as 1357, having regaled a cardinal at a banquet in Cesena.

Ingredients

4 Tablespoons fresh butter	Pinch of pepper
4 Tablespoons flour	⅛ teaspoon nutmeg
2 cups milk	⅛ teaspoon thyme
⅛ teaspoon salt	

Method

1. Melt the butter in a heavy soup pot.
2. Slowly add the flour, stirring constantly.
3. In another pan, gently heat the milk until it is hot but not boiling.
4. Add the hot milk to the butter and flour in small amounts, stirring constantly.
5. Add the condiments and stir. Slowly simmer 5 minutes. Serve warm or cool over meats or vegetables.

MULLED APPLE OR PEAR CIDER

Ingredients

2 quarts fresh apple cider or pear juice	½ teaspoon ginger powder
¼ teaspoon nutmeg	7 sticks of cinnamon
⅛ teaspoon thyme	*Garnish*
	1 Tablespoon finely crushed sweet basil

Method

1. In a large enameled pot, gently simmer the juice with the spices for 7 minutes.
2. Break the cinnamon sticks, placing a portion in each tankard or chalice or glass. Pour on warmed cider. Sprinkle sweet basil sparingly on top.

MAUMENYE BASTARDE
A PRODIGIOUSLY MULLED WINE

"Bastarde" refers not to paternity but to type of wine, the popular medieval vintage, generally imported from Spain. The quantities listed here, from a fifteenth-century manuscript, suggest the magnitude of pot and production required by the noble household. Here "vinegar" refers to a wine which has just "turned" *slightly* acidic. (The following is presented more as a curiosity than a recipe.)

Ingredients

1 pottel (2 quarts) clarified honey

1 pound pine nuts

1 pound currants

Plus

3 pounds almonds

1 gallon wine

1 "good gallon" vinegar

1 pound sandalwood

1 pound powdered cinnamon

2 gallons wine (or ale)

1 pound pepper

Plus

Powdered ginger

Salt

Saffron

Method

Mix all of these in one gigantic pot. Heat for 10 minutes. To "season it up," strew powdered ginger on the surface.

WYNE POTAGE
SPICED WINE BROTH

Ingredients

1 cup freshly squeezed orange juice

2 cups water

2 cups dry white wine

4 Tablespoons honey

½ teaspoon salt

3 Tablespoons lemon juice

2 cinnamon sticks

2 Tablespoons flour

Garnish

6 egg whites (or 1 pint heavy cream)

½ teaspoon nutmeg

½ teaspoon ginger powder

Method

1. Bring to boil and then gently simmer for 3 minutes the orange juice, water, wine, honey, salt, lemon juice, and cinnamon.
2. Remove ½ cup of broth and stir the flour into it.
3. Add this to broth and simmer another 4 minutes. Remove cinnamon sticks.

4. Blend the nutmeg and ginger with the egg white (or with the heavy cream) and whip until the mixture "peaks."
5. Pour the broth into individual bowls. Garnish with a generous dollop of spiced froth (or cream) immediately before serving. This is either a soup or a drink.

SPICY POMEGRANATE DRINK

Ingredients

1½ cups water

1 cup sugar

½ teaspoon cinnamon

¼ teaspoon nutmeg

⅛ teaspoon ginger

4 whole cloves

½ unblemished lemon

1 quart fresh pomegranate juice or 6 to 8 medium-sized pomegranates, skinned, the pith removed, seeds squeezed, pulverized, and strained

Method

1. In a large enameled pot combine water, sugar, and all spices. Bring to boil and gently simmer for 7 minutes. Remove the whole cloves.
2. Finely grate the lemon peel and reserve it. Squeeze the juice from the lemon.
3. Add the pomegranate juice and lemon juice to the spiced hot fluid. Bring to slow boil, then simmer 2 minutes.
4. Serve warm with a garnish of grated lemon peel for each glass. Or serve cool, garnishing each glass with peel and a small wedge of fresh lemon.

YPOCRAS
Hippocras: A Spiced Red Wine

Many medieval and Renaissance recipes for *hippocras* utilize prodigious amounts of spicery. A comprehensive description of the total process—including the three pewter basins, the three "boulting-cloth" strainer bags, the fabric sieve called "Hippocrates' Sleeve" from which the drink gets its name—is presented in John Russell's *Boke Of Nurture*, lines 121–76, appearing on the following page. The recipe below follows medieval sources and Russell's ideas but reduces the labor as well as the quantity.

Ingredients

½ teaspoon ginger powder (or 5 slivers of fresh ginger)

4 cinnamon sticks, broken in thirds

4 grains of cardamon, coarsely ground

½ cup sugar

⅛ scant teaspoon pepper (optional)

1 quart good red dry wine

4 blue heliotrope blossoms ("turnsole") for coloring

Garnish

1 unblemished lemon, cut in small slivers

Method

1. Place spices in a large enameled pot. Pour in red wine.
2. Bring the wine and spices to a boil and simmer, tightly covered, for 7 minutes.
3. Add heliotrope blossoms and slowly simmer another 3 minutes.
4. Remove all whole spices and flowers.
5. Serve warm in individual chalices, goblets, or mazers (small glass bowls will do); garnish each portion with a sliver of fresh lemon.

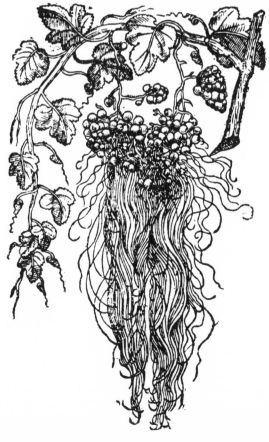

YPOCRAS

Good son, to make ypocras, hit were gret lernynge,
and for to take the spice therto aftur the proporcionynge,
Gynger, Synamome / Graynis, Sugar / Turnesole, þat is good colourynge;
For commyn peple / Gynger, Canelle / longe pepur / hony aftur claryfiynge.
look ye haue of pewter basonsoon, two, & thre,
For to kepe in youre powdurs / also the licour therin to renne when that nede be;
to iij. basouns ye must haue iij. bagges renners / so clepe ham we,
& hange them on a perche, & looke that Sure they be.
Se that youre gynger be welle y-pared / or hit to powder ye bete,
and that hit be hard / with-owt worme / bytynge, & good hete;
For good gynger colombyne / is best to drynke and ete;
Gynger valadyne & maydelyn ar not so holsom in mete.
looke þat your stikkes of synamome be thyn, bretille, & fayre in colewre,
and in youre mowthe, Fresche, hoot, & swete / that is best & sure,
For canelle is not so good in this crafte & cure
Synamome is hoot & dry in his worchynge while he wille dure.
Graynes of paradise, hoot & moyst they be:
Sugre of iij. cute / white / hoot & moyst in his propurte;
Sugre Candy is best of alle, as y telle the,
and red wyne is whote & drye to tast, fele, & see,
Graynes / gynger, longe pepur, & sugre / hoot & moyst in worchynge,
Synamome / Canelle / red wyne / hoot & drye in theire doynge;
Turnesole is good & holsom for red wyne colowrynge:
alle these ingredyentes, they ar for ypocras makynge.
Good son, youre powdurs so made, vche by tham self in bleddur laid,
hange sure youre perche & bagges that they from yow not brayd,
& that no bagge touche other / do as y haue yow saide;
the furst bag a galoun / alle other of a potelle, vchon by other teied.
Furst put in a basoun a galoun ij. or iij. wyne so red;
then put in youre powdurs, yf ye wille be sped,
and aftyr in-to the renners so lett hym be fed,
than in-to the second bagge so wold it be ledde.
loke thou take a pece in thyne hand euermore amonge,
and assay it in thy mouthe if hit be any thynge stronge,
and if thow fele it welle both with mouthe & tonge,
than put it in the iij. vesselle / & tary not to longe.
And than yiff thou feele it be not made parfete,
that it cast to moche gynger, with synamome alay that hete;
and if hit haue synamome to moche, with gynger of iij. cute;
than if to moche sigure ther be / by discressioun ye may wete.
Thus, son, shaltow make parfite ypocras, as y the say;
but with thy mowthe to prove hit, / be thow tastynge alle-way;
let hit renne in iiij. or vj bagges; gete them, if thow may,
of bultelle clothe, if thy bagges be the fynere withowten nay.
Good son loke thy bagges be hoopid at the mothe above,
the surere mayst thow put in thy wyne vn-to thy behoue,
the furst bag of a galoun / alle other of a potelle to prove;
hange thy bagges sure by the hoppis; do so for my loue;
And vndur euery bagge, good son, a basoun clere & bryght;
and now is the ypocras made / for to plese many a wight.
the draff of the spicery / is good for Sewes in kychyn diyt;
and yiff thow cast hit away, thow dost thy mastir no riyt.
Now, good son, thyne ypocras is made parfite & welle;
y wold than ye put it in staunche & a clene vesselle,
and the mouthe þer-off y-stopped euer more wisely & felle
and serue hit forth with wafurs bothe in chambur & Celle.

Breads and Cakes

PARSLEY BREAD

One of the few extant bread recipes, this makes excellent eating fresh and is splendid, when aged, for trenchers.

Ingredients

2 packages active dry yeast

1¾ cups warm water

6 Tablespoons honey

7 to 8 cups (or more) unbleached white wheat bread flour

6 small whole eggs plus one yolk

⅔ cup currants, softened in warm water

1⅔ Tablespoons coarse salt

6 Tablespoons melted butter or oil

1½ teaspoons dried rosemary

1½ teaspoons dried basil

⅔ cup finely chopped fresh parsley

1½ teaspoons cinnamon

Several drops green vegetable color (see *Food Paints and Pigments*)

Butter for greasing bowls and cookie sheet

Method

1. Sprinkle yeast on ½ cup of the warm water; stir in honey. Let proof for 5 minutes.
2. Add remaining warm water; beat in about 2½ to 3 cups of flour. Beat with wooden spoon for about 200 strokes. Cover with damp towel, put in warm place, and allow this sponge to rise for 30–45 minutes, or until doubled.

3. Stir down.
4. Beat 5 whole eggs plus one yolk. Stir in currants. (Or add them later, before rise in Step 8.) Beat in salt and melted butter or oil. Mix into the dough.
5. In a mortar crush the dried herbs and chopped parsley to a paste. Mix in cinnamon. Add to batter and beat well. (Bread should be a delicate green hue. If color from parsley isn't strong enough, add green food color—sparingly.) Add remaining flour first with a spoon, then with hands, until dough comes away from the side of the bowl.
6. Turn out onto lightly floured board or marble and knead until smooth, shiny, and elastic, about 10–12 minutes, adding small amounts of flour if necessary.
7. Place in buttered bowl; cover with damp towel. Let rise in warm place until doubled in bulk, about 50 minutes.
8. Punch down. Cover; let rise again until doubled in bulk, about 30 minutes. (This rise, though unnecessary, gives the bread a finer texture.)
9. Punch down. Turn out onto floured surface. Let rest for five minutes. Shape into one or two free-form curls or twists. Place on buttered cookie sheet. Cover lightly with damp towel and let rise in warm place to double, about 25 minutes.
10. Preheat oven to 375°. Brush loaf or loaves with remaining whole egg, beaten. Bake for about 50 minutes, or until nicely browned and loaf sounds hollow when rapped on top and bottom. Cool on rack.
11. Serve with hard cheese, fresh butter, and white wine.

BURREBREDE
SHORTBREAD

Ingredients

3 cups all-purpose unbleached white flour	½ teaspoon powdered ginger
½ cup superfine sugar	¾ teaspoon allspice
2 teaspoons cinnamon	½ teaspoon salt
½ teaspoon powdered cardamon	1 cup butter at room temperature

Method

1. Preheat oven to 350°.
2. Combine sugar, spices, and salt evenly. Separate into 2 equal portions, reserving one.
3. On strong, clean kneading surface (breadboard, butcher block, or counter) mix gently, by hand, one-half the spice mixture into the flour.
4. Squeeze butter in hands, and bit by bit add spiced flour by working it into butter on the board. Take time to thoroughly integrate dry and butter mixture.
5. Press batter into 8″ square, shallow pan.
6. Score the surface of the batter to make "fingers" (2 inches by 1 inch) of shortbread. Also make several shallow fork pricks on each "finger."
7. With reserved spice mixture, evenly strew all cuts.
8. Bake 1 hour or less until firm and yellow, not brown.
9. Cool in pan; break into shortbread fingers and serve. Often tasting better several days old, this keeps beautifully if stored in an airtight tin or tightly wrapped in tinfoil.

FLOTERES
SALMON AND CURRANT DUMPLINGS

Ingredients

  1 cup flour

1½ teaspoons baking powder

  ½ teaspoon cinnamon

  ½ teaspoon salt

  ¼ teaspoon crushed fennel seed

  ⅛ teaspoon thyme

  ⅔ cup milk

  2 well-beaten eggs

  ½ cup cooked salmon, finely flaked

  ½ cup currants

  4 quarts boiling water

  1 Tablespoon salt

Method

1. Mix thoroughly the flour, baking powder cinnamon, salt, fennel, and thyme. Stir in ½ cup milk, making a smooth batter.
2. Beat the eggs to a lemon hue. Add the eggs to the batter.
3. Stir in the salmon and currants. Add more milk if mixture is too dry.
4. With fingers lightly wet in warm water, form small balls of less than a teaspoon volume. Drop these into briskly boiling salted water in a wide, deep soup pot. Reduce heat to a slow boil. Cover.
5. In about 7 minutes the "floaters" will rise to the top of the water. Remove with a skimmer and serve warm. These "dumplings" or "knaidlach" are splendid in clear soups, wine broths, or plain.

RYSBRED
RICE PANCAKES

Ingredients

  3 teaspoons finely minced onion

¼ to ½ cup oil for frying

  2 Tablespoons flour

  ¼ teaspoon mace

  ½ teaspoon salt

  ½ cup coarsely ground almonds

  2 cups cold cooked rice

  4 raw eggs

Garnish

"Cinnamon honey":

  2 Tablespoons honey,

  ⅔ teaspoon cinnamon

Method

1. Heat 2 Tablespoons of oil in deep skillet and lightly sauté onions until golden. Skim off onions, drain, and reserve. Allow skillet to cool for reuse later.
2. Mix mace and salt with flour.
3. Add flour and almonds to the cooked rice in a mixing bowl, stirring thoroughly.
4. Beat the eggs with a fork. Stir in the onions.
5. Mix eggs into rice.
6. In the skillet, gently heat the remaining oil along with any residual from the onions sautéing.
7. Form small "rice balls" of about 1 and ½ inch in diameter and then flatten them in the hand to "pancake" shape. Or drop batter by Tablespoonful, making silver dollar-sized cakes.
8. Fry rice cakes on both sides until golden brown. Drain on paper towel on cooling rack, briefly.
9. Stir cinnamon into honey, and drizzle on rice cakes. Serve warm.

SOPPES DORRE
Spiced Toast with Almond Sauce

The name means either: "golden sops" (*d'or*), or "The King's Sops" (*du roi*); it is a simple savory dish.

Ingredients

½ cup ground almonds

1 cup white wine

⅛ teaspoon saffron

1 Tablespoon brown sugar

½ teaspoon salt

4 slices white bread, toasted lightly

4 Tablespoons butter

Dredge:

¼ teaspoon powdered ginger

½ teaspoon white granulated sugar

½ teaspoon cinnamon

¼ teaspoon cloves

⅛ teaspoon mace

Method

1. Prepare a spice dredge by uniting ginger, white sugar, cinnamon, cloves, and mace. Reserve.
2. Boil ground almonds with wine for 7 minutes, making "almond syrup."
3. Add saffron, brown sugar, and salt. Stir, simmer 2 minutes. Keep syrup warm.
4. Cut slices of toast into long "fingers" (about 4 to each slice) and butter on both sides.
5. Reheat toast briefly on grill or in frying pan.
6. Sprinkle toasts with spice dredge, allowing spices to penetrate the butter.
7. Pour almond syrup over bread fingers on serving platter. Serve warm.

TANSY CAKE WITH PEPPERMINT CREAM

Ingredients

2 cups gritty brown-bread crumbs (a stone-ground whole wheat or mixed-grain brown bread makes a particularly tasty tansy)

3 Tablespoons flour

½ teaspoon nutmeg

¼ teaspoon powdered ginger

½ teaspoon salt

½ cup pitted and minced dates

½ cup diced dried apricots (or currants)

½ cup heavy sweet cream

4 large raw eggs

6 Tablespoons butter for frying

Mint Cream

1 cup heavy cream

2 Tablespoons sugar

1 teaspoon dried peppermint

Several drops green food coloring, optional (see *Food Paints and Pigments*)

Method

1. Sprinkle bread crumbs with flour, nutmeg, ginger, and salt, and stir.
2. Mix fruits, cream, and eggs until evenly blended.
3. Combine egg and crumb mixtures. Separate into 2 or 3 portions for frying.
4. Fry each in a well-buttered skillet, turning if possible, as for a large pancake.
5. Serve cool, cut in wedges, topped with green peppermint cream.
6. To prepare cream, whip until stiff, slowly blending in the sugar, peppermint, and green coloring. When cream "peaks" either spoon onto tansy cake, or pipe several green peaks from a pastry tube with a serrated nozzle.

NUTTERBREDE

NUSTORT OR NUTCAKE FOR THE JEWISH FESTIVAL OF PASSOVER

This flourless "nustort" appears in various medieval cookeries, German and English. This congenial modernization comes from the family archives of Mrs. Emile Flesch, whose Hungarian-Jewish heritage includes this "Kosher for Pesach" cake.

Ingredients

8 egg yolks and 8 egg whites, separated

3 cups sugar

2 cups coarsely ground walnuts

¼ teaspoon cloves

½ teaspoon cinnamon

3 drops lemon juice

4 Tablespoons heavy, sweet, red wine

1 cup raspberry preserves

Butter for greasing 2 tort pans

Glaze:

½ fresh lemon

2 cups confectioner's sugar

¼ teaspoon salt

2 to 4 Tablespoons warm water

Method

1. Preheat oven to 425°, then reduce to 350°.
2. Beat egg yolks until lemon-colored.
3. Mix yolks with sugar.
4. Beat egg whites until stiff.
5. Fold in sugared yolks.
6. Add cloves and cinnamon to nuts.
7. Combine lemon juice with wine.
8. Evenly sprinkle wine over nuts. Allow to settle for 3 minutes.
9. Fold egg mixture into the wined nuts.
10. Pour into two well-greased tort pans, approximately 8 inches in diameter and 1½ inches deep.
11. Bake at 350° for ¾ of an hour. Remove from pans to rack and cool.
12. Spread raspberry preserves on top of one tort and place the other on top to form the second layer.
13. Prepare the simple lemon glaze by grating finely the lemon peel; squeeze lemon juice into water and stir with salt into sugar, making a thin white fluid.
14. Pour over cake, allowing to run down over sides. Serve cool.

OREOLES
Elderberry Funnel Cakes

The American "Pennsylvania Dutch" still make this pleasant, simple fried "cruller." Because the batter is piped through a funnel or tube, amusing or fantastic shapes are possible with pleasantly edible results.

Ingredients

3 beaten eggs

½ teaspoon salt

2 cups milk

4 cups flour

2 scant teaspoons baking powder

½ cup elderberry preserves or Damson-plum preserves (from "Damascus," whence came many a medieval shipment of plums)

1 to 2 cups vegetable oil for "deep frying"

a funnel (½-inch diameter nozzle or pastry tube with serrated edge)

Garnish

4 to 6 Tablespoons honey

Method

1. Add salt to the beaten eggs; stir the eggs briskly into the milk.
2. Stir the baking powder into the flour.
3. Mix most of the milk and the eggs with the flour.
4. Add elderberry or plum preserves to the mixture. If the resulting batter is too thick to run easily through the funnel or large nozzled pastry tube, add a small amount of milk; if too thin to hold its shape—consistency ought to be a reasonably thick pancake batter—add a small amount of flour.
5. Into hot oil in a deep, wide, frying vessel, pipe the elderberry (or plum) batter in spiral or any imaginative shapes, making initials or designs. Fry until golden.
6. Remove from oil; drain; lightly drizzle with honey, and serve warm.

CIRCLETES
ALMOND-CARDAMON CAKES

Ingredients

1 cup butter

⅔ cup brown sugar

1 beaten egg

2½ cups flour

½ teaspoon grated lemon peel

¾ teaspoon crushed cardamon

½ cup ground almonds

1 cup currants

Butter for greasing cookie sheets

Method

1. Preheat oven to 350°.
2. Cream butter. Blend in sugar, beating with a spoon until frothy.
3. Whip in the beaten egg.
4. Stir peel, cardamon, sugar, almonds, and currants into the flour.
5. Beat the dry mixture into the sweetened butter.
6. Chill dough for at least 1 hour.
7. Using well-floured fingers, shape dough into small balls (1 inch in diameter) placing them 1 inch apart on greased cookie sheets.
8. Bake 7–10 minutes until light golden. Cool on racks.

FOYLES
LAYERED, SPICED PANCAKES

Ingredients

½ teaspoon salt

1 cup flour

1 cup milk

3 raw eggs

½ cup oil for sautéing

⅔ cup brown sugar

¼ cup slivered, candied ginger, or shaved, candied red anise or licorice

Garnish: crushed sprigs of parsley

Method

1. Sift the salt with the flour.
2. Slowly add the milk, making a smooth batter.
3. Beat the eggs until frothy. Add the eggs to the batter.
4. Thoroughly coat the bottom of a heavy skillet with oil, and heat; pour off excess, reserving it to be used again.
5. Pour a small amount of the very thin batter into the hot skillet, tilting it from side to side in order to thoroughly coat the bottom. When the "pancake" browns, carefully flip it to cook the other side. (Each side browns in about 30 seconds.)
6. Keep this and the subsequent pancakes warm on a cookie sheet in a slow oven, about 225°.
7. Repeat the process for making thin pancakes until you have about 14.
8. Make 2 stacks, 7 in each, and lightly strew between each layer an even mixture of brown sugar and candied ginger.
9. Cut a wedge of the 7-layered pancake for each portion. Garnish with parsley. Serve warm.

Meats

CUSTARD LUMBARDE
Marrow and Fruit Tart

Ingredients

9-inch pie shell, unbaked

2 cups boiling, salted water

8 pieces bone marrow

2/3 cup heavy cream

6 eggs

1/4 cup dates, rinsed and quartered, pits discarded

1/4 cup prunes, pits removed, quartered

1/4 cup sugar

1/2 teaspoon cinnamon

1/2 teaspoon salt

Method

1. Preheat oven to 400°.
2. Bake empty pie shell "blind" for 10 to 15 minutes. Dried lima beans or other reusable beans, on a round sheet of waxed paper placed on the bottom of the pie shell, will prevent its bubbling. Reset oven to 375°.
3. Boil marrow in salted water for 20 minutes; drain. Cut the cooked marrow into small strips.
4. Stir eggs with a fork. Beat in heavy cream.
5. Add salt, cinnamon, and sugar to evenly mixed dates and prunes.
6. Distribute fruits evenly over the bottom of the pie shell. Pour on the egg-and-cream mixture.
7. Arrange marrow strips evenly over surface of pie.
8. Bake for about 30 minutes until custard is set and pie crust browned.

MAWMENYE
LENTILS AND LAMB

Ingredients

1¼ pounds lean lamb, cut into small
    pieces ½ by ½ inch

 ¼ teaspoon pepper

 ½ teaspoon salt

  2 Tablespoons butter for sautéing

  1 cup chicken broth

  1 cup dry lentils

  4 cups beef broth

 ¼ teaspoon cinnamon

 ¼ teaspoon salt

 ½ teaspoon dried basil

  1 cup diced turnip or squash

  1 cup currants

 ⅔ cup coarsely cut figs

Garnish

"gold" leaves of any edible plant—such
as young celery leaves or 6 to 8 yellow
dandelion flowers

Method

1. Salt and pepper lamb and then brown in melted butter.
2. Add the cup of chicken broth; gently simmer for 45 minutes or until lamb is tender. Drain.
3. Wash and pick over lentils to eliminate any stray stones.
4. Bring lentils to boil in 4 cups of beef broth, reducing heat to low; simmer for 15 minutes.
5. Combine cinnamon, salt, and basil, and stir into diced turnips.
6. Add turnips, currants, and figs to the lentils and cook very slowly for 10 minutes.
7. Stir lamb into lentils. Turn out into attractive serving bowl and garnish with gold leaves or "plant" with dandelions.

GALANTINE PIE

Ingredients

Same ingredients as for *Galantine Sauce*.

Plus

½ cup lean beef, minced small

½ cup chicken breast, minced small

 2 Tablespoons butter for sautéing

⅔ cup bog berries or cranberries

⅔ cup currants

½ cup dates, pits removed,
  cut fine

 1 9-inch pie shell and lid

Method

1. Prepare galantine sauce and reserve. Preheat oven to 400°.
2. Briefly sauté beef and chicken in hot butter. Remove from pan and drain.
3. Combine evenly the meats and the fruits.
4. Place in pie shell and pour on 1½ cups of the galantine sauce.
5. Cover pie with pastry lid, carefully sealing and crimping the edges. Prick top in several places.
6. Bake at 400° for 30 to 40 minutes until well browned.

A ROSTE
Beef Roast with Crisps

Ingredients

4 or more Tablespoons oil or butter for searing meat

5 pounds beef roast tied with butcher's cord

½ cup flour

1 teaspoon cinnamon

1 teaspoon salt

1 teaspoon dried sweet basil, crushed

½ teaspoon dried rosemary, crushed

¼ teaspoon thyme

1 cup dates, pits removed, cut in halves

1 cup dried figs, stems removed, cut in strips

½ cup dried apple rings, cut in halves

2 Tablespoons brown sugar or honey

1½ cups beef stock

Batter

1 cup flour

1 egg

⅔ cup milk

¼ teaspoon salt

½ scant teaspoon baking powder

¼ cup chopped fresh parsley, crushed

Method

1. Preheat oven to 350°.
2. In Dutch oven or cast-iron pot (either having tight covers) melt the butter.
3. Dredge the roast with the mixture of flour, cinnamon, and salt, and thoroughly sear in the heated butter, browning all sides.
4. Mix basil, rosemary, and thyme. Mix spices with combined dates, figs, and apples.
5. Arrange spiced fruits around the meat. Sprinkle sugar or drizzle honey on fruits.
6. Carefully pour on beef stock around edges of the pot so as to avoid "flooding" any food surfaces. Cover tightly.
7. Bake at 350° for 3 hours, or until tender. Remove from oven to cool for 30 minutes. Increase oven heat to 450°.
8. Prepare a very thick batter by vigorously stirring all ingredients, except parsley. Add extra flour if necessary.
9. Add chopped parsley to the batter.
10. Pour batter over roast allowing the excess to trickle into the gravy. Return meat to hot oven (450°) for 5 to 10 minutes so that coating browns nicely.
11. Cut the roast in its dough "jacket" (somewhat reminiscent of the modern Beef Wellington). Serve the "crisps," which formed in the juices, along with the gravy and fruit.

CANELYNE
CANELINE BEEF PIE

Ingredients

1 pound lean beef, cut into very small cubes

2 Tablespoons vegetable oil for sautéing

2/3 cup boiling water

1 Tablespoon cinnamon

1/2 teaspoon nutmeg

1/4 teaspoon thyme

1/4 teaspoon sage

9-inch unbaked pastry pie shell and lid

1 cup raw cranberries, stems removed

2 Tablespoons honey

2/3 cup currants

Garnish

"Cinnamon sugar" (1 teaspoon sugar to 1/2 teaspoon cinnamon)

For Sauce

1/2 cup ground almonds

1/2 cup dry white wine

Method

1. In heavy skillet sauté the meat pieces in hot oil.
2. In boiling water dissolve cinnamon, nutmeg, thyme, and sage. Add to the sautéed meat. Simmer slowly for about 15 minutes until meat is not quite tender for eating.
3. Remove from fire, drain, reserving cooking liquid both for the pie and a side sauce.
4. Preheat oven to 425°. Line the bottom of the pie shell with the washed cranberries.
5. Evenly drizzle the honey over the berries.
6. Evenly distribute the currants.
7. Arrange the meat pieces over all. Add about 7 Tablespoons of the reserved cooking liquid to the pie.
8. Cover with the pastry lid, carefully crimping edges to seal. Pierce several times with a fork.
9. Sprinkle edges of crust with blended cinnamon sugar. Bake at 400° for about 40 minutes until crust is well browned. Serve hot.
10. Add almonds and white wine to the residual caneline broth and simmer 7 minutes to make a side sauce. (If you find this too "heavy" to serve with the pie, try it poured over a hard cheese or over ricotta perched on top of a bread trencher.)

DILLED VEAL BALLS

Ingredients

1 pound chopped veal

1/2 pound dried figs, stems removed, minced fine

1/2 teaspoon cinnamon

2 Tablespoons dried dill weed

1/4 teaspoon nutmeg

1/2 teaspoon salt

1/2 cup toasted dark-wheat bread crumbs

3 eggs

1/4 cup oil for sautéing

Garnish

1/2 cup raspberry preserves

Method

1. In large mixing bowl, evenly mix veal with figs.
2. Combine cinnamon, dill, salt, and nutmeg with crumbs.
3. Stir in spiced crumbs to veal and figs.
4. Beat the eggs, reserving about 1 Tablespoonful.
5. Add eggs to meat mixture, molding it by hand or spoon until it holds shape.
6. With egg-wet fingers, form small meatballs 1½ inch in diameter and sauté in hot oil about 10 minutes, or until crisp on the outside. Drain and serve, with a dollop of raspberry preserves on each meatball.

NOMBLYS DE ROO (OR VENYSON)
"HUMBLE PIE" OR SPICED TRIPE

Although other "garbage" fancied a delicacy in the Middle Ages is often a garnish for waste bins today, tripe was served to all classes of feasters from the most humble through the most noble. Most animals' gastrointestinal systems as well as urino-genital tracts were used by inventive medieval cooks for several spectacular dishes. This particular pie is the origin of our modern expression for submission, "to eat humble pie." (The word "numble" comes from "an umble" in which the *n* was transferred to the word from the article.)

Ingredients

2½ to 3 pounds honey-comb tripe

3 cups water

1 teaspoon salt

2 cups beef broth

1 cup wine

2 Tablespoons cumin seeds

¼ teaspoon pepper

1 Tablespoon cinnamon

1 teaspoon powdered ginger

1 Tablespoon vinegar

2 eggs

9-inch pastry shell

Garnish

"Cinnamon sugar" (1 teaspoon sugar to ½ teaspoon cinnamon)

Method

1. Boil tripe in water and ½ teaspoon salt for ½ hour. Preheat oven to 275°.
2. Drain tripe and discard boiling water. Cut tripe into small bite-size pieces, about 1 inch across.
3. In a heavy covered casserole, combine broth, wine, spices, vinegar, and tripe. Bring to slow simmer.
4. Bake at slowest simmer for 10 hours until tripe is tender. Reset oven to 400°.
5. With a slotted spoon, remove tripe to pastry shell, reserving the liquid.
6. Beat 2 eggs with ⅔ cup of the reserved liquid in which the tripe had been simmered.
7. Pour over tripe in pastry shell.
8. Bake for 40 minutes until pie is "set" and crust nicely browned.
9. Before serving, sprinkle cinnamon sugar on crust of pastry.

VISORYE
VEAL CUSTARD PIE

Ingredients

2/3 cup raw veal, minced small

2/3 cup water

1/2 teaspoon finely chopped parsley

1/8 teaspoon sage

1/8 teaspoon hyssop

1/4 teaspoon crushed rosemary

1/4 teaspoon powdered ginger

1/2 teaspoon salt

1 teaspoon vinegar

2/3 cup red wine

1/8 teaspoon pepper

1/4 teaspoon cinnamon

1/8 scant teaspoon ground cloves

1/8 teaspoon mace

1/8 teaspoon saffron

4 eggs

1/2 cup dates, cut into small slivers

1/4 cup prunes, cut into small slivers

8-inch pie shell

Method

1. Preheat oven to 400°.
2. In heavy pot, simmer the minced veal with water, parsley, sage, hyssop, rosemary, ginger, salt, and vinegar for 7 minutes.
3. In small saucepan simmer wine for 3 minutes with the remaining spices: pepper, cinnamon, cloves, mace, and saffron.
4. Add spiced wine to veal broth. Simmer 2 minutes.
5. Remove herbed meat with a skimmer or slotted spoon and let broth cool. (Add water, if necessary, to make 1¼ cups of wine-broth.)
6. Strain the eggs or lightly beat them and add to the broth so that it thickens.
7. Place veal in pie shell along with an even arrangement of the dates and prunes.
8. Pour on the custard broth.
9. Bake until custard is puffed and set, and crust is browned, about 30 minutes.

Fish

PORPOISE PUDDING
Oat-stuffed Pike

Ingredients

4 pound pike, whole, with head and tail intact

½ cup fish blood, or fish stock or dry white wine

2 cups oatmeal (gritty "Irish oatmeal" is best)

⅔ cup raisins

¾ teaspoon salt

¼ teaspoon pepper

½ teaspoon ginger or 1 teaspoon finely chopped candied ginger

6 Tablespoons butter

4 Tablespoons melted butter for basting

Method

1. Preheat oven to 400°.
2. If you obtain the fish complete, make an incision into the underbelly to allow the fish to bleed into a deep bowl. Reserve ½ cup of blood. (Otherwise, obtain fish boned and gutted by the fish market, though still looking "whole.")
3. Mix oatmeal, raisins, salt, pepper, and ginger.
4. Melt butter in baking dish large enough to accommodate the pike.
5. Pour off half the melted butter into the oatmeal mixture.
6. Add fish blood (or stock or white wine) and stir.
7. Stuff the pike about two-thirds full with this "pudding," allowing for its expansion in cooking and for complete closure of the fish. Carefully sew the fish closed with needle and heavy thread.
8. Shape leftover pudding into small balls.
9. Place fish in buttered baking pan. Arrange pudding balls around the fish so that they bake until crisp. Brush fish and pudding balls with melted butter. Baste 4 times during baking.
10. Bake for 30 minutes or until fish is tender and juicy. Serve warm.

VYAND DE CYPRIS IN LENT
ALMOND FISH STEW

Ingredients

1 cup coarse-ground almonds

3 cups milk

1 cup cooked crabmeat, minced

1 cup cooked salmon, minced

4 Tablespoons of flour

1 teaspoon salt

½ cup white wine ("Vernage," i.e., Vernaccia)

½ cup sugar

Garnish

¼ cup pomegranate seed or thin slices of pomegranate

Method

1. In large enameled porcelain pot, gently simmer the ground almonds with milk.
2. Add the crabmeat and salmon, stir, and simmer two minutes.
3. Add flour and salt to ½ cup of the hot milk; stir this into the pot and simmer 2 minutes until mixture thickens.
4. Briefly heat wine with sugar and add to the creamed fish. Simmer another 2 minutes.
5. Pour into serving bowl and garnish with pomegranate seeds or sliced pomegranate so that each portion has some red pomegranate decoration and taste.

LUCE WAFERS
A DELICATE FISH CAKE

Fish stomachs generally grace the garbage cans of fish markets, not their display cases. However, with such fish maws, as with other "giblets" modern cooks tend to waste, medieval cooks created delicacies.

Ingredients

1 cup of luce or salmon or flounder "stomachs," or fresh fish fillets, cut small (about ½ pound)

1 cup or more of beef broth

½ cup grated cheddar cheese

½ cup all-purpose flour

½ teaspoon brown sugar

¼ teaspoon salt

½ teaspoon powdered ginger

3 egg whites

3 egg yolks

1 whole egg

1 teaspoon milk

2 Tablespoons each, oil and butter combination for frying

Garnish

Fresh parsley or dill, chopped

Method

1. In large heavy frying pan or skillet gently poach fish in enough beef broth to cover, until just done, about 7 minutes.

2. Drain fish or fish stomachs, discarding broth. Gently flake with a fork or cut into small slivers. (If using fillets, be sure to eliminate all bones.)
3. Combine grated cheese, flour, sugar, salt, and ginger.
4. Combine fish with dry mixture.
5. Beat egg whites until light and frothy.
6. Carefully fold into fish-and-cheese mixture.
7. Slowly heat oil and butter in heavy skillet.
8. Beat the yolks, whole egg, and milk.
9. Wetting hands in egg, form thin fish wafers or patties. Immediately sauté in skillet, turning once, until golden brown.
10. Drain (on paper towel) and serve warm. Garnish wafers with chopped fresh parsley or dill.

PYKE EN DOUCETTE
SMOKED PIKE SALAD IN PASTRY

Ingredients

  1 onion, diced small

  2 Tablespoons butter for sautéing

  2/3 teaspoon dried sweet basil, crushed

  1/4 teaspoon rosemary, crushed

  1/4 teaspoon salt

  1/4 teaspoon sage

  1 pound smoked pike (ready for eating)

  1 Tablespoon heavy cream

  1/2 cup finely shredded lettuce

  1/2 cup dates, pits removed, finely minced

  12 small baked pastry shells about 1 1/2 inches in diameter

Garnish

  Small fresh fennel sprigs

Method

1. Preheat oven to 400°.
2. Lightly sauté onion until light gold and not brown. Drain.
3. Mix basil, rosemary, salt, and sage. Add to onions.
4. Flake pike.
5. Stir into pike the cream, spiced onions, lettuce, and dates to evenly distribute ingredients.
6. Spoon or pipe with pastry tube (with wide nozzle) into baked pastry tarts.
7. Bake for 5 minutes, or until piping hot. Serve hot or cold with fennel garnish.

SAUMON ROSTED
ROAST SALMON IN ONION WINE SAUCE

Ingredients

6 salmon steaks for broiling	4 small onions, finely minced
1½ cups red wine	1 Tablespoon vinegar
1 Tablespoon cinnamon	*Garnish*
1 teaspoon powdered ginger	6 foils of parsley wet in vinegar

Method

1. Broil salmon steaks, or as the fifteenth-century recipe suggests, "roast on a grid iron" about 5 minutes each side.
2. Slowly simmer wine with spices, onions, and vinegar, about 12 minutes.
3. Pour the hot syrup over the salmon and serve. Wet parsley foils in vinegar to garnish each salmon steak.

SAUMON PIE
SALMON AND FRUIT TART

Ingredients

1 pound fresh cooked salmon, cut into 1-inch chunks	⅛ teaspoon ginger
½ lemon	¼ teaspoon salt
1 cup figs, stems removed, cut small	¼ cup raisins
1 cup wine, red or white	¼ cup currants
½ cup dates, pits removed, cut in quarters	1½ Tablespoons pine nuts
⅛ teaspoon pepper	1 unbaked 9-inch pie shell and lid
½ teaspoon cinnamon	*Pastry Glaze*
¼ teaspoon ground cloves	¼ teaspoon pulverized almonds
⅛ scant teaspoon mace	⅛ teaspoon saffron
	2 Tablespoons milk

Method

1. Preheat oven to 375°.
2. Squeeze lemon onto chunks of salmon.
3. Simmer figs in wine for 10 minutes until soft. Remove figs to mixing bowl.
4. In same wine, briefly simmer dates 3 minutes. Reserve dates in a separate bowl.
5. To the figs, add all spices except the pine nuts. Add raisins and currants and mix evenly.
6. Place this mixture in the bottom of the pie shell, evenly distributing the fruits.
7. Scatter pine nuts evenly over the mixture.
8. Alternate drained salmon pieces with dates on the surface of the pie.

9. Close the pie with its pastry lid, crimping the edges to tightly seal. Pierce the lid with fork four times. Make a small vent hole in the center.
10. Glaze with mixture of milk, almonds, and saffron, well mixed.
11. Bake 30–40 minutes until well browned.

PLAYCE YSOD
POACHED PLAICE WITH MUSTARD SAUCE

Ingredients

Fresh whole plaice, about 3 pounds

3 cups water

½ cup chopped parsley

½ teaspoon salt

½ cup ale

Sauce

1 cup spicy mustard

4 Tablespoons ale

½ teaspoon salt

½ cup white bread crumbs

Optional

¼ cup oil or clarified butter for frying instead of boiling

Method

1. Boil water, parsley, salt, and ale.
2. Poach plaice in that broth for 12 to 15 minutes, until it nearly flakes.
3. Meanwhile, mix mustard, ale, salt, and crumbs to make a sauce. Briefly heat to a simmer.
4. Serve fish with warm mustard sauce poured on.

GYNGERE
GINGERED CARP

Ingredients

1½ pounds smoked carp or about 12 slices

½ cup candied ginger, slivered or coarsely grated

½ teaspoon rosemary

¾ teaspoon dried sweet basil

½ teaspoon crushed pine nuts

½ cup beef or fish stock

Garnish

Parsley sprigs

Method

1. Preheat oven to 350°.
2. Place carp slices side by side in baking dish.
3. Combine spices and herbs with stock. Pour the thick spiced stock onto the sliced carp.
4. Bake for 10 minutes. Serve hot or cold, being sure flakes of ginger accompany each portion. Garnish with parsley.

ROSEYE
FRIED LOACHE WITH ROSES AND ALMONDS

Ingredients

½ cup roasted almonds

1 Tablespoon brown sugar

1½ cups whole milk

¼ cup rice flour or all-purpose
white flour

3 Tablespoons white sugar

¼ teaspoon salt

⅛ teaspoon saffron

½ cup red rose hips or washed red
rose petals (If using fresh petals,
be sure they have not been sprayed
with an insecticide.) Or 4 Tablespoons rose-hip powder

½ cup flour for dredging

2 to 3 pounds filleted loache or similar
white fish, cut into small serving
portions (about 2 inches by 1 inch)

3 Tablespoons butter and 3 Tablespoons oil for sautéing

Spice Powder

½ teaspoon brown sugar

¼ teaspoon cinnamon

¼ teaspoon nutmeg
(stirred together)

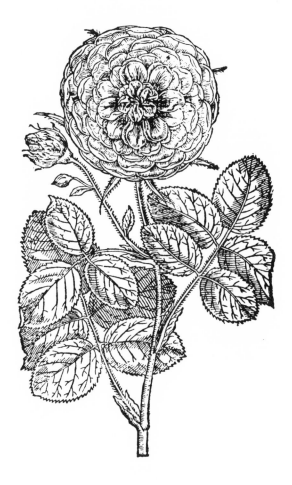

Method

1. Coarsely grind roasted almonds in mortar or blender. In porcelain pot, slowly simmer the ground almonds with 1 Tablespoon brown sugar and 1½ cups of milk.
2. Pour off approximately ½ cup of the almond milk and reserve.
3. Mix white sugar, salt, and saffron with ¼ cup flour.
4. Slowly add this spiced flour to the 1 cup of warm almond milk in the pot.
5. In mortar or blender, crush the rose hips or rose leaves with ½ cup almond milk, making a pleasant pink fluid, "roseye." If the roses have not imparted enough of a "hot pink" hue, then add 1 or 2 drops of red food coloring. (See *Food Paints and Pigments*.)
6. Add rose milk to almond milk. Gently strew on the "spice powder" of mixed sugar, cinnamon, and nutmeg, and slowly heat but do not boil. Keep warm while cooking fish.
7. Flour loache pieces, coating thoroughly, and fry in ½ butter and ½ oil until tender, less than 7 minutes.
8. Drain fried fish and arrange on platter. Pour the thick "roseye" over the loache and serve hot.

LAMPROI
BAKED LAMPREY

Ingredients

2 cups pumpernickel or whole grain brown bread, crumbed or cut into small pieces

½ cup red wine vinegar

1 cup wine

1 teaspoon cinnamon

⅛ teaspoon pepper

¼ teaspoon salt

1½ pounds lamprey or eel, skinned, cleaned and cut into 3-inch pieces

2 cups boiling water

8-inch pastry pie shell and pastry lid, uncooked

Extra Lamprey Syrup

½ cup wine

½ teaspoon ginger powder

2 to 3 slices white bread, crusts removed

Method

1. Preheat oven to 400°.
2. In shallow bowl, pour vinegar over bread until absorbed. Place sodden bread in strainer and press out excess vinegar.
3. In mixing bowl, beat spices into wine with rotary beater.
4. Stir vinegared bread into spiced wine.
5. Place lampreys in large frying pan and pour on enough boiling water to cover; poach gently for 9 to 12 minutes. Drain. Cut lampreys into bite-sized pieces.
6. Arrange these "gobbets" evenly over bottom of unbaked pie shell and pour the "wine-bread stew" over all, allowing about ⅛ inch above surface of filling for closure of the pie.
7. Carefully apply pie lid, sealing edges securely. Pierce a small hole in the center. (The original recipe suggests blowing through that "little hole in the middle" with a "good blast of wind from the mouth." Suddenly "stop the hole, the air still within," in order to keep the lid raised above the pie filling. That is still a reasonable modality.) When the crust is slightly hardened but not yet brown, prick the "coffin" with a pin or a fork in several places and bake until browned to taste, about 25 minutes.
8. Serve lamprey cold. If you wish to follow a medieval nobleman's recipe for the leftovers, reserve the lamprey liquid and much of the pie crust.
9. After most of the lamprey is eaten, any remaining is to be boiled with wine and powdered ginger. Lay bread fingers in the remaining pastry; pour on the newly made lamprey syrup and heat the new recycled lamprey pie, once again a lordly dish, a "gode lordys mete."

Fowl

MAWMENYE RYALLE
Spiced Capon or Pork or Partridge in Nutted Wine Sauce

Ingredients

 2 cups Vernaccia or strong, sweet wine

 2 Tablespoons powdered cinnamon

10 pine nuts, crushed fine

 3 Tablespoons sugar

 1/8 teaspoon sandalwood

 1/8 teaspoon ground cloves

1 1/2 cups shredded raw capon or pork or partridge

 2 Tablespoons butter for sautéing

 4 Tablespoons quince preserves or plum preserves

 1/8 teaspoon ginger powder

 1/4 teaspoon salt

 1/8 scant teaspoon saffron

 1 cup coarsely cut or slivered almonds

1 1/2 cups ale

Garnish

 2 Tablespoons brown sugar

Method

1. Heat Vernaccia and cinnamon in heavy enameled saucepan.
2. Add pine nuts, sugar, sandalwood, and cloves. Simmer gently for 10 minutes.
3. Sauté meat in butter until flesh turns white.
4. Add meat and quince preserves to the spiced wine; season with ginger, salt, and saffron, slowly cooking for 15 minutes, if fowl is used; 20 minutes if pork.
5. In another pot, gently simmer almonds in ale for 12 minutes.
6. Mix aled nuts into the meat and wine.
7. Serve in individual small bowls. Strew brown sugar on surface just before serving warm.

VYAND DE CIPRYS RYALLE
Spiced Minced Chicken Relish

Ingredients

8 egg yolks

1 cup honey

½ teaspoon clove powder

½ teaspoon salt

½ cup raisins

1 cup cooked capon or chicken, minced small

1 cup dry white wine

2 teaspoons sugar

1 Tablespoon flour

⅔ teaspoon cinnamon

Method

1. In a heavy saucepan, stir the egg yolks and honey. Add clove powder, salt, raisins, and chicken.
2. Simmer *very* slowly for 10 minutes, stirring constantly. Remove from heat.
3. Briefly heat wine, sugar, flour, and cinnamon, making a syrup.
4. Pour a small amount of spiced wine into a small decorative serving bowl, coating all its surface. Pour any excess back into the pot. Pour the syrup into a "gravy boat" for service.
5. Spoon the *vyand de ciprys* into the wine-coated bowl.
6. Serve with white-wine syrup as a relish for a plain roast or broiled fowl.

BLANKMANGERE
Chicken with Cumin and Cream

Ingredients

20 small individual pastry shells

4 chicken breasts, skinned and boned

4 Tablespoons for sautéing

1 cup chicken broth

1 cup ale

½ teaspoon salt

1 cup slivered almonds

1 cup heavy cream

1 teaspoon cumin seeds

1 teaspoon rosemary, finely ground

Method

1. Bake pastry-tart shells at 425° so that they are crisp for serving.
2. In heavy skillet, sauté chicken in butter until white on all sides.
3. Cut chicken into small cubes.
4. Add broth and simmer with chicken on low flame for 20 minutes or until tender.
5. Drain broth. Sprinkle salt on chicken. Reset oven to 400°.
6. Heat ale; pour hot ale over chicken. Let steep 20 minutes; drain off ale.
7. Roast almonds for 5 minutes at 400° on well-greased cookie sheet.
8. Add cream, almonds, rosemary, and cumin to chicken. Stir thoroughly.
9. Gently heat, but do not boil, for 7 minutes.
10. Spoon into crisp, warm tart shells. Or reheat for 5 minutes in warm oven before serving.

NEKKESAN
Swan-Neck Pudding or Capon or Turkey-Neck Pudding

Swans are rarely sold for food, raised in America more as ornamental birds than poultry. While the turkey is of course a New World fowl, introduced to Europe only in the sixteenth century, its size and taste are similar enough to the medieval swan to make its neck a fine substitute for swan neck; 2 large chicken necks also would do.

Ingredients

Gizzard, liver, heart, and neck of large bird

½ cup fresh chopped parsley

2 cups chicken broth

¼ teaspoon mace

¼ teaspoon cloves

⅛ teaspoon saffron

¼ teaspoon salt

⅛ teaspoon pepper

⅔ cup currants

3 raw eggs

1 Tablespoon melted butter

Method

1. Preheat oven to 375°.
2. Carefully remove the neck skin from the flesh, tendons, and bones beneath, making a cylindrical sheath. Sew one end to seal it, creating a long sausagelike container for filling.
3. Boil giblets with parsley and broth until tender, about 15 minutes. Discard parsley broth.
4. Carefully remove meat from neck, discarding all bone and gristle. Finely shred the neck meat. Chop gizzard, heart, and liver and mix with neck meat.
5. Stir all spices together with the currants; mix with giblets.
6. Beat raw eggs and stir into giblets.
7. Stuff the neck skin about ¾ full with mixture and sew the open end.
8. If you are baking a chicken or other large bird, arrange the stuffed neck on the back of the roasting bird with toothpicks, being careful to prick only the sewn ends, not the filled sheath itself. Otherwise, place neck in lightly greased baking pan.
9. Roast 25 minutes at 375° until pleasantly crisp, brushing several times with melted butter.
10. Serve the neck pudding in rounds, cut with an exceedingly sharp knife, on a parsley-bread trencher.

SMALLE BYRDES
Bird Stuffed with Dates and Mustard

Variations upon this recipe appear in several medieval cookeries for preparing such birds as the plover, baby crane, dove, snipe, "smalle hennes," and similar "smalle byrdes." The easily available cornish hen is a congenial bird for such cooking.

Ingredients

8 cornish hens, slightly over 1 pound each

1½ pounds pitted dates

4 Tablespoons spicy mustard

2 teaspoons salt

4 egg yolks for "endoring"

½ teaspoon yellow dandelion pollen or crushed petals

Method

1. Place dates, pits removed, in a colander and run them under hot water for several moments to soften. With fingers, separate each date into 2 or 3 pieces.
2. In a mixing bowl stir in mustard and ½ teaspoon salt to the softened dates.
3. Stuff each "smalle byrde" with the date mixture, approximately 1 large Tablespoon per bird.
4. Arrange birds in 1 or 2 baking dishes and sprinkle remaining salt evenly over all.
5. Bake at 275° for 50 minutes; intermittently baste and check to be sure the legs and wings do not burn. The birds will be dry. Remove from oven and tipping pan, pour off natural juices into heat-resistant pitcher or cup and then pour onto the birds. Repeat this basting several times. Remove from heat and partially cool, for about 20 minutes. Reset oven to 400°.
6. Beat egg yolks and stir in dandelion; paint onto cooling birds to gild them before serving. Bake for 4 to 6 minutes at 400° and serve hot.

FESAUNT AND GELYE
Baked Pheasant or Chicken with Cold Herbed Giblet Jelly

Ingredients

2 large, unblemished juice oranges	1 teaspoon basil, crushed
Large pheasant or roasting chicken, 5 to 6 pounds	½ teaspoon dill weed
All giblets of the bird	½ teaspoon salt
¼ cup oil for sautéing	¼ teaspoon pepper
½ pound dates, pits removed	2 Tablespoons cinnamon
1 teaspoon rosemary, crushed	1 cup ale

Method

1. Preheat oven to 325°.
2. Grate the peel from the two oranges. Squeeze the juice and pulverize the pulp, keeping juice and pulp separate from the grated peel. Reserve all three.
3. Sauté giblets and neck in oil for 5 minutes. Drain. Pick off neck meat and discard bones.
4. In a large bowl, mix sautéed giblets with dates, rosemary, basil, dill weed, salt, pepper, and orange peel.
5. Stuff the bird with this mixture. Place in deep roasting pan.
6. Pour the orange juice over the bird and arrange the orange pulp around it.
7. Liberally coat the bird with cinnamon. Pour ale between bird and walls of pan.
8. Bake 2 to 2½ hours until done.
9. Remove bird from juices and reserve it for reheating. Pour all juices from pan into a large mixing bowl.
10. Remove stuffing from cavity. Discard any bones and extraneous gristle; mince giblets and mix them back with dates.
11. Evenly distribute giblet-and-date mixture in the "juices."
12. Chill for 2 hours in a shallow dish.
13. Skim off fat. Serve the giblet jelly cold, cutting criss-cross lines through the planes so that the amber shapes reflect light.
14. Reheat bird at 425° for about 15 minutes or less until skin is crisp. Serve hot, along with the cold jelly, placed on parsley-bread trenchers for each guest.

FARSED CHYCKEN
CHICKEN STUFFED WITH LENTILS, CHERRIES, AND CHEESE

Ingredients

1 large roasting chicken, about 5 pounds, or two smaller fryers

½ cup dry lentils

1½ cups ale

1 cup chicken broth

½ to ⅔ pound cherries

½ pound ricotta cheese

⅔ cup oats

½ teaspoon salt

½ teaspoon sweet basil, dried

2 Tablespoons butter

Sauce

⅔ cup white wine

3 to 4 slices white bread, crumbed

¼ teaspoon salt

Method

1. Soak lentils in ale overnight. Boil lentils in residual ale plus broth for 15 minutes. Drain lentils and reserve 1 cup of fluid.
2. Remove pits from cherries and cut each in half, or, if very large, in quarters.
3. Mix lentils, cherries, ricotta, and oats. Sprinkle on salt and basil.
4. Stuff the bird, rub the skin with butter, and bake at 350° for about 2 hours or until flesh is tender and skin crisp. Prepare a "gravy" with 1 cup of reserved lentil fluid, wine, bread, and salt, gently simmering all for 10 minutes.

FARSED FESAUNT
PHEASANT OR CHICKEN STUFFED WITH SPICED APPLES AND OATS

Ingredients

½ teaspoon basil

½ teaspoon rosemary, crushed fine

½ teaspoon thyme

⅔ teaspoon salt

2 cups oats, uncooked

⅔ cup dried apples, cut small

⅔ cup figs, cut small

½ cup beef stock or dry white wine

pheasant or large roasting chicken, about 5 pounds (or 2 smaller birds)

2 Tablespoons butter

2 raw apples

½ lemon

Method

1. Mix basil, rosemary, thyme, and salt with the oats. Preheat oven to 375°.
2. Mix in dried apples and figs.
3. Stir stock into oats and fruit.
4. Stuff bird with mixture. Rub skin with butter.
5. Bake at 375° for 2 hours or until very tender.
6. Grate apple peel and reserve. Remove core and discard. Chop or cut raw apple into small slivers and mix well with apple peel. Squeeze lemon juice onto apple to prevent its browning.
7. Remove stuffing from bird. Mix in raw apples and serve immediately with warm fowl.

HENNE DORRE
GOLDEN CARDAMON CHICKEN

Ingredients

1 large roasting chicken cut into small serving portions

¼ cup walnuts, coarsely ground

¼ cup filberts, coarsely ground

4 Tablespoons butter for sautéing

3 tart apples, cored and peeled

⅔ cup golden raisins

½ cup currants

½ teaspoon cinnamon

¼ teaspoon fresh rosemary, finely crushed

pinch of thyme

7 cardamon berries (or ¾ teaspoon crushed cardamon)

½ teaspoon salt

¼ cup wine

½ cup chicken broth

Glaze

6 egg yolks

⅛ teaspoon saffron

2 Tablespoons honey

Method

1. Preheat oven to 350°.
2. In a Dutch oven or shallow covered baking dish, sauté the chicken and nuts in butter until the meat is white. Leave in dish and remove from heat.
3. Cut apples into thin slivers. Mix raisins and currants with apples.
4. Stir together all spices and salt, and mix with fruits.
5. Distribute the spiced fruit amongst the chicken and nuts.
6. Pour on mixed wine and chicken broth. Bake covered in slow oven for 45 to 55 minutes, until the chicken is tender. Remove from oven while preparing golden glaze. Turn over to 400°.
7. Beat the egg yolks, saffron, and honey thoroughly. Evenly pour over chicken so as to coat each piece. Or use a pastry brush to "paint" each portion gold. Return to oven uncovered for 5 to 7 minutes to let endoring "set." Serve warm.

GARBAGE PYE
GIBLET CUSTARD PIE

Having none of the modern pejorative implications of refuse, "garbage" in medieval England simply meant animal innards or giblets.

Ingredients

8-inch pie shell

4 Tablespoons rendered goose fat or chicken fat or butter (or 1 cup of chicken broth for boiling)

giblets from a goose or a large chicken

4 Tablespoons flour

½ cup white wine

½ cup cream

3 eggs

½ teaspoon salt

⅛ teaspoon pepper

½ teaspoon cinnamon

½ teaspoon dried basil, crushed

Method

1. Preheat oven to 400°.
2. Bake the pie shell "blind" for 10 minutes to harden it.
3. In a heavy skillet, heat half of the fat, and slowly sauté the giblets for 12 minutes. Mince the giblets, shred the neck meat finely, discard all bones and gristle, and reserve. (Or, boil the giblets in broth for 20 minutes; drain well, mince, and reserve.)
4. In the same skillet, heat the remaining 2 Tablespoons of fat; stir in the flour over a low heat until frothy. Remove from heat.
5. Stir into the roux the wine, cream, and giblets.
6. Beat 3 eggs with salt, pepper, cinnamon, and basil. Add to the creamed giblets. Stir.
7. Pour all into pie shell. Bake until "set" and crust is golden brown (about ½ hour).

Vegetables and Vegetarian Variations

FRUYTES RYAL RICE
ARTICHOKES WITH BLUEBERRY RICE

Ingredients

6 artichokes	½ teaspoon dill leaves, chopped fine
1 lemon	¼ teaspoon powdered ginger
1 cup uncooked white rice	½ pound blueberries (or strawberries)
2 cups chicken broth	¼ pound fresh butter
½ teaspoon rosemary, chopped fine	2 Tablespoons parsley, chopped fine

Method

1. Cut off the roots of the artichokes. With scissors, snip prickly leaf tips off, cutting approximately ½ inch off tips. Place 6 artichokes, root side down, snugly in a pot with 2 to 3 inches of water plus the lemon cut in eighths. Boil on very low heat for ½ hour. Gently remove the artichokes from the pot.
2. Carefully remove each "choke," the thistle covering of the artichoke "heart," and gently spread the leaves so as to make a commodious well for the stuffing. Cool.
3. In a large pot boil rice, broth, rosemary, dill, and ginger, until water is almost completely absorbed, approximately 15 minutes.
4. Add washed and stemmed blueberries (or strawberries) for another 5 minutes of cooking.
5. Stir gently. The purple blueberry dye ought to permeate most rice granules. Stir until a pleasing color is uniform.
6. Stuff the artichokes with "royal rice" mixture, by carefully spooning it into the "well."
7. Melt butter and chopped parsley over low heat, about 2 minutes.
8. Serve artichokes cool with parslied butter in separate dish for dipping artichoke leaves.

A variation, in several manuscripts, adds flaked cooked salmon to the lavender rice, making a startling contrast in color between the delicate orange-pink of the fish and the purple-blue of the rice. Use ½ cup cooked salmon and stir into rice with utmost care so that purple dye does not color the fish; or make a well within the rice and spoon in salmon. Make a thin glaze of ricotta cheese on top of the stuffed artichokes. Bake for 12 to 15 minutes at 350° and serve warm.

LEMONWHYT
LEMON RICE WITH ALMONDS

Ingredients

1 large unblemished lemon	²⁄₃ cup coarsely ground almonds
1 cup raw rice	²⁄₃ cup currants
2 cups water	1 cup dry white wine
½ teaspoon salt	1 cup fresh peas
½ teaspoon cinnamon	*Garnish*
1 Tablespoon butter	12 teaspoons honey

Method

1. Finely grate the skin from the lemon. Then cut the lemon, thoroughly squeezing its juice and removing most of the pulp. Reserve the skin, juice, and soft pulp, discarding the membranes and pits.
2. In a large enameled pot bring to a brisk boil the water, rice, salt, cinnamon, butter, and lemon, reducing heat to simmer until most fluid is absorbed (about 10 minutes). Stir once or twice while simmering; otherwise keep pot tightly covered. Remove covered pot from heat.
3. Slowly simmer the almonds and currants in white wine for 7 minutes.
4. Fluff rice gently with a fork. Add the wined almonds to the lemon rice.
5. Stir in fresh peas. Very slowly simmer for 5 to 7 minutes. If the rice begins to stick to the bottom of the pot, add small amounts of boiling water.
6. Garnish with 1 teaspoon honey for each portion.

RAPES
LENTIL CRISPS

Ingredients

1½ cups oatmeal	½ teaspoon salt
²⁄₃ cup almonds, skinned, slivered or ground	6 eggs, hard-boiled and chopped
²⁄₃ cup coconut	¾ teaspoon salt
4 Tablespoons honey	½ cup raisins, chopped (or currants)
1 cup lentils	½ cup dates, pitted and chopped
2 cups beef broth	1 teaspoon dried sweet basil
½ pound ricotta or small-curd cottage cheese	Vegetable oil for frying in a heavy, deep skillet

Method

1. Mix oats, almonds, and coconut and spread evenly on 2 well-greased cookie sheets. Drizzle honey over all, and bake in 425° oven for approximately 10 minutes. The result ought to

resemble "granola." Cool. Reserve in 2 shallow bowls.

2. Wash lentils. Boil them in beef broth and ½ teaspoon salt for 15 minutes in a large pot. Drain.
3. Mix cheese, eggs, salt, raisins, dates, and sweet basil together, and unite with lentils.
4. Roll the lentil-cheese mixture into teaspoon-size balls and immediately roll each into oat crumbs until evenly coated.
5. Gently fry in oil until golden brown.
6. Drain on paper towel and serve crisps warm.

If prepared in advance and frozen, reheat for 5 minutes in hot oven (425°) until recrisped.

SALLAT
A MEDIEVAL SALAD

Ingredients

turnips, quartered

parsnips, sliced

beets, quartered

St. John's bread (carob)

almonds

filberts

cabbage, shredded

large prunes

figs

dates

golden raisins

dried apple rounds

dried honeyed pineapple, cut in small wedges

Lumbard or sharp mustard

brown sugar

Method

1. In lightly salted water boil the turnips and parsnips for 5 to 7 minutes so that they retain their firmness but lose their hardness. Similarly boil the beets, separately.
2. Arrange artistically all elements of the "sallat" so that repetitive patterns of color and shape please. Oftentimes an armorial or coat of arms was formed from such edible "quarterings." The long pods of the St. John's bread are particularly useful uncut as well as broken.
3. An alternative to the raw salad is a design covered in aspic.
4. The salad elements should be dipped in Lumbard mustard and brown sugar, each of which ought to appear in a separate spice bowl.

FLORE FRITTOURS
Fried Squash Flowers

Ingredients

2 cups fresh flowers from zucchini or other squash

2/3 cup ricotta cheese

1/8 teaspoon ginger

1/2 teaspoon dried basil, crushed

1/4 teaspoon salt

1/2 cup flour

2 eggs, well beaten

1/2 cup oil (or more) for sautéing

Method

1. Wash the delicate flowers carefully, removing the stamens and stems. Gently pat dry with a towel.
2. Mix ginger, basil, and salt into the cheese.
3. Carefully spoon a small portion of cheese into each flower.
4. Slowly heat the oil in a heavy skillet.
5. Roll each stuffed flower in the flour.
6. Briefly immerse each flower in the beaten egg.
7. Sauté in the hot oil (gently turning to brown all sides) for 1 to 2 minutes. Drain, and serve warm.

AMYNDOUN SEAW
A Vegetable Gruel

Ingredients

2 cups *amyndoun* or wheatgerm or buckwheat groats or "gritty" cereal (such as the easily available "Grape Nuts")

2 Tablespoons butter

4 cups milk

1 cup fresh carrots, scraped and sliced into "rounds" about 1/2 inch thick

1/2 cup fresh parsnip, scraped and diced

1 cup raisins

8 to 10 prunes, pits removed

1/2 teaspoon salt

1/4 teaspoon ginger powder

1/4 teaspoon cinnamon

1/2 teaspoon dried sweet basil, crushed (or grated candied ginger)

6 Tablespoons honey

3 Tablespoons purple-plum preserves

Method

1. In deep, covered skillet melt butter and "toast" the *amyndoun* or groats for 2 to 3 minutes by tossing it in butter over low flame.
2. Mix all other ingredients together—except for basil (or grated ginger), honey, and preserves—and add to the toasted cereal. Slowly simmer for 20 minutes.
3. Spoon into individual serving bowls.
4. Garnish each bowl with a dollop of honey in the center, a small circle of plum preserves on top, plus basil or candied ginger sprinkled round the edges. Serve warm.

ST. JOHN'S RICE
CURRANT RICE WITH CAROB CREAM

This exquisite dish requires a rich brown cream over the white rice. Yogurt, making a fine variation, is not anachronistic; it was familiar in the medieval East and could have been introduced to Europe by returning Crusaders and traders. Various creams, cheeses, and diverse milk products made from cow, sheep, and goat milk were cultivated as the "white-meat" substitute for animal flesh. Thus, it is impossible to be sure what type of "cream" is the most "historically correct."

Ingredients

1 Tablespoon butter

1 cup rice

1 cup currants

1½ teaspoons dried sweet basil, ground fine

½ teaspoon salt

2¼ cups chicken broth

2 heaping Tablespoons ground carob or St. John's bread powder

2 cups clotted cream (or sour cream or yogurt)

4 Tablespoons honey

Method

1. In a large heavy pot, melt the butter and then mix rice, currants, basil, salt, and broth. Boil for 12 to 15 minutes until all fluid is absorbed by the rice. Fluff rice with fork and cool in a shallow serving bowl or rimmed platter.
2. Mix carob into cream.
3. Pour the carob cream onto the rice, covering the surface evenly.
4. Drizzle honey over all in a labyrinthine pattern and serve.

CAUDELE ALMAUNDE
A NUT DISH SERVED AS A VEGETABLE

Apparently served as today we would eat "stuffing" accompanying a roast capon or turkey, almond caudle was neither soup nor sauce, but a "side dish" for sliced meat or hard cheese.

Ingredients

2 cups coarse-ground almonds

2 cups ale

1 cup water

¼ teaspoon saffron

⅔ cup brown sugar

½ teaspoon salt

½ cup toasted bread crumbs

1 cup currants

Garnish

1 Tablespoon fresh basil or dill, snipped finely

Method

1. Bring to boil, then slowly simmer the almonds, ale, and water in a soup pot for 30 minutes.
2. Add saffron, sugar, salt, bread crumbs, and currants. Continue simmering for 10 minutes, stirring occasionally.
3. Serve hot, garnished with basil or dill.

MARY CABOGES
CABBAGE WITH MARROW

Ingredients

8   marrow bones, split lengthwise

5   cups beef broth

1   large head of cabbage

1   cup grated toasted bread crumbs

¼   teaspoon saffron

½   teaspoon salt

⅛   teaspoon thyme

Method

1. Boil marrow bones in beef broth until marrow is soft, about ½ hour. Skim grease from surface of the broth; remove bones, reserving broth in pot.
2. Knock out marrow from bones and cut it into small pieces with a sharp knife. Reserve.
3. Wash and cut cabbage in eighths, and then chop coarsely.
4. Add cabbage to bone marrow broth, bring to boil and then simmer for 5 minutes.
5. Combine saffron, salt, and thyme, with grated bread. Stir in reserved marrow.
6. Add to cabbage; stir, and simmer gently 5 more minutes. Serve warm either from a large serving bowl or in individual soup bowls. Place several small pieces—"gobbettys"—of marrow on top of each portion.

JOUTES
HERBED BEETS (OR, WHEN THINNED WITH BROTH, A SPLENDID "BORSCHT")

This recipe suggests serving the herbed beets with boiled bacon (or ham) just as one serves "frumenty" with venison—as a "relish" or mixed vegetable or sauce. If you have fresh herbs available, obtain several sprigs of each of five types whose tastes or aromas please, making a "bouquet garni." Tie these in a cheesecloth, allowing the pouch of herbs to cook with the beets. Dried herbs work best when utilizing ¼ to ½ teaspoon for each of five herbs, simply sprinkled into the broth.

Ingredients

4   cups beef broth

2   pounds beets

½   teaspoon salt

4   marrow bones, split lengthwise

2   cups white bread crumbs

¼   teaspoon saffron

A *bouquet garni* composed of such herbs as violet, mallows, parsley, "young worts," bennet, ox-tongue wort, and orach; or a similarly fragrant though more accessible combination including violet, dill, rosemary, sweet basil, parsley, and dandelion.

Method

1. Wash and cut beets into small chunks (about ½ inch by ½ inch).
2. Wash all herbs and mince small.
3. Bring beef broth to boil, and then very slowly simmer.
4. Add beets, salt, marrow bones, and herbs to beef broth and simmer slowly for 25 minutes.
5. Add bread crumbs and simmer 5 minutes more. Remove herb pouch.
6. Remove from heat. Sprinkle saffron on surface. Stir well, letting stand at least 10 minutes before serving, so that saffron gold enriches the red beet color.
7. Knock out marrow from bones, and finely chop it. (Discard bones.) Stir marrow into the *joutes*. Serve warm in small side dishes or on thick bread trenchers.

VEGETARIAN CUSTARD LUMBARDE
ALMOND AND FRUIT TART

For Lent and for meatless days of the year, favorite foods had vegetarian variations in which almonds often substituted for the forbidden flesh. This recipe follows in the manuscript the *Custard Lumbarde* instructions with the words: "when it is in Lent . . ." (Compare this with the recipe for *Custard Lumbarde*.)

Ingredients

1 9-inch pie shell, unbaked

1 cup coarsely ground almonds

1 Tablespoon ground pine nuts

½ teaspoon dried sweet basil, crushed finely

¼ cup sugar

½ teaspoon cinnamon

½ teaspoon salt

½ cup dates, pits removed, rinsed and quartered

¼ cup figs, stems removed and minced

¼ cup prunes, pits removed and quartered

2 eggs, beaten

⅔ cup heavy cream

¼ teaspoon nutmeg

Method

1. Preheat oven to 400°.
2. Bake pie shell "blind" for 10 to 15 minutes. Cool. Reset oven to 375°.
3. In mixing bowl, stir in all spices (except nutmeg) to the almonds.
4. Line the pie shell with the spiced almonds.
5. Evenly distribute the dates, figs, and prunes on surface.
6. Stir the cream with the eggs and pour on pie.
7. Sprinkle nutmeg on edges of pie crust.
8. Bake until custard is set and crust browned, about 30 minutes.

Fruit and Flower Desserts

QUYNADE
QUINCE SAUCE

Ingredients

8 medium quinces	⅛ teaspoon saffron
1 cup rose water or beef broth (rose water is available ready-made in health-food shops; or see recipe for it, below)	⅛ teaspoon ground cloves
	¼ teaspoon ginger
½ cup ground almonds	2 cardamon grains, crushed ("grains of paradise")
½ cup heavy cream	½ cup sugar
¼ cup white wine	
¼ teaspoon salt	*Garnish*
	"foils of silver," decorative silver leaves, either edible or artificial

Method

To make rose water: On low flame, boil the petals of 6 roses (which have not been sprayed with chemicals) in 1¼ cups of water and 2 Tablespoons of honey for 20 minutes. Remove the sodden petals and crush in mortar or with fork, and return to the fluid.

1. Wash, quarter, and core the quinces. (Peel them if you wish a smoother sauce; leave skin on if you prefer a varied texture.)
2. Boil the quinces in rose water until very soft, 15 to 20 minutes. Place quinces in colander and pour off residual rose water, reserving about ½ cup of fluid.
3. In enameled pot, simmer almonds in cream and wine for 5 minutes. The almond cream will be thick, so stir intermittently.
4. Add the quinces and simmer 5 minutes. The texture ought to resemble thick apple sauce. Add some reserved rose water if the mixture tends to stick to the pot.
5. Blend salt and all spices with the sugar.
6. Stir the spiced sugar into the sauce.
7. Serve warm or cool in individual dessert dishes, each portion garnished with a silver leaf—a "foil of silver," says the recipe.

CHARDWARDON
Spiced Pear Sauce

This spiced confection is said to be "comfortable for a mannys body and namely fore the stomak." It is particularly pleasant after or with boiled beef or roast chicken.

Ingredients

10 pears, cored and quartered, skin on

1 cup beer or ale

2 cups honey (or 1 cup honey and 1 cup sugar)

½ teaspoon pepper

1 teaspoon ginger powder

1 teaspoon galingale

1 teaspoon cinnamon

3 Tablespoons dry white wine

Garnish

½ teaspoon powdered ginger

½ teaspoon cinnamon

Method

1. Simmer pears in beer until very soft, 15 to 20 minutes. Pour pears and beer through a colander into a large bowl, straining the pears, or press through coarse mesh of food mill, returning pulp and skin, finely cut, to sauce in bowl.
2. Slowly heat honey mixed with pepper in a large pot and stir in the pear sauce. Simmer very slowly for 10 minutes. Remove from heat.
3. Mix ginger, galingale, and cinnamon with white wine. Stir spiced wine into the cooling pear-and-honey sauce.
4. Pour into large bowl. Cool thoroughly. Sprinkle mixed ginger and cinnamon on surface as a garnish.

DAMSON
Plum and Currant Tart

Ingredients

Marrow from 4 large beef bones

1 cup boiling water

½ teaspoon salt

½ cup sugar

2 beaten eggs

⅔ cup heavy cream

1 cup fresh purple plums, cut into quarters (½ to ¾ pound)

⅔ cup currants

1 8-inch unbaked pie shell

Method

1. Preheat oven to 400°.
2. Boil bones for 25 minutes and knock out marrow; or boil marrow for 15 minutes. Drain and cut marrow into 12 even pieces.
3. Add salt and sugar to beaten eggs; stir in cream.
4. Pour it over plums and currants evenly mixed in a bowl.
5. Pour mixture into the pie shell, distributing fruits fairly evenly.
6. Arrange pieces of marrow evenly around the surface of the tart.
7. Bake for 40 minutes or until the fruit custard is set and the pastry shell is browned.

FRUYTE FRITTOURS
PARSNIP AND APPLE FRITTERS

Ingredients

4 parsnips

4 large firm apples

2 cups boiling water

2 cups flour

2 eggs

2 Tablespoons ale (more as needed)

½ teaspoon dill seeds, crushed

¼ teaspoon salt

4 Tablespoons butter

4 Tablespoons oil

4 Tablespoons brown sugar

Garnish

Red anise or red licorice

Method

1. Pare the apples; cut them in quarters and seed, then cut in sixteenths or until moon-shaped slices remain firm, not flimsy. Trim parsnips; cut longitudinal strips of white flesh, making "bars" (about ½ inch thick).
2. Parboil parsnip bars for 3 minutes. Drain, and reserve.
3. Beat eggs. Add eggs, ale, dill, and salt to flour and stir until evenly blended. (Add more ale if mixture is too dry; it should be the consistency of thick pancake batter.)
4. Generously coat apple slices and parsnip strips with batter.
5. Sauté in hot butter and oil combination in skillet until golden brown.
6. Remove to rack.
7. Strew each "frittour" with brown sugar while still warm.
8. Arrange crescents and bars artistically on platter, garnished with red anise or red licorice.

FYGEYE
A TRICOLORED FIG CONFECTION

Ingredients

30 large, fresh figs, stems removed

2 cups beef broth

¼ teaspoon salt

¾ teaspoon cinnamon

2 cups coarse white bread or cracker crumbs

2 cups ale

2 Tablespoons ground pine nuts

½ teaspoon ground cloves

White powder

4 teaspoons sugar

1 teaspoon nutmeg

1 teaspoon cinnamon

½ teaspoon sandalwood powder (or 4 drops of red food color)

½ teaspoon saffron (or 4 drops of yellow food color)

Method

1. In large heavy saucepan, simmer figs in broth until very soft, about 15 minutes. Remove figs and mash or grind in mortar. Return to pot without broth.
2. Mix salt and cinnamon with crumbs.
3. Stir ale into spiced crumbs. Add pine nuts and cloves.
4. Pour mixture over figs.
5. Simmer 10 minutes.
6. Stir in well-mixed *white powder:* sugar, nutmeg, and cinnamon.
7. Separate the fig sauce into 3 equal parts. With one, mix sandalwood or red food color; with the second mix saffron or yellow food color. Leave the third brownish, "itself."
8. On each platter or trencher, serve equal amounts of each of three colors, laid side by side in small stripes. Pipe these out with a large, serrated-nozzled pastry tube.

BLAK PERYS
PEARS WITH CAROB CREAM

Ingredients

6 fresh pears, hard but edible

1 fresh lemon, juice of

2 heaping Tablespoons carob powder (obtainable from any health-food or gourmet shop as a substitute for chocolate, tasting astonishingly like that confection)

2 Tablespoons sugar or honey

¼ teaspoon salt

1 cup heavy whipping cream

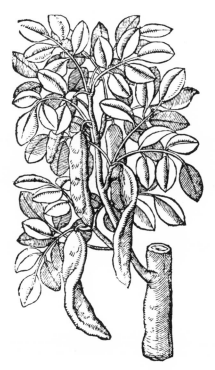

Method

1. Cut the pears in half longitudinally, keeping the skin on, and carefully scoop out the core area utilizing either a sharp spoon or grapefruit knife.
2. Generously coat each pear-half with lemon juice.
3. Either allow the pears to remain raw or bake pears for 7 to 10 minutes in 350° oven and then cool.
4. Beat the carob powder, sugar, and salt with the cream until the mixture either peaks, or, depending upon the type of carob powder you use, has the thick consistency of chocolate mousse.
5. Spoon or pipe the carob cream into the craters of each pear-half with a pastry tube. Chill in refrigerator for at least ½ hour before serving.

PERYS COFYNS
Lentil- and Berry-filled Pears

Since this recipe calls for pear "coffers" or "coffins" which contain the lentil-and-"bog-berry" filling, three separate preparations are convenient: 1. baking the pears; 2. cooking the lentils; 3. steaming the berries. Since tart "bog berries" are called for in the manuscript, cranberries (a New-World berry) are suggested. But one variation suggests raspberry (for that, reduce the sugar by half). Both are delightful.

Baking the Pears

Ingredients

10 fresh hard pears

1 fresh lemon, juice of

¾ teaspoon ground cinnamon

Method

1. Cut pears in half on long axis making boat-shaped "coffers." Carefully cut out or scoop out the pits and core, allowing about ½- to ¾-inch uniform wall to remain.
2. Thoroughly coat with lemon juice to prevent discoloring.
3. Sprinkle lightly with ground cinnamon.
4. Bake in 350° oven for 5 to 10 minutes allowing pears to go from hard to firm. If they become too soft, they will not retain their filling. Set aside to cool.

Cooking the Lentils

Ingredients

½ cup lentils

1 small stalk of celery, finely chopped

½ teaspoon salt

1 cup beef broth, or more

¼ cup dates, pits removed, finely chopped

½ teaspoon dried sweet basil, crushed

Method

1. Wash the lentils and place in deep pot with celery, salt, dates, and basil, plus beef broth to cover by two inches.
2. Bring to boil and cook over very low heat for 15 to 20 minutes. Add stock or boiling water if necessary to prevent sticking. Lentils should be just tender, still holding their shape but double their raw size.

Steaming the Berries

Ingredients

1 cup fresh whole "bogberries" or cranberries (or raspberries)

2 Tablespoons brown sugar or honey

¼ cup and 1 Tablespoon water

Method

1. Wash raw cranberries and remove any residual stems.
2. In deep pot, bring berries, sugar, and water to quick boil. Berries will rise to the surface and pop. As the medieval manuscript warns, sound, odor, and sight of pink broth are delightful;

but watch inquisitive eyes: berry innards pop high and hot. Remove immediately when one-third of berries have popped. Cool.
3. Scoop about 1 Tablespoon of lentils into pear crater.
4. Top with 1 teaspoon of cranberry (or raspberry).

BOLAS
Wild Plum and Stuffed Pear Dessert

A culinary variation upon the old Russian egg-doll or Chinese-box technique of the smaller treasure within the larger, this dessert demands careful spooning during eating, making it possible to unite plum, pear, and spiced dates in one mouthful.

Ingredients

15 to 18 bullace or wild plums, washed and pits removed

1¼ cups red wine

½ cup rice or wheat flour

½ cup sugar

½ teaspoon ginger

¼ teaspoon cloves

⅛ teaspoon mace

½ teaspoon cinnamon

9 very firm pears

2 lemons

2 cups water

24 dates, pits removed

White powder

4 teaspoons sugar

1 teaspoon nutmeg

1 teaspoon cinnamon

Method

1. Place plums in enameled pot and pour on wine to just cover. Simmer gently until the plum pulp is soft, about 7 minutes. Remove skins, mince skins and flesh, and return to wine in pot.
2. Stir in flour to ½ cup of the hot wine; then stir this into the pot and simmer 4 minutes. Remove from heat.
3. Evenly blend the sugar with ginger, cloves, mace, and cinnamon and stir into plums. Reserve.
4. Snugly fit the pears (cores in) into a pot. Squeeze the juice of one lemon over the pears; add water and slowly boil for 7 minutes or less until pears go from hard to firm. Remove pears from water. When they are slightly cool, peel off the skins and carefully remove the cores with an apple corer. Coat each pear with juice of the second lemon.
5. Moisten the dates in hot water to make them softer and easier to handle. Split and fill each with ¼ teaspoon of the evenly blended *white powder*.
6. Gently stuff each pear with 2 or 3 spiced dates, making a new pear core with the dark dates. (If pears are small and dates large, 1 or 2 stuffed dates will do.)
7. Spoon out the plum sauce into 9 flat plates; place one decorated pear in the center of each. (Extra spiced dates may be cut in slices and arranged radiating out from the pear.)

TROYCREM
Tri-Cream

Several variations of this colorful dessert appear in medieval cookbooks, calling for cream or "crudded milk," or a light "loose" cheese such as ricotta. It is particularly delightful with ricotta thinned with milk or sour cream; or blend the colors and tastes with yogurt; or with whipped heavy cream.

Ingredients

3 pints of heavy cream (or yogurt, or ricotta cheese thinned with milk or cream)

3 Tablespoons dark-brown spicy mustard

3 Tablespoons red-raspberry preserves

3 Tablespoons honey

(For another variation in taste and color:

3 Tablespoons quince preserves

3 Tablespoons honey)

Method

1. In one pint of cream, mix the mustard; in a second, mix the red-raspberry preserves; leave the third plain and white.
2. Whip each cream until it thickens.
3. Arrange all three side by side in a large attractive serving dish, making three "stripes."
4. With a knife dipped once in warm water, gently swirl or "enmarbleize" until a pleasant design as well as an interesting blend of colors is achieved. Drizzle honey over surface, embellishing the design of the creams.
5. When serving, each portion in a small bowl ought to allow tasting of all three juxtaposed creams, the gold, red, and white colors artistically set forth.

The quince-and-honey version, though somewhat less colorful, is no less tasty. The russet quince is well complemented by the golden honey and plain white creams.

FAUN TEMPERE
Gilli Flower Pudding

Ingredients

2½ cups milk

½ cup beef broth

¼ cup rice flour (or white flour)

½ cup ground almonds

½ cup sugar

¼ teaspoon ginger

¼ teaspoon galingale

½ teaspoon cinnamon

½ teaspoon basil

½ teaspoon rosemary

¼ teaspoon dill weed

5 egg yolks

¼ teaspoon mace

2 cubeb berries, finely ground (or ¼ to ½ teaspoon cubeb powder)

8 to 10 gilli flowers (or dandelions)

Method

1. In the top of a double boiler, slowly heat the milk and broth. Mix flour, sugar, almonds, ginger, galingale, cinnamon, basil, rosemary, and dill. Slowly add to milk stock and simmer for 12 minutes, stirring constantly.
2. Beat 5 egg yolks with a fork. Remove ½ cup of hot spiced stock and stir yolks in. Add this to pot and simmer for 3 minutes, stirring, as pudding thickens.
3. Pour the pudding into a serving bowl and cool.
4. Strew combined mace and cubebs evenly over the surface of pudding.
5. Shred gilli flowers or dandelion petals and liberally sprinkle over the pudding. Serve cool.

VALENCYE
FRIED VALENCIA ORANGES

Ingredients

 4 large seedless eating oranges

 4 Tablespoons brown sugar

 ⅛ teaspoon nutmeg

 ⅛ teaspoon mace

 ¼ teaspoon cinnamon

 1 cup flour

1½ teaspoons baking powder

 ¼ teaspoon salt

 3 Tablespoons brown sugar

 1 cup oil for sautéing

 1 raw egg

 ½ scant cup milk

Garnish

 4 Tablespoons mustard

 4 Tablespoons brown sugar

Method

1. Carefully peel the oranges and separate the sections. Strew on mixed sugar, nutmeg, mace, and cinnamon.
2. Prepare a thick batter by uniting the flour, baking powder, salt, and brown sugar. Blend 2 Tablespoons of oil, the egg, well beaten, and the milk. Thoroughly stir this liquid into the dry mixture. If the batter is thin, add a scant amount more of flour. If it is too thick to evenly coat the orange sections, then dilute with more milk. Chill batter for 1½ hours.
3. Heat the remaining oil in a heavy skillet until hot, not smoking.
4. Dip orange sections in batter to coat thoroughly. Drop into hot oil and fry until nicely browned. Serve warm, with mustard and brown sugar in separate spice dishes.

Spectacle, Sculpture, and Illusion Food

HASLET
Mock Entrails

Haslet was the noble reward of the courtly hunt—the roasted entrails and genitalia of the deer or boar or other animal of the pursuers' fancy. This illusion food emulates haslet by utilizing dried fruits and nuts to imitate the shapes and textures of the real thing. Noble hunters particularly favored this feast delicacy.

Ingredients	Batter	Garnish
24 very large prunes, pits removed	1 cup flour	½ cup honey
24 very large dates, pits removed	¾ cup milk	
24 dried figs, stems removed	1 beaten egg	
24 the largest almonds and filberts available	1 Tablespoon ale	
	1 teaspoon sugar	
24 dried pear halves	½ teaspoon cinnamon	
12 pineapple rings, dried and honey-dipped, cut in quarters	¼ teaspoon saffron	

Method

1. Soak dried fruit in hot water for ½ hour. Drain and dry thoroughly.
2. On strings about 1 foot long of heavy butcher's thread, knotted at one end and attached to stout needles, alternate the fruits and nuts, creating two or three repeated configurations on each string. Knot the sewing end of the haslet cord, after removing the needle.
3. Prepare the golden batter by mixing all batter ingredients to form a thick coating.
4. Carefully dip each string of haslet into the batter so as to thoroughly coat each fruit and nut.
5. In a shallow greased baking dish bake each string for 12 minutes at 350° or until golden brown.
6. Drizzle honey over the baked haslet.
7. Serve either one whole string or at the very least two repeated configurations of the baked fruit, preferably upon a green parsley-bread trencher.

GELYE DE FYSSHE
An Elaborate Jelly Design

This major "spectacle" for a feast table creates a fanciful design or heraldic emblem in jelly. Thus initiative and ingenuity are as significant as the recipe: color, shape, and intricacy of design are at the fancy of the modern feast enthusiast. For appropriate display, one needs a large, attractive platter with a deep rim or a fish mold, about 9-cup capacity.

Ingredients

4 cups beef-flavored gelatin (or see the Medieval gelatin recipe, below)

2 to 4 cups white wine

½ pound pike, cut into small pieces, ½ to ¾ inch

½ pound perch, similarly cut small

½ pound tench, similarly cut small

¼ pound small shrimp or cut eels

½ teaspoon salt

⅛ teaspoon pepper

½ teaspoon saffron

2 Tablespoons wine vinegar

Garnish

¼ cup slivered almonds, roasted

1 teaspoon shaved or powdered cloves

2 Tablespoons coarsely grated candied ginger

Method

1. Use a favorite beef-flavored gelatin or an unflavored gelatin seasoned with 3 beef bouillon cubes or with concentrated beef stock. Whatever your recipe, substitute white wine for one-half the required water. Or follow these medieval preparations for the meat gelatin in which to stew the fish.

"Jelly" Ingredients & Method

2 calves' feet

2 "veal hooves"

4 cups white wine

2 cups water

Boil calves' feet in water until the flesh turns white, about 4 minutes. Drain. Discard water. Soak veal hooves in warm water until all blood runs out. Discard water.
Boil feet and hooves in white wine for 20 minutes. Discard feet and hooves. Skim off top of jellied wine. Cool.

2. Gently heat all 4 types of fish in the jellied broth so that each piece keeps its shape and yet does not break, about 4 minutes of simmering, a few more minutes for eel.
3. With slotted spoon carefully remove all fish, keeping like pieces with like, and cool.
4. Remove jelly from fire. Add salt, pepper, and saffron, to make a good amber color. If you have prepared the medieval gelatin, strain the jelly through a cheesecloth, discarding the "sediment." Otherwise, pour or spoon off about ⅓ of the jelly onto the bottom of the serving platter or mold.
5. Artistically arrange fish pieces on the partially congealed jelly so that whichever way it will be cut, each portion will have at least one piece of each of the four types of fish. Create a geometric design, an armorial pattern, or a short motto.
6. Pour remaining amber jelly to cover completely. Chill for at least 1 hour.
7. Complete the artistic decoration with the almond slivers, grated ginger, and clove shards, integrating these into the total design.

COCKENTRICE
A MARVELOUS BEAST

The extraordinary "beasts" created by these instructions never were seen on land or sea. A bestiary pair, these chicken and pork visual as well as edible delights were intended to startle as well as feed. The creation of such illusion foods was an important contribution of the medieval cook to the flamboyant art forms of the medieval feast.

Ingredients

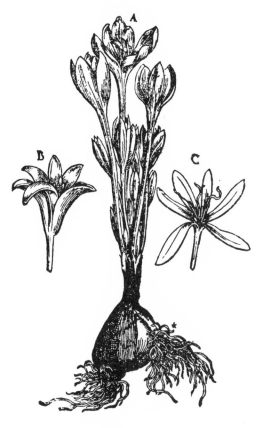

  1 suckling pig, about 7 pounds

  1 large roasting chicken, about 6 pounds

  6 egg yolks

  ¼ teaspoon powdered saffron

  ½ cup all-purpose flour

  ¼ cup white wine

  1 Tablespoon fresh parsley leaves, very finely chopped

  1 Tablespoon flour

Method

1. Bake the chicken and the suckling pig separately at 375° until tender; the chicken ought to take 2 hours, the suckling pig closer to 3.
2. Cut the chicken in half with the incision running around the body behind the wings. The forward half is thus separated from the hindparts. Similarly cleave the pig so that the "head and shoulders" are cut from the back half of the animal.
3. With a strong butcher's thread or "carpet" thread sew the forward half of the chicken to the back half of the pig; sew the pig's "head and shoulders" to the hind half of the capon. Each is now a *cockentrice*! Turn oven up to 400°.
4. Lightly beat the egg yolks. Mix in the saffron and flour to make a thick fluid. Paint this on the suture lines as well as various parts of either the "face" or appendages—gold snout and gold nails were typical adornments.
5. Return these marvelous animals to the oven so the gold "endoring" may set and the final creatures appear resplendent.
6. Mix parsley in white wine with flour until the green color well permeates the fluid. If not a bright green, add two drops of green food coloring. Paint on "feathers" or designs for final embellishing of the *cockentrice*, your fancy guiding your hand.

POUMES or POMME DOREE
Golden Apples of Meat

These golden (or green) apples are meant happily to deceive the feaster who bites into them expecting the taste of fruit, but finding veal instead.

Ingredients

- 1 cup dates, minced
- 1 cup raisins
- ½ teaspoon salt
- ⅛ teaspoon pepper
- ½ teaspoon cinnamon
- ¼ teaspoon ginger
- ¼ teaspoon clove powder
- ⅛ teaspoon saffron
- 1 pound chopped veal
- 4 eggs
- 1 teaspoon oil for greasing baking sheet

Batter

- 1 cup flour
- 2 raw egg yolks
- ¼ teaspoon ginger powder
- 1 pinch powdered saffron
- 1 teaspoon fresh parsley, finely chopped (or 1 Tablespoon for greener "apples")

Optional

Green food coloring (see *Food Paints and Pigments*)

Method

1. Mix the dates and raisins.
2. Mix salt, pepper, cinnamon, ginger, cloves, and saffron; mix spices with dried fruits.
3. Thoroughly stir spiced fruits with veal.
4. Beat eggs, reserving about 1 Tablespoon of the beaten egg mixture for later use; add to meat mixture, stirring until meat holds its shape.
5. Wetting fingers in the residual egg, form "meat balls" of "small-apple" size. These later will be covered with batter so that a size larger than a silver dollar is useful.
6. On lightly oiled baking sheet, bake meat balls for 20 minutes at 375°. Cool.
7. Prepare a thick batter by uniting ingredients thoroughly. Reset oven to 400°.
8. Coat each ball on all sides and return to oven for 7 minutes or until golden, not brown. The "apples" will appear either green or gold, depending upon the amount of pigment in your local parsley. If you wish, "paint" stems and apple leaves, following your exuberant intuition.

MARCHEPANE
Basic Marzipan for Food Sculpture

Some spectacular feast sculptures were made of such edible confections as marzipan. This basic recipe, yielding about 4 pounds of tasty sculpture material, ought to allow fanciful excursions into illusion food. Animals, human figures, allegorical and symbolic creatures, heraldic devices, architectural and imaginative constructions all are feasible with marzipan plus ingenuity. Every medieval feast deserves at least one culinary spectacle.

Ingredients

  2 pounds skinned, blanched whole almonds

     Ice water

  4 egg whites

$2\frac{2}{3}$ cups confectioner's sugar

$\frac{1}{2}$ cup orange juice

Colors

(Natural, or, if necessary, artificial):
parsley or mallow for green
sandalwood or alkanet for red
saffron or dandelion for yellow
blue turnsole for light blue
violets for lavender

Method

1. In a mortar and pestle or a blender, grind the almonds to a thick paste. Add small amounts of ice water, about $\frac{1}{2}$ teaspoon at a time, to prevent the almonds from becoming too oily. Place almond paste in a large mixing bowl.
2. In another bowl, beat egg whites until they peak. Gradually beat in the sugar.
3. Add the sweetened egg whites to the almond paste. With fingers wet in orange juice, knead the resulting mixture. If the mixture is too sticky to handle, add small amounts of orange juice, 1 teaspoon at a time. Thoroughly knead for about 10 minutes.
4. Separate the marzipan into several sections, one for every color required for your sculpture.
5. In a separate small mixing bowl for each color, place the marzipan portions and cover the bowl tightly with a clean cloth tied securely or with aluminum foil. Allow these to ripen or "age" in refrigerator for at least 24 hours. (One fifteenth-century recipe recommends aging for a fortnight.) Two days ought to suffice.
6. Mix the natural coloring agents, such as the parsley, sandalwood, and saffron (or the drops of vegetable food coloring) into the aged marzipan. The stiff confection will be easier to knead if allowed to return to room temperature.
7. Sculpture the paste according to your wildest fancy. Use fingers for molding, preferably wet in ice water, or use icewater-dipped sharp knives as sculpturing instruments.
8. If the sculptured multicolored castles or coats of arms or fanciful scenes require designs or lettering, use pastry-decorator tubes with a simple confectioner's-sugar-and-milk "writing fluid." Or cut out from paper a "pierced" design (or use an intricately designed paper doily); place this upon the surface to be embellished. Gently rub confectioner's sugar through a finely meshed sieve over the cutout or doily. The sugar will fill all crevices. Carefully raise the paper. The design will appear on the "bare" colored marzipan, accentuated by the white surrounding it.

APPRAYLERE
THE PITCHER THAT IS NOT WHAT IT SEEMS

This chopped beef or pork "sculpture" requires the use of a crockery pitcher for baking and then breaking. Since this seems a somewhat profligate use of costly modern cooking gear, some reusable mold, 8- or 9-cup capacity, such as easily available fish or gingerbread-man molds, serve superbly. The purpose of this illusion food is to force the feaster to expect one sensation or taste, but to receive yet another. Therefore, the more outlandish and exuberant the effect, the more surprising the ultimate taste.

Ingredients

¼ teaspoon ginger powder

½ teaspoon cinnamon

¼ teaspoon salt

⅛ teaspoon galingale

1 cup well-aged cheddar cheese, grated

1 cup gritty brown bread (pumpernickel or stone-ground wheat) crumbs

3 cups ground lean beef (or pork)

⅛ teaspoon saffron

4 raw eggs

2 Tablespoons oil for greasing mold

⅛ teaspoon saffron

¼ teaspoon cinnamon

¼ cup brown sugar

½ cup milk

¼ teaspoon baking powder

Garnish

Candied fruits (citron, orange, or lime), or pickled vegetables (as pickled cucumbers or squash)

Batter

1 cup flour

2 raw eggs

¼ teaspoon allspice powder

Method

1. Blend ginger, cinnamon, salt, and galingale evenly and stir into grated cheese.
2. Mix in bread crumbs.
3. Add bread crumbs and cheese to ground meat, and evenly unite.
4. Beat raw eggs and stir into meat so that the whole mixture keeps its shape.
5. In a well-oiled mold, tightly pack the meat mixture and securely cover the exposed area with tinfoil.
6. Bake at 375° until not only done but slightly dry, approximately 2 hours. Let cool in mold for ½ hour.
7. Unmold and cool. Preheat oven to 400°.
8. Prepare a thick sticky batter by thoroughly stirring all batter ingredients.
9. Spread on top and sides of the molded meat.
10. Bake 10 minutes or more until golden.
11. Set out on large platter garnished with parsley or candied fruits (such as citron) or pickled vegetables (such as squash or melon).
12. If you have used a pitcher form for making this food sculpture, decorate it with some geometric design "painted on" with food color. If you have used a fish, embellish it with eyes, scales, and fins, lavishly utilizing imaginary "food color" pigments. If you have created a meat "gingerbread man," make him flamboyantly gaudy.

FOUR AND TWENTY SINGING BLACKBIRD PIE
or
LIVE FROG AND TURTLE PIE

The nursery rhyme *Sing a Song of Sixpence* suggests that the blackbirds were baked *in* a pie to make a dainty dish to set before the King. Actually, the pies were baked before the birds were tethered within! As an ardent conservationist, I will not encourage the making of spectacle foods that might endanger the animals within the pastry. However, the Medieval method was essentially safe for the birds, some of which were raised for the very purpose of adorning either feast spectacles or, indeed, the feast trenchers. I have made such pies with wind-up, mechanical "birds," which also were popular in the Middle Ages as feast adornments; medieval automata and table toys were exceedingly popular amongst the nobility and those who aped their habits.

Ingredients

Prepare the largest pie shell and top lid which your pastry pans and oven will accommodate.

A "spring-mold pan" or one allowing easy removal of the pie crust is best to use.

Butter for greasing baking pan

2 or more cups of dried beans or such a "heavy" cereal as Grape Nuts

Live tethered birds or frogs or turtles or wind-up animals

2 egg yolks

½ teaspoon cinnamon

Method

1. Preheat oven to 425°.
2. Very lightly grease the large pie pan, then dust with flour.
3. Reserving sufficient dough for a top crust, press in a reasonably thick bottom pie crust.
4. Fill the pie shell with dried beans, or other reusable filler, to weight down the crust as it bakes to avoid bubbling. Apply and carefully seal the upper crust to the lower.
5. Glaze with egg yolk mixed with cinnamon.
6. Bake 40 minutes at 425° or until golden brown.
7. When cool, carefully gain access to the bottom crust and cut a large hole—3-to-4-inch diameter—through which remove all bean or cereal filler, reserving the piece of cut crust.
8. Into the well-cooled shell, insert the live or wind-up animals immediately before serving. If possible, replace the pastry cut so as to "close the hole." (I have not been able to do so; but the medieval cooks apparently could.)
9. Scrupulously carefully, cut around the circumference of the crust at time of serving, about one-quarter way around the pie. Equally gently, cut toward the center, taking extreme care not to touch the animals (or mechanical toys). Lift out upper-crust portion.
10. The birds or frogs will happily "liberate" themselves on the table in order to amaze and amuse the feasters.
11. This pie makes a dramatic finale to a formal feast.

Bibliography

This list appears formidable but ought to prove pleasant and easy to use. It consists of three unequal sections, each of which has several subdivisions. The first part lists *MANUSCRIPTS*. Since more than eight hundred original sources were studied for Chapter III alone, this list represents only a fraction of the total consulted; but it ought to make happy scavenging for any who care to read the delightful documents. Separated here according to subject, numerous manuscript sources pertain not only to cookery in general but to such specific commodities as *bread, wine, water, animals,* and *fish.*

The second section of the bibliography suggests *ARCHIVE AIDS* to those who welcome an English guide through the labyrinth of Latin, Old French, and Medieval-English sources. Calendars and compilations of laws and references will lead the avid quester to the correct volumes for beginning original research in this remarkably various subject. The final items in this section are the standard international bibliographies on cookery.

Last and longest is the list of printed secondary sources called *READINGS.* Each entry has a code letter which represents a general classification for the book or paper; of course, numerous volumes could be classed several ways; potential usefulness forced certain eccentric groupings under the rubrics:

> *A for ART*
> > (food scenes in painting, sculpture, architecture, tapestry, decoration)
>
> *G for GASTRONOMY*
> > (cookeries, food serving, eating, and special social effects)
> > *G a* for agriculture, herbals, food production, bread, and fish
> > *G e* for gastronomic education, etiquette, and table manners
> > *G n* for nutrition, health, and medicine
> > *G u* for table utensils
> > *G v* for wine, viticulture, and drinks
>
> *L for LITERATURE*
> > (food scenes in literature, banquet pageantry, and courtly table theater)
>
> *M for MUSIC*
> > (musical instruments, songs, dances, and techniques associated with food and feasting)
>
> *T for THE TIMES*
> > (historical surveys, technological, philosophical, theological, and economic analyses placing food in the context of the eras)
> > *T c* for commerce and markets
> > *T e* for education for courtliness
> > *T h* for hydrodynamics, waters, and sanitation
> > *T s* for general surveys of ideas and customs

One desiring a bibliography for medieval knives, forks, and table gear simply finds all entries with the code *G u* for Gastronomy, Utensils.

Collectively, these three groups of sources make a fabulous feast for the intellect. Taste and delight!

MANUSCRIPTS

The 19 classes of documents appearing in the charts pertain to:

Cookery	*Fish*	*Wine*	*Markets and Merchants*
Gastronomy and	*Nets*	*Drink*	*Weights and Measures*
Food Legislation	*Water*	*Fruits and Vegetables*	*Utensils*
Animals	*Bread*	*Cheese*	*Time*
Poultry	*Hay*	*Spices*	*Kitchens*

Cookeries

late 14th-15th century

Middle English

British Museum
Harleian MS 279

Harleian MS 4016

Cottonian MS
Claudius D II

Oxford University
Bodleian Ashmole
MS 1439

Bodleian Douce
MS 55

Bodleian Laud
MS 553

Dr. Curt Bühler
The Morgan Library

Galeria Medievalia,
Tenafly, New Jersey
MS C 3

The Camelot Collection,
Ft. Lauderdale, Fla.
MS 107

Dr. Justen Rudshield
London
MS IFD 22

Gastronomy and Food Legislation

12th-16th century

Middle English
Norman French
Medieval Latin

London
Guildhall
Letter Books
A, B, C, D, E, F, G, H
Journal I

Liber Albus

Liber Horn

Liber Custumarum

The Public Record
Office

Close Rolls

Patent Rolls

Coroner's Rolls

Miscellaneous
Wills and Memoranda

An entry listed under the heading *Animals,* which reads:

4 Edward II D cxxii L
1311

represents a document whose subject is animals used for food, dated the 4th year of the reign of King Edward the Second, or the calendar year 1311. It is found in the London Guildhall, *Letter Book D,* entry 122, written in Latin. All such listings refer to manuscripts in the London Guildhall owned by the Corporation of London; those referring to *Rolls* and *membranes* (e.g., Roll A 27, membr. 8b) come from the Public Record Office in London. L equals Latin; NF, Norman French; and E, Middle English documents.

Animals

Date	Reference	
20 Edward I 1292	C ii	L
4 Edward II 1311	D cxxii	L
4 Edward II 1311	D cxxvii	L
5 Edward II 1312	D cxlix	L
6 Edward II 1312	D clv	L
13 Edward II 1319	E xciv	L
14 Edward II 1320	E cv	L
14 Edward II 1320	E cv	L
14 Edward II 1320	E cxv	L
5 Edward III 1331	E ccxviii	N L
17 Edward III 1343	F lxvii	L
19 Edward III 1345	F cii	L
19 Edward III 1345	F ciii	L
22 Edward III 1348	F clii	L
27 Edward III 1353	G vi	L
31 Edward III 1357	G lxxi	L N
37 Edward III 1363	G cvii	N
43 Edward III 1369	G ccxxxiii	L
48 Edward III 1375	G cccxxvi	L
2 Richard II 1378	H xcvii	N
2 Richard II 1378	H xcix	N
2 Richard II 1379	H cxiv	L N
3 Richard II 1379	H cxvii	N
12 Richard II 1388	H ccxxxvii	N
15 Richard II 1391	H cclx	L
1 Henry V 1414	I cxxxiii	L
3 Henry V 1415	I clii	L

Poultry

Date	Reference	
19 Edward III 1345	F cii	N
19 Edward III 1345	F ccii	L
19 Edward III 1345	F ciii	L
24 Edward III 1351	F cxciv	L
31 Edward III 1357	G lxxi	L N
37 Edward III 1363	G cvii	N
39 Edward III 1365	G cxxxviii	L
48 Edward III 1375	G cccxxvi	L
49 Edward III 1375	H xxii	L
49 Edward III 1375	H xv	L N
3 Richard II 1379	H cxvii	N
4 Richard II 1381	H cxxxiii	L
4 Henry V 1416	Journal 1 fols. 2, 3	L
4 Henry V 1416	I clxxxv	L

Fish

Date	Reference	
4 Edward II 1311	D cxxiii	L
6 Edward II 1312	D clxviii	N
8 Edward II 1315	E xxxii	L
9 Edward II 1315	E xxxix	L
13 Edward II 1320	E xcix	L
19 Edward III 1345	F cii	L
24 Edward III 1351	F ccviii	N
46 Edward III 1372	G ccxcii	L
3 Richard II 1379	H cxvi	N
5 Richard II 1382	H cxxxix	N
5 Richard II 1382	H cxliii	L
5 Richard II 1382	H cxlv	L
6 Richard II 1382	H cliv	N
6 Richard II 1382	H cliv	L N
6 Richard II 1382	H cliv	L
7 Richard II 1383	H clxxii	E
12 Richard II 1388	H ccxxxvii	N
13 Richard II 1390	H ccxlvii	L
4 Henry IV 1402	I xxiii	L
13 Henry IV 1412	I cxi	L N
1 Henry V 1413	I cxxvi	L
1 Henry V 1414	I cxxxiii	L
3 Henry V 1415	I clii	L
3 Henry V 1416	I clxiv	L
6 Henry V 1418	Journal 1 fol. 51	L
29 Feb. 1384	Roll A 27 membr. 9b	F
8 Aug. 1382	Roll A 25 membr. 9b	F
21 Aug. 1394	Roll A 33 membr. 6	F
30 Jan. 1386	Roll A 27 membr. 28	F
20 June 1386	Roll A 27 membr. 28	
21 July 1386	Roll A 27 membr. 28-28b	
4 May 1386	Roll A 27 membr. 29	
4 July 1415	Roll A 39 membr. 9b	
13 Aug. 1406	Roll A 39 membr. 17	

Date	Reference	
9 May 1387	Roll A 28 membr. 5	
8 Aug. 1382	Roll A 25 membr. 9b	
21 Aug. 1394	Roll A 33 membr. 6	

Nets

Date	Reference	
6 Edward II 1313	A lxci	L
13 Edward II 1320	E xcix	L
3 Edward II 1329	E cxciv	L
17 Edward III 1343	F lxxi	L
18 Edward III 1344	F xci	L
18 Edward III 1344	F xcii	L
23 Edward III 1349	F clxv	L
8 Richard II 1385	H clxxxvi	L
9 Richard II 1386	H cxcviii	L
12 Richard II 1388	H ccxxxvii	N
30 Jan. 1386	Roll A 27 membr. 28	F
·13 Aug. 1406	Roll A 39 membr. 17	
21 July 1386	Roll A 27 membr. 28-28b	
15 Jan. 1384	Roll A 27 membr. 8	
30 Jan. 1386	Roll A 27 membr. 28	F
30 Jan. 1386	Roll A 27 membr. 28	
20 June 1386	Roll A 27 membr. 28	
26 March 1384	Roll A 27 membr. 9	

Water

Date	Reference	
9 Edward I 1281	A cxxx	N
10 Edward I 1282	C liii	L
16 Edward I 1288	A cxxx	L
19 Edward I 1291	A lxxxiv	L
21 Edward I 1293	C vii	L
25 Edward I 1297	B xxxii (old numeration)	L
26 Edward I 1298	B 34	L
28 Edward I 1300	C xlvii	L
28 Edward I 1300	C xlviii	L
2 Edward II 1309	C xcvi	N
4 Edward II 1310	C cx	L
4 Edward II 1310	D cxiv	L
6 Edward II 1312	D clix	L
15 Edward II 1322	E cxxxvi	L
19 Edward II 1325	E clxii, iii	L
11 Edward III 1337	F xix	L
11 Edward III 1337	F xx	L
19 Edward III 1345	F cvii	L
24 Edward III 1350	F clxxxvi	L
24 Edward III 1350	F cxcv	N
24 Edward III 1350	F ccxxxvii	L N
29 Edward III 1355	G xxxix	L
31 Edward III 1357	G lxiv	L
43 Edward III 1369	G ccxxiv	L
43 Edward III 1369	G ccxxx	L
46 Edward III 1372	G ccxcii	L
47 Edward III 1373	G ccxvi	L
48 Edward III 1374	G cccxvi	L
48 Edward III 1374	G cccxviii	L
49 Edward III 1375	H xxi	L
49 Edward III 1375	H xv	L N
50 Edward III 1376	H xlix	N
1 Richard II 1377	H lxxiii	L
1 Richard II 1378	H lxxxiv	L
3 Richard II 1379	H cxvi	N
4 Richard II 1380	H cxxv	L
6 Richard II 1383	H clxiv	N
11 Richard II 1388	H ccxxvi	L
14 Richard II 1390	H cclii	L
22 Richard II 1398	H cccxviii	N
5 Henry IV 1404	I xxix	L N
10 Henry IV 1409	I lxxx	L N
14 Henry IV 1413	I cxviii	N
3 Henry V 1415	I clii	L
3 Henry V 1415	I cliv	N
5 Henry V 1417	I cxciii	N
5 Henry V 1417	I cc	L
7 Henry V 1419	Journal I, 61	L N

Bread

Date	Reference	
26 Edward I 1298	B 85	L
3 Edward II 1310	D clxxi	L
5 Edward II 1311	D clxxv	L
6 Edward II 1313	D clxxx	L
9 Edward II 1316	D clxxxviii	L
9 Edward II 1316	D clxxxviii	L

9 Edward II 1316	D clxxxix	L
9 Edward II 1316	D cxc	L
10 Edward II 1316	D cxc	L
12 Edward II 1318	E lxxxii	L
1 Edward III 1327		L
5 Edward III 1331	E ccxxi	L N
21 Edward III 1347	F cxxxix	L
37 Edward III 1363	G cxiii	L
38 Edward III 1364	G cxxxii	L
39 Edward III 1365	G cxxxv	N
40 Edward III 1366	G clxxxiii	L
45 Edward III 1370	G cclv	N
2 Richard II 1378	H xcix	N
2 Richard II 1379	H cxiv	L N
5 Richard II 1382	H cxlii	L
11 Richard II 1387	H ccxxiv	L
4 Henry V 1417	Journal 1 fol. 12	L
4 Henry V 1417	I cxc	L
25 April 1383	Roll A 26 membr. 3b	
11 March 1384	Roll A 27 membr. 8b	
8 Feb. 1391	Roll A 30 membr. 4	

Hay

1 Edward III 1327	E clxxix	L N
37 Edward III 1363	G cxiii	L

Wine

44 Edward III 1370	G ccxliii	L N
21 Feb. 1393	Roll A 32 membr. 3-3b	F

29 Nov. 1381	Roll A 25 membr. 2	F
6 Dec. 1383	Roll A 27 membr. 7	
3 Nov. 1384	Roll A 27 membr. 12b	
25 Nov. 1386	Roll A 28 membr. 2b	
6 July 1389	Roll A 29 membr. 11-11b	
10 Feb. 1383	Roll A 25 membr. 30	
9 July 1387	Roll A 28 membr. 5b	
25 April 1383	Roll A 26 membr. 3b	

Drink

4 Edward II 1311	D cxvii	N
6 Edward II 1312	D clxviii	N
13 Edward II 1320	E cviii	L
5 Edward III 1331	E ccxxi	L N
8 Edward III 1335	E ccxxvii	L
16 Edward III 1342	F lxiii	L
19 Edward III 1345	F cvii	L
27 Edward III 1353	G iii	L
38 Edward III 1364	G cxli	L
44 Edward III 1370	G ccxliii	L N
48 Edward III 1374	G cccxxiv	L
49 Edward III 1375	H xxvi	L
1 Richard II 1377	H lxii	L
10 Richard II 1386	H ccix	L
12 Edward II 1319	E xxv	N
17 Richard II 1394	H ccxci	L
19 Richard II 1396	H cccii	L N

4 Henry IV 1402	I xxiii	L
3 Henry V 1415	I cliv	N
4 Henry V 1416	Journal 1 fol. 5	L
7 Henry V 1419	I ccxxvi	E
7 Henry V 1419	I ccxxvii	E
16 Dec. 1383	Roll A 27 membr. 10b	
23 May 1384	Roll A 27 membr. 1	
21 Feb. 1387	Roll A 28 membr. 3	
4 Dec. 1393	Roll A 33 membr. 2-2b-3	

Fruits and Vegetables

19 Edward III 1345	F cxi	L N

Cheese

51 Edward III 1377	H lxii	L N

Spices

9 Edward II 1316	E liii	N
6 July 1394	Roll A 33 membr. 6	
13 Dec. 1387	Roll A 28 membr. 6b-7	

Market and Merchants

25 Edward I 1297	B xxx (old numeration)	L
33 Edward I 1305	C lxviii	L
3 Edward II 1310	D cv	N
20 Edward III 1346	F cxxvi	N
31 Edward III 1357	G lxxi	L N
43 Edward III 1369	G ccxxx	N
16 Richard II 1393	H cclxxviii	L N

Liber Albus; Liber Custumarum; Liber Horn; Cottonian MS Claudius D.II; in Munimenta Gildhallae Londonienses, ed. Henry Thomas Riley. London, 1860.

Annales Londoniensis and Annales Pauline, ed. W. Stubbs. Rolls Series 76, London, 1882.

Liber de Antiques Legibus, ed. Thomas Stapleton. London, 1846.

Chambers, R. W., and Marjorie Daunt. *A Book of London English: 1384–1425.* Oxford, 1931.

Calendar of Early Mayor's Court Rolls, 1298–1307, ed. A. H. Thomas. Cambridge, 1924.

Calendar of the Close Rolls Preserved in the Public Record Office, ed. W. H. B. Bird. 1399–1402, London, 1927; 1402–05, London, 1929; 1408–09, London, 1938; 1409–13, London, 1932; Index 1399–1413, London, 1938.

Calendar of Letter Books of the City of London, ed. R. R. Sharpe. *Letter Book A and B,* London, 1899; through *Letter Book H,* London, 1907.

Calendar of the Patent Rolls Preserved in the Public Record Office from Edward I thru Henry VII, ed. R. C. Fowler. London, 1907.

Calendar of Plea and Memoranda Rolls of the City of London, ed. A. H. Thomas. 1323–64, Cambridge, 1926; 1364–81, Cambridge, 1929; 1381–1412, Cambridge, 1932; 1413–37, Cambridge, 1943.

Calendar of Plea and Memoranda Rolls of the City of London, 1437–57, ed. Philip E. Jones. Cambridge, 1954.

Calendar of Select Pleas and Memoranda of the City of London, 1381–1412, ed. A. H. Thomas. Cambridge, 1932.

Historical Charters and Constitutional Documents of the City of London, ed. Walter De Gray Birch. London, 1887.

The Register of Henry Chichele, Archbishop of Canterbury, 1414–43, ed. E. F. Jacob. 4 vols. Oxford, 1937–47.

Select Pleas from the Rolls of the Exchequer of the Jews. London, 1902.

Riley, H. T. *Memorials of London and London Life.* London, 1868.

Coote, H. C. *Ordinances of Some Secular Guilds of London, 1354–96.* London, 1871.

Hall, Hubert. *Select Cases in the Law Merchant II.* London, 1930.

Cross, C. *Select Cases in the Law Merchant I.* London, 1903.

Stow, John. *A Survey of London,* ed. C. L. Kingsford. Oxford, 1908.

Biting, K. G. *Gastronomic Bibliography.* San Francisco, 1939.

Simon, Andre L. *Bibliotheca Gastronomica.* London, 1953.

Vicaire, Georges. *Bibliographie gastronomique.* Paris, 1890.

Lord Westbury. *Handlist of Italian Cookery Books.* Florence, 1963.

Gn Abel, Mary W. *Practical Sanitary and Economic Cooking.* Rochester, 1890.

Ts Abrahams, Israel. *Jewish Life in the Middle Ages.* 1896; New York, 1969.

Ts Abram, A. *English Life and Manners in the Later Middle Ages.* London, 1913.

Gn Accum, Fredrick. *A Treatise on Adulterations of Food and Country Poisons.* London, 1820.

Gn Allen, E. Elliston. *British Tastes: An Enquiry into the Likes and Dislikes of the Regional Consumer.* London, 1968.

Gv Allen, H. Warner. *A History of Wine.* London, 1961.

Gn Ambro, Richard D. "Dietary-Technological-Ecological Aspects of Lovelock Cave Coprolites," *Reports of the University of California Archaeological Survey* 70 (1967), 37–47.

G *American Heritage Cookbook and Illustrated History of American Eating and Drinking.* New York, 1964.

Ga Amherst, A. M. [See Cecil, A. M.]

G Anderson, John L. *A Fifteenth Century Cookery Book.* New York, 1962.

G André, J. *L'Alimentation et la cuisine à Rome.* Paris, 1961.

Th Andreae, S. J. Fockena. "Embanking and Drainage Authorities in the Netherlands during the Middle Ages," *Speculum* 27 (1952), 158–67.

Ga Andrewe, Lawrens. *The Noble Lyfe & Natures of Man, of bestes serpentys, fowles & fisshes y be moste knowen.* London, 1531.

L Anglo, Sydney. "Le Camp du Drap d'Or et les Entrevues d'Henri VIII et de Charles Quint," *Les Fêtes de la Renaissance,* ed. J. Jacquot. Paris, 1960, 113–34.

L ———. "The Court Festivals of Henry VII: A Study based upon the Account Books of John Heron, Treasurer of the Chamber," *Bulletin of the John Rylands Library* 43 (1960), 12–45.

A ———. "The Foundation of the Tudor Dynasty: the Coronation and Marriage of Henry VII," *The Guildhall Miscellany* 2 (1960), 3–31.

L ———. "La Salle de banquet et le théâtre construits à Greenwich pour les fêtes franco-anglaises de 1527," *Le Lieu Théâtral à la Renaissance,* ed. J. Jacquot. Paris, 1964, 273–88.

L ———. *The Great Tournament Roll of Westminster.* Oxford, 1968.

L ———. *Spectacle, Pageantry, and Early Tudor Policy.* London, 1969.

L *Anglo-Saxon Poetical Records,* eds. George P. Krapp and E. V. K. Dobbie. New York, 1931–42.

Ga Angress, S. and Reed, C. A. *An Annotated Bibliography on the Origin and Descent of Domestic Mammals, 1900–1955.* Chicago, 1962.

T Anon. *Annales, economies, sociétés, civilisations.* Paris, 1929.

T Anon. *Our English Home: Its Early History and Progress,* 2nd ed. Oxford, 1861.

G Apicius. *De re coquinaria/culinaria,* trans. as *The Roman Cookery Book* by Barbara Flower and Elisabeth Rosenbaum. London, 1958.

G Aresty, Esther B. *The Delectable Past.* New York, 1964.

G Arrington, L. R. "Foods of the Bible," *Journal of the American Dietetic Association* 35 (1959), 816–20.

Te Ascham, R. *The Scholemaster,* ed. J. E. B. Mayor. London, 1934.

Gu Ash, D. *How to Identify English Silver Drinking Vessels: 600–1830.* London, 1964.

Ga Ashley, Sir William. *The Bread of Our Forefathers: An Inquiry in Economic History.* Oxford, 1928.

Th Ashton, J. *The Fleet: Its River, Prison and Marriages.* London, 1939.

G Athaneus. *The Deipnosophists,* trans. Charles Burton Gulik. Cambridge, 1927.

Gn Austin, Gertrude Ellen. "English Food in the Thirteenth Century," *Medieval Forum* 3 (1935–36), 117–33.

G Austin, Thomas, ed. *Two Fifteenth Century Cookery Books.* London, 1888.

Gn Avinon, Juan de. *Sevillana Medicina* [1418]. Society of Andalusian Bibliophiles, 1885.

M Azzaiolo. *Villotte alla padoana.* Bologna, 1953.

Gu Bailey, C. T. P. *Knives and Forks.* London, 1927.

M Baines, Anthony. *Woodwind Instruments and Their History.* New York, 1963.

T Baldwin, F. E. *Sumptuary Legislation and Personal Regulation in England.* Baltimore, 1926.

Ts Balsdon, J. P. V. D. *Life and Leisure in Ancient Rome.* London and New York, 1969.

A Baltimore. Walters Art Gallery. *The International Style: The Art in Europe Around 1400.* Baltimore, Oct.–Dec. 1962.

A Banchereau, J. "Travaux d'agriculture sur un chapiteau de Vézélay," *Bulletin Monumental* 77 (1913), 403–11.

T Barber, R. W. *Arthur of Albion.* London, 1961.

L Bargagli, Girolamo. *La Pellegrina,* ed. Florindo Correta. Biblioteca dell' Archivum Romanicum. Rome, 1971.

Gn Barker, T. C., J. C. McKenzie and John Yudkin, eds. *Our Changing Fare: Two Hundred Years of British Food Habits.* London, 1966.

T Barraclough, Geoffrey, ed. *Eastern and Western Europe in the Middle Ages.* London, 1970.

Gu Barretlet, James. "Le Verre de tables au moyen-âge, d'après les manuscrits et peintures," *Cahiers de la céramique du verre et des arts du feu* 16 (1959), 194–225.

T Barron, Caroline M. *The Medieval Guildhall of London.* London, 1974.

Th Barton, N. J. *Lost Rivers of London.* London, 1962.

L Baskervill, Charles Read, ed. *Pierre Gringoire's Pageants for the Entry of Mary Tudor into Paris.* Chicago, 1934.

Tc Beardwood, Alice. *Alien Merchants in England, 1350–77.* Cambridge, 1931.

T Beatty, Nancy Lee. *The Craft of Dying.* New Haven and London, 1970.

Ga Becher, K. *Early Herbals from the Library of*

   Dr. Karl Becher. Karlsbad, n.d.

M Bedford, Arthur. *Thes Great Abuse of Musick.* New York, 1965.

Gu Bedford, J. *Pewter.* New York, 1966.

L Beijer, Agne. "La Naissance de la Paix. Ballet de cour de René Descartes," *Le Lieu théâtral à la Renaissance,* ed. J. Jacquot. Paris, 1964, 409–22.

Gu Bell, M. *Old Pewter.* London, 1905.

Th Bell, W. G., F. Cottrell, and C. Spon. *London Wall Through Eighteen Centuries.* London, n.d.

Th Bennett, C. E., and C. Herschel, eds. *Frontinus: The Stratagems and the Aqueducts of Rome.* London, 1925.

Gn Bennett, H. S. "Science and Information in English Writings of the 15th Century," *Modern Language Review* 39 (1944), 1–8.

Ts ———. *Life on the English Manor. A Study of Peasant Conditions 1150–1400.* Cambridge, 1937.

L Benson, Larry D. *Art and Tradition in Sir Gawain and the Green Knight.* New Brunswick, 1965.

L ———. ed., *The Learned and the Lewd.* Cambridge, 1974.

L *Beowulf,* ed. Fr. Klaeber. Boston, 1950.

T Bergeron, David M. *English Civic Pageantry, 1558–1642.* London, 1971.

Te Berges, W. *Die Fürstenspiegel des höhen und späteren Mittelalters.* Stuttgart, 1938.

A Berti, Luciano. *Santa Croce, Firenze.* Bologna, 1967.

Ts Besant, Sir Walter. *Medieval London, Historical and Social.* London, 1906.

Tc Best, Henry. *Rural Economy in Yorkshire, Being the Farming and Account Books of Henry Best, 1641.* London, 1857.

Gv Bickerdyke, J. *The Curiosities of Ale and Beer.* London, 1965.

Ga Biggs, H. E. J. "Mollusca from Prehistoric Jericho," *Journal of Conchology* 24 (1960), 379–87.

Gn Billingham, J. "Snail Haemolymph, an Aid to Survival in the Desert," *Lancet* I (1961), 903–06.

A Birch, W. de Gray. *Catalogue of Seals in the Department of Manuscripts in the British Museum.* London, 1885–1900.

Ts Bishop, Morris. *The Middle Ages.* New York, 1970.

L Bjurström, Per. *Giacomo Torelli and Baroque Stage Design.* Stockholm, 1961.

L Bleeth, K. A. ". . . Merchant's Tale," in *The Learned and the Lewd,* ed. L. Benson. Cambridge, 1974.

L Bloomfield, Morton. *The Seven Deadly Sins.* Michigan, 1952.

A Blum, Shirley Neilsen. *Early Netherlandish Tryptichs: A Study in Patronage.* Berkeley and Los Angeles, 1969.

T Boase, T. S. R. *Death in the Middle Ages.* New York, 1972.

Gn Bodenheimer, F. S. *Insects as Human Food.* The Hague, 1951.

Gn ———. *Animal and Man in Bible Lands.* Leiden and New York, 1960.

A Boeckler, Albert. *Das goldene Evangelienbuch Heinrichs III.* Berlin, 1933.

M Boetticher, Wolfgang. *Orlando di Lasso und seine Zeit, 1532–1594.* Basel, 1958.

A Bonavia, F. *The Flora of the Assyrian Monuments.* London, 1894.

Ga Bonnefons, Nicolas de. *The French Gardiner.* London, 1695.

Gn Boorde, Andrew. *A Compendyous Regyment, or a Dyetary of Helth,* 1542. ed. F. Furnivall, London, 1870.

Te Born, L. K. *Erasmus. The Education of the Christian Prince.* New York, 1936.

Te ———. "The Perfect Prince," *Speculum* 3 (1928), 420–504.

A Borsook, E. "Art and Politics at the Medici Court. I: The Funeral of Cosimo I de' Medici," *Mitteilungen des kunsthistorischen Institutes in Florenz* 12 (1965), 31–54.

A ———. "Art and Politics at the Medici Court. IV: Funeral Decor for Henry IV of France," *Mitteilungen des kunsthistorischen Institutes in Florenz* 15 (1969), 201–43.

Ga Boswell, Victor R. "Our Vegetable Travelers," *The National Geographic Magazine* 96 (1949), 145–217.

M Bottrigari, Hercole. *Il Desiderio,* trans. Carol MacClintock. New York, 1962.

M Bowles, Edmund A. "Musical Instruments at the Medieval Banquet," *Revue belge de musicologie* 12 (1958).

M Boyd, Morrison C. *Elizabethan Music and Musical Criticism,* 2nd ed. Philadelphia, 1967.

T Boyer, M. N. "A Day's Journey in Medieval France," *Speculum* 26 (1951).

Tc Braudel, Fernand. *Capitalism and Material Life 1400–1800.* New York, 1974.

A Braun, H. "The Hall" and "Private Houses," in his *An Introduction to English Medieval Architecture,* 2nd ed. New York, 1968.

Ge Brett, G. *Dinner is Served: A Study of Manners.* Hamden, 1969.

Tc Bridbury, A. R. *England and the Salt Trade in the Later Middle Ages.* Oxford, 1955.

Gn Brillat-Savarin, Jean-Anthelme. *La Physiologie du goût,* trans. Anne Drayton. Harmondsworth, 1970.

A Brinton, S. J. C. *Francesco di Giorgio Martini of Siena, 1439–1502.* London, 1934.

M *British Union Catalogue of Early Music Printed Before the Year 1801: A Record of the Holdings of One Hundred Libraries Throughout the British Isles.* ed. Edith B. Schnapper. London, 1957.

T Bromley, J., and H. Child. *The Armorial Bearings of the Guilds of London.* London, 1961.

Ts Brooks, C. E. P. *Climate Through the Ages.* London, 1926.

G Brooks, R. *The Natural History of Chocolate.* London, 1725.

Gn Brothwell, D. R. "Teeth in Earlier Human Populations," *Proceedings of the Nutrition Society* 18 (1959), 59–65.

G Brothwell, Don and Patricia. *Food in Antiquity. A Survey of the Diet of Early Peoples.* London, 1969.

T Brothwell, D. R. and E. S. Higgs, eds. *Science in Archaeology.* London and New York, 1963.

M Brown, H. M. "The Music of the Strozzi Chansonnier," *Acta musicologica* 40 (1968).

M ———. *Instrumental Music Printed Before 1600.* Cambridge, 1965.

M ———. *Sixteenth Century Instrumentation.* American Institute of Musicology, 1974.

M ———. *Embellishing Sixteenth Century Music*. Oxford, 1975.

M ———. "A Cook's Tour of Ferrara in 1529," Paper presented at University of Notre Dame, Renaissance Conference (April, 1975).

T Bruce-Mitford, R., ed. *Recent Archaeological Excavations in Britain*. London, 1952.

A Bruges. Sroeninge Museum. *Anonieme Vlaamse Primitieven*. Bruges, 14 June – 21 Sept. 1969.

A Brussels. Bibliothèque royale de Belgique. *Medieval Miniatures*. New York, 1965.

A Brussels. Palais des Beaux-Arts. *Le Siècle d'or de la miniature flamande*. Amsterdam, 26 June – 13 Sept. 1959.

G Bruyerin, Jean Baptiste. *De re cibaria . . .* Lyon, 1630.

Ts Bühler, C. F. *The Fifteenth Century Book*. Philadelphia, 1960.

Gu ———. "Rondels," *Renaissance News* 9 (1956), 146f.

M Bukofzer, Manfred F. *Studies in Medieval and Renaissance Music*. New York, 1950.

T Bullough, D. A., and R. L. Storey, eds. *The Study of Medieval Records: Essays in Honor of Kathleen Major*. Oxford, 1971.

Ga Burckhardt, Titus. *Die Jagd*. Olten and Freiburg-im-Breisgau, 1964.

Tc Burnett, John. *A History of the Cost of Living in England*. Harmondsworth, 1969.

Gn ———. *Plenty and Want: A Social History of Diet in England from 1815 to the Present Day*. London, 1966.

Gn Callen, E. O., and T. W. M. Cameron. "A Prehistoric Diet Revealed in Coprolites," *New Scientist* 8 (1960), 35–40.

T Calthorp, D.C. *English Costume*. London, 1906.

Tc *Cambridge Economic History of Europe*, I–IV. Cambridge, 1941–67.

A Cames, Gérard. *Allégories et symboles dans L'Hortus Deliciarum*. Leiden, 1971.

T Campbell, Anna. *The Black Death and Men of Learning*. New York, 1931.

Ga Campbell-Thompson, R. *The Assyrian Herbal*. London, 1924.

M Carpenter, Nan Cooke. *Music in the Medieval and Renaissance Universities*. New York, 1972.

Ts Carcopino, Jerome. *Daily Life in Ancient Rome: The People and the City at the Height of the Empire*. London, 1941; 1967.

Ga Carefoot, G. L., and E. R. Sprott. *Famine on the Wind. Plant Diseases and Human History*. New York, 1967.

T Carletti, Francesco. *Ragionamenti, 1594–1606*, trans. as *My Voyage Around the World* by Herbert Weinstock. New York, 1964.

M Carse, Adam. *Musical Wind Instruments*. London, 1939.

Tc Carus-Wilson, E. M. *Medieval Merchant Adventurers*. Ann Arbor, 1967.

M Case, J. *Praise of Musicke*. London, 1588; 1870.

Te Castiglione, B. *The Book of the Courtyer*, 1561, trans. T. Hoby. London, 1932, or any modern version.

T Catalano, Michele. *Vita di Lodovico Ariosto*. Geneva, 1930.

L Cauley, A. C. "The 'Grotesque' Feast in the Prima Pastorum," *Speculum* 30 (1955).

Tc Cave, R. C., and H. N. Coulson. *A Source Book for Medieval Economic History*. Milwaukee, 1936.

T Cavendish, George. *The Life and Death of Cardinal Wolsey*, ed. R. S. Sylvester. London, 1957.

Ga Cecil, Hon. Alicia M. [Amherst]. "A Fifteenth Century Treatise on Gardening by Mayster Ion Gardener," *Archaeologia* 54 (1844), 156–72.

Ga ———. *A History of Gardening in England*. London, 1895–96.

Ts Chamberlin, E. R. *Life in Medieval France*. New York, 1967.

Ts ———. *Everyday Life in Renaissance Times*. London, New York, 1965.

L Chambers, E. K. *The Medieval Stage*. London, 1903.

A Chamban, R. "Influence vénitienne sur la production verrière de la Belgique à la fin du XVᵉ et au XVIᵉ Siècle," *Cahiers de la céramique du verre et des arts du feu* 18 (1960), 120–34.

A Champier, J. *Rosa Gallica*. Paris, 1514.

Gn Chaney, Ralph W. "The Food of 'Peking Man'," *Carnegie Institution Bulletin* 3 (1935), 199–202.

Ga Chaplain, Raymond E. "Animals in Archaeology," *Antiquity* 39 (1965), 204–11.

Th Chapman, Carlton B. "The Year of the Great Stink," *The Pharos* (July 1972), 90–105.

M Chappell, William. *Popular Music of the Olden Time*. London, 1859.

A Charcot, J. M., and Paul Richer. *Les Difformes et les malades dans l'art*. Paris, 1889.

L Chartrou, Joseph. *Les Entrées solennelles et triomphales à la Renaissance, 1484–1551*. Paris, 1928.

L Chaucer, Geoffrey. *The Works of Geoffrey Chaucer*, ed. F. N. Robinson. Boston, 1957.

T Chaucer Society. *Analogues of Chaucer's Canterbury Pilgrimage*, eds. F. J. Furnivall and A. Kirk. London, 1903.

T Chevalier, A. "Medieval Dress," *Ciba Review* 57 (June, 1947).

A Chew, Samuel C. "Spenser's Pageant of the Seven Deadly Sins," *Studies in Art and Literature for Belle Da Costa Greene*. Princeton, 1954.

T *Chronicon Monasterii de Melsa*. ed. E. A. Bond. Public Records Series, London, 1866–68.

M Christout, Marie-Françoise. *Le Ballet de Cour de Louis XIV 1643–1672*. Paris, 1967.

Ts Cimber, Louis Lafaist, and F. Danjou. *Archives curieuses de l'histoire de France, Louis XI-Louis XVII*. Paris, 1834–40.

Tc Cipolla, C. M. *Money, Prices, and Civilization in the Mediterranean World*. Princeton, 1956.

Ga Clark, Colin. *Population Growth and Land Use*. London, 1967.

Ga Clark, J. G. D. "Radiocarbon Dating and the Spread of Farming Economy," *Antiquity* 38 (1964), 45–48.

Tc ———. *Prehistoric Europe. The Economic Basis*. London, 1952; Stanford, 1966.

Gu Clair, Colin. *Kitchen and Table*. London and

New York, 1965.

L   Clephan, R. *The Tournament, its Periods and Phases.* London, 1919.

T   Cobbett, William, ed. *Parliamentary History of England.* London, 1742.

M   Cocks, William A. "The Phagotum: An Attempt at Reconstruction," *Galpin Society Journal* 12 (1959).

M   Collaer, Paul, and A. Vander Linden. *Atlas historique de la musique.* Paris, 1960.

L   Collier, J. P. *The History of English Dramatic Poetry . . . and the Annals of the Stage.* London, 1879.

Ga   Collins, J. L. "Antiquity of the Pineapple of America," *Southwestern Journal of Anthropology* 7 (1951), 145–55.

G   Colombié, Auguste. *Histoire du repas à travers les âges,* 2nd ed. Paris, 1895.

Ga   Columella. *De re rustica,* trans. as *On Agriculture* by E. S. Forster and E. H. Heffner. London, 1941.

A   Colvin, Sidney. *Early Engraving and Engravers in England.* London, 1905.

M   *Compositione di Meser Vincenzo Capirola,* ed. Otto Gombosi. Neuilly-sur-Seine, 1955.

G   *Compost et Kalendrier des bergères.* Paris, 1499.

Ga   Cooke, A. O. *A Book of Dovecotes.* London and Boston, 1920.

T   Cook, S. F., and E. E. Treganza. "The Quantitative Investigation of Indian Mounds," *University of California Publications on American Archaeology and Ethnology* 40 (1950), 223–62.

Ts   Coon, Carleton S. *The History of Man: From the First Human to Primitive Culture and Beyond.* New York, 1954.

Ts   ———. "Race and Ecology in Man," *Cold Spring Harbor Symposia on Quantitative Biology* 24 (1959), 153–59.

Gu   Cooper, Charles. *The English Table in History and Literature.* London, 1929.

T   Cosman, M. P., and L. Pelner. "Elias Sabot and King Henry IV," *New York State Journal of Medicine* (1964).

Te   Cosman, M. P. *Education of the Hero in Arthurian Romance.* Chapel Hill, 1966; Oxford, 1967.

Gu   Cotterell, H. H. *Pewter down the Ages.* London, 1932.

T   Cotton, Charles. *The Compleat Gamester, or, Instructions How to Play at All Manner of Usual and Most Genteel Games,* 1674. Bane, Mass., 1970.

Ts   Coulton, G. G. *Life in the Middle Ages.* New York, 1935.

M   Cowling, G. H. *Music on the Shakespearian Stage.* New York, 1964.

M   Cox, F. A., ed. *English Madrigals in the Time of Shakespeare.* London, 1899.

T   Cox, Harvey. *Feast of Fools.* Cambridge, Mass., 1969.

Ga   Crane, Eva, ed. *Honey, A Comprehensive Survey.* New York, 1975.

A   Crisp, Frank. *Medieval Gardens.* London, 1924.

Ga   Crescentius, Petrus. *Commodorum ruralium.* Speyer, 1490–95.

L   Cross, Tom Peete, and C. H. Slover. *Ancient Irish Tales.* New York, 1936.

A   Crossley, F. H. *The English Abbey.* New York, 1936.

Gu   Curle, A. O. "Domestic Candlesticks from the Fourteenth to the Eighteenth Century," *Proceedings of the Society of Antiquaries of Scotland* 11 (1925–26).

G   Curtis-Bennett, Sir Noel. *The Food of the People.* London, 1949.

L   Curtius, E. *European Literature in the Latin Middle Ages,* trans. Willard Trask. New York, 1953.

Ga   Curwen, E. Cecil, and G. Hatt. *Plough and Pasture: The Early History of Farming.* New York, 1953.

Ga   Cutting, Charles L. *Fish Saving: A History of Fish Processing from Ancient to Modern Times.* New York, 1956.

A   d'Allemagne, Henry René. *Decorative Antique Ironwork: A Pictorial Treasury,* trans. Vera K. Ostoia. New York, 1968.

A   d'Ancona, Paulo, et al. *Dictionnaire des Miniaturistes du Moyen-Age et de la Renaissance,* 2nd ed. Milan, 1949.

G   Darenne, E. *Histoire des métiers de l'alimentation.* Meulan, 1904.

T   David, F. N. *Games, Gods, and Gambling.* Griffin, 1962.

Ga   Davidson, Alan. *Mediterranean Seafood.* Harmondsworth, 1972.

Gn   Dawson, Warren R. *A Leechbook or Collection of Medical Receipts of the Fifteenth Century.* London, 1934.

M   Deakin, Andrew. *Musical Bibliography: A Catalogue of the Musical Works Published in England During the 15th, 16th, 17th and 18th Centuries.* Birmingham, 1892.

Ge   Dean, Ruth, and M. Dominica Legge, eds. *The Rule of Saint Benedict.* Oxford, 1964.

Ts   de Givry, Emile G. *Illustrated Anthology of Sorcery, Magic and Alchemy,* 1929. New York, 1973.

Ts   de Calonne, Alberic (Baron). *La Vie municipale au XVᵉ siècle dans le nord de la France.* Paris, 1880.

Ga   DeCandolle, A. *Origin of Cultivated Plants.* London, 1886.

Ga   De Castro, J. *Geography of Hunger.* London, 1955.

Ga   Deerr, Noel. *The History of Sugar.* London, 1949.

T   Deevey, Edward S. "The Human Population," *Scientific American* 203 (1960), 194–204.

Gn   De Kruif, Paul Henry. *Hunger Fighters.* New York, 1928.

M   De Lafontaine, Henry. *The King's Musick. A Transcript of Records Relating to Music and Musicians, 1460–1700.* New York, 1973.

A   Delaporte, Y., and E. Houvet. *Les Vitraux de la cathédrale de Chartres.* Chartres, 1926.

Ge   Della Casa, Giovanni. *Galateo, or the Book of Manners,* 1558, trans. R. S. Pine. Harmondsworth, 1958.

Gu   de Navarro, A. *Causeries on English Pewter.* New York, 1911.

L   de Nolhac, P., and A. Solerti. *Il Viaggio in Italia di Enrico III.* Turin, 1890.

A   Denny, Norman, and J. Filmer-Sankey. *The Bayeux Tapestry. The Story of the Norman Conquest: 1066.* New York, 1966.

M   Dent, E. J. "Social Aspects of Music in the Middle Ages," *Oxford History of Music*. London, 1929.

T   Derry, T. K., and T. Williams. *A Short History of Technology from the Earliest Time to A.D. 1900*. Oxford, 1960.

A   Detroit. Institute of Arts. *Flanders in the Fifteenth Century, Art and Civilization.* Detroit, Oct.–Dec., 1960.

A   Deuchler, Florens. "Looking at Bonne of Luxembourg's Prayer Book," *Metropolitan Museum of Art Bulletin* 29 (Feb. 1971), 267–78.

A   ———. *Gothic Art*. New York, 1973.

T   ———. *Die Burgunderbeute*. Bern, 1963.

L   Devoto, Daniel. "Folklore et politique en Château Ténébreux," *Les Fêtes de la Renaissance*, ed. J. Jacquot (1960), 311–28.

A   Didot, A. F. *Essai typographique sur l'histoire de la gravure sur bois*. Paris, 1863.

Gn   di Lullo, Orestes. *El folklore de Santiage del Estero, medicina y alimentacion*. Santiago del Estero, Argentina, 1944.

Ga   Dimbleby, Geoffrey. *Plants and Archaeology*. London and New York, 1967.

Ga   Dodge, B. S. *Plants That Changed the World*. London and Boston, 1962.

A   Dodwell, C. R. *The Canterbury School of Illumination, 1066–1200*. Cambridge, 1954.

M   Dolmetsch, Mabel. *Dances of Spain and Italy from 1400–1600*. London, 1954.

Ts   Douglas, David C. *The Norman Achievement 1050–1100*. London and Berkeley, 1969.

G   Drummond, J. C., and Anne Wilbraham. *The Englishman's Food. A History of Five Centuries of English Diet*. London, 1939.

G   Druetti, Giuseppe. "Dai mezzi di alimentazione . . . ," *Istituto superiore di sanità*. Rome, 1947.

G   Dubarry, Armand. *Le Boire et le manger*. Paris, 1884.

Tc   Duby, Georges. *Rural Economy and Country Life in the Medieval West*. London and Columbia, South Carolina, 1968.

Ts   Duby, Georges, and R. Mandrou. *A History of French Civilization*. London, 1965.

T   Duckett, Eleanor. *Death and Life in the Tenth Century*. Ann Arbor, 1967.

Gv   Dufour, Phillippe Sylvestre. *Traitez nouveaux et curieux du café, du thé, et du chocolat*. Lyon, 1685.

A   Dupont, Jacques, and Cesare Grudi. *Gothic Painting*. Geneva, 1954.

G   *Early English Recipes. Selected from the Harleian MS. 279 of about 1430*. Cambridge, 1937.

G   Edelstein, Ludwig. *Antike diätetik*. Berlin and Leipzig, 1931.

Tc   Edwardes, Michael. *East-West Passage; The Travel of Ideas, Arts and Inventions Between Asia and the Western World*. London and New York, 1971.

M   Einstein, Alfred. *The Italian Madrigal*. Princeton, 1949.

Te   Elyot, T. *The Boke Named the Governor*. London, 1531; London, 1907.

Gn   Emery, W. B. *A Funerary Repast in an Egyptian Tomb of the Archaic Period*. Leiden, 1962.

L   *Enciclopedia dello Spettacolo*. Rome, 1954–66.

G   Engle, Fannie, and Gertrude Blair. *The Jewish Festival Cookbook*. New York, 1973.

Gn   Eokmann, Gerhard. *Ueber die praktische Rolle der Diätetik in der hippokratischen Medizin*. Berlin, 1936.

T   *The Register of Eudes of Rouen*, ed. J. F. O'Sullivan, trans. Sydney Brown. New York, 1964.

A   Evans, Joan. *Art in Medieval France, 987–1498. A Study in Patronage*. London, 1948.

Ts   ———. *Life in Medieval France*. New York, 1925, 1969.

T   ———. *English Jewellery from the Fifth Century A.D. to 1800*. London, 1921.

A   Evans, M. W. *Medieval Drawings*. London and New York, 1969.

Ga   Evelyn, John. *Acetaria. A Discourse of Sallets*. London, 1706.

Gn   Faber, Hugo. *Eine diätethik aus Montpellier*. Leipzig, 1921.

Ts   Faral, Edmond. *La Vie quotidienne au temps de Saint Louis*. Paris, 1942.

M   Farmer, J. S., ed. *The Return from Parnassus*, 1606. London, 1910.

Ga   Farrar, W. V. "Tecuitlatl; a Glimpse of Aztec Food Technology," *Nature* 211 (1966), 341–42.

M   Fellowes, E. H. *The English Madrigal*. London, 1925.

M   ———. *William Byrd*. London, 1936.

M   ———. *The English Madrigal Composers*. London, 1950.

Gn   Filby, Frederick A. *A History of Food Adulteration and Analysis*. London, 1934.

G   Fitz Stephen, William. "A Description of London," ca. 1183, trans. H. E. Butler, in F. M. Stenton, *Norman London*. London, 1934.

Ga   Flannery, Kent V. "The Ecology of Early Food Production in Mesopotamia," *Science* 147 (1965), 1247–56.

A   Flinn, Elizabeth Haight. "A Magnificent Manuscript—A Historical Mystery," *Metropolitan Museum of Art Bulletin* 29 (Feb. 1971), 257–60.

Th   Foord, Alfred Stanley. *Springs, Streams and Spas of London*. London, 1920.

Ts   Forbes, R. J. "Metallurgy," *A History of Technology* 2, ed. C. Singer *et al*. Oxford, 1957.

Ts   ———. *Studies in Ancient Technology*. Leiden, 1955–58; New York, 1969.

Gn   Francis, C. A. *A History of Food and Its Preservation*. Princeton, 1937.

Ts   Franklin, A. *Vie privée des français, 12e à 18e siècles*. Paris, 1887–1902.

G   Franklin, Alfred. *La cuisine*. Paris, 1888.

G   ———. *Les repas*. Paris, 1889.

T   Fraser, A. *A History of Toys*. London, 1966.

Ga   Fraser, H. M. *Beekeeping in Antiquity*. London, 1931.

T   Fraser, J. T., ed. *The Voices of Time*. New York, 1966.

T   ———. *Of Time, Passion, and Knowledge*. New York, 1975.

Ga   Freeman, Margaret B. *Herbs for the Medieval Household for Cooking, Healing and Divers Uses*. New York, 1943.

A   Friedlander, Max. *Der Holzschnitt*. Berlin, 1917.

T   Froissart, Jean. *Chronicles*. eds. Gillian and William Anderson. Carbondale, 1963.

T   Frothingham, A. "Apothecaries' Shops in Spain," *Notes Hispanic* (1941).

L   Furniss, W. Todd. "Ben Johnson's Masques," *Yale Studies in English* 138 (1958).

Ge   Furnivall, Frederick J. *Early English Meals and Manners*. London, 1868.

Ge   ———. *Manners and Household Expenses in 13th Through 15th Century England*. London, 1861.

Te   ———, ed. *The Babees Book*, Early English Text Society 32. London, 1868.

Te   ———, ed. *A Book of Precedence*. London, 1869.

Tc   Gabel, Creighton. *Analysis of Prehistoric Economic Patterns*. New York, 1967.

G   Galavaris, George. *Bread and the Liturgy*. Madison, Wis., and London, 1970.

M   Galpin, Francis. "The Romance of the Phagotum," *Proceedings of the Royal Musical Associations* 67 (1941).

Gu   Gask, N. *Old Silver Spoons of England*. London, 1926.

T   Gallaeus, Joannes. *Speculum diversarum imaginum speculativarum*. Antwerp, 1638.

A   Gardner, A. H. *Outline of English Architecture*. London, 1945.

A   Gasparetto, Astone. "Aspects de la verrerie vénitienne antérieure à la Renaissance," *Cahiers de la céramique du verre et des arts du feu* 17 (1960), 30–48.

A   Gauthier, M. M. *Emaux du moyen-âge occidental*. Fribourg, 1972.

G   Gellerey, William. *The London Cook*. Dublin, 1762.

G   Gérard, Charles. *L'ancienne Alsace à table*. Colmar, 1862.

Ga   *Geoponika*, trans. R. T. Owen. London, 1805.

G   Glasse, Hannah. *The Art of Cookery . . .* London, 1748.

M   Glyn, Margaret Henrietta. *About Elizabethan Original Music and Its Composers*. London, 1924.

Tc   Goitein, S. D. *Letters of Medieval Jewish Traders*. Princeton, 1973.

T   Goodman, W. L. *The History of Woodworking Tools*. London, 1964.

Ga   Gomez Miedes, Bernardo. *Alographia* [Salt]. Ursel, 1605.

L   Gordon, D. J. "Poet and Architect: the Intellectual Setting of the Quarrel Between Ben Jonson and Inigo Jones," *Journal of the Warburg and Courtauld Institutes* 12 (1949), 152–78.

Gn   Gottschalk, Alfred. "L'alimentation humaine depuis la préhistoire jusqu'à nos jours," *Hippocrate* (1946).

M   Gosson, S. *An Apologie for the Schoole of Abuse*. 1597; ed. Ed Arber, London, 1930.

A   Grabar, Andre, and Carl Nordenfalk. *The Great Centuries of Painting. Early Medieval Painting*. Geneva, 1957.

A   ———. *Romanesque Painting*. Geneva, 1958.

Ga   Gray, W. D. *The Relation of Fungi to Human Affairs*. New York, 1959.

Th   Griffiths, Roger. *A Description of the River Thames*. London, 1758.

G   Grigson, Jane. *Good Things*. New York, 1971.

L   Guenée, Bernard, and F. Lehoux. *Les Entrées Royales françaises de 1328 à 1515*. Paris, 1968.

M   Gundesheimer, Werner, ed. *Art and Life at the Court of Ercole 1 d'Este*. Geneva, 1972.

Ga   Günther, R. T. "The Oyster Culture of the Ancient Romans," *Journal of the Marine Biological Association* 4 (1897), 360–65.

Ts   Gurney, O. R. *The Hittites*. Harmondsworth, 1961.

A   Gutkind, Curt Sigmar. *Das Buch der Tafelfreuden*. Leipzig, 1929.

L   Guyer, Foster Erwin. *Chrétien de Troyes: Inventor of the Modern Novel*. New York, 1957.

Gv   Hackwood, Frederick W. *Inns, Ales, and Drinking Customs of Old England*. New York, 1909.

Ts   Halle, Edward. *Chronicle: Containing the History of England during the Reign of Henry the Fourth*. London, 1548. New York, 1965.

Gu   Hampson, John. *The English at Table*. London, 1944.

M   Haraszti, Emile. "La Technique des improvisateurs de langue vulgaire et de latin au quattrocento," *Revue belge de musicologie* 9 (1955).

Th   Harrington, Sir John. *A New Discourse on a Stale Subject Called the Metamorphosis of Ajax*. ed. Elizabeth Donno. New York, 1962.

Ts   Harrington, J. H. *The Production and Distribution of Books in Western Europe to the year 1500*. New York, 1956.

Ga   Harrison, S. G., G. Masefield and M. Wallis. *The Oxford Book of Food Plants*. Oxford, 1969.

Gn   Hart, James. *The Diet of the Diseased*. London, 1633.

Ts   Hartley, Dorothy, and Mary Elliot. *Life and Work of the People of England*. New York, 1926–29.

G   Hartley, Dorothy. *Food in England*. London, 1954.

Th   ———. *Water in England*. London, 1964.

Ts   Haskins, Charles Homer. *The Renaissance of the Twelfth Century*. Cambridge, Mass., 1927.

Ga   Hauseleiter, Johannes. *Der vegetarismus in der antike*. Berlin, 1935.

Gu   Hayward, J. F. *English Cutlery: Sixteenth to Eighteenth Century*. London, 1956.

T   Hazlitt, W. C. *Faith and Folklore of the British Isles*. London, 1813; repr. 1965.

G   ———. *Old Cookery Books*. London, 1886.

Ga   Hedrick, U. P., ed. *Sturtevant's Notes on Edible Plants*. Albany, 1919.

T   Henry VIII, Court of. *Privy Purse Expenses (1529–32)*. London, 1827.

Ts   Heer, F. *The Medieval World*. Cleveland, 1962.

Gn   Helbaek, Hans. "Studying the Diet of Ancient Man," *Archeology* 14 (1961), 95–101.

Ga   ———. "Early Crops in Southern England," *Proceedings of the Prehistoric Society* 18 (1952), 194–233.

Ga   ———. "Domestication of Food Plants in the Old World," *Science* 130 (1959), 365–72.

A   Hell, Vera and Hellmut. *Die grosse Wallfahrt des Mittelalters*. Tübingen, 1964.

Ts   Hellyer, B. *Under Eight Reigns*. London, 1937.

Gn   Hemardinquer, J. J., ed. *Pour une histoire de l'alimentation*. Paris, 1972.

Gv   Henderson, A. *History of Ancient and Modern Wines*. London, 1824.

A   Henderson, George. *Gothic*. Harmondsworth and Boston, 1967.

Gn   Henslow, G. *Medical Works of the Fourteenth Century*. London, 1899.

L   Herbert, W. *History of the Twelve Great Livery Companies.* London, 1834.

G   Herman, Judith, and Marguerite Shallett. *The Cornucopia. English Cookery 1390–1899.* New York, n.d.

Th   Herschel, Clemens. *Frontinus and the Water Supply of the City of Rome.* Boston, 1899. [See also Bennett, C.]

Ga   Higgs, E. S., and J. P. White. "Autumn Killing," *Antiquity* 37 (1963), 282–89.

L   Himmelheber, G. *Spiele.* Munich, 1972.

A   Hind, Arthur M. *An Introduction to a History of Woodcut.* New York, 1963.

A   ———. *Engraving in England in the Sixteenth and Seventeenth Centuries.* Cambridge, 1952–64.

Tc   Hirth, F. "Notes on the Early History of the Salt Monopoly in China," *Journal of the [North] China Branch of the Royal Asiatic Society* 12 (1887).

Th   Hodder, Michael. "The Waterworks of Canterbury," *Scholia,* Fall, 1975. [The Institute for Medieval and Renaissance Studies, C.C.N.Y. of C.U.N.Y.]

A   Hoffeld, Jeffrey. "The Art of the Medieval Blacksmith," *Metropolitan Museum of Art Bulletin* 28 (Dec. 1969), 161–73.

L   Holmes, Urban Tigner. *Chrétien de Troyes.* New York, 1970.

Ts   ———. *Daily Living in the Twelfth Century.* Madison, Wis., 1970.

T   Hone, Nathaniel J. *The Manor and Manorial Records.* London, 1912.

Ga   Homans, George C. "Men and the Land in the Middle Ages," *Speculum* 11 (1936), 338–51.

M   Honigsheim, Paul. *Music and Society.* ed. K. Peter Etzkorn. New York, 1973.

Gu   Hope, W. H. "On the English Medieval Drinking Bowls Called 'Mazers'," *Archaeologia* 50 (1887), 129–93.

L   Horrell, Joe. "Chaucer's Symbolic Plowman," *Speculum* 14 (1939), 82ff.

Ga   Houghton, W. "Notices of Fungi in Greek and Latin Authors," *Annals and Magazine of Natural History* 5 (1885), 22–49.

A   *The Hours of Catherine of Cleves.* Introduction and Commentaries by John Plummer. New York, 1966.

Th   Howe, E. *A Short Guide to the Fleet River.* London, 1921.

Ga   Howes, F. N. *Nuts, the Production and Everyday Uses.* London, 1948.

T   Hudson, A. *Leet Jurisdiction in Norwich.* London, 1891.

T   Huizinga, Johan. *Homo Ludens.* Boston, 1955.

Ts   ———. *The Waning of the Middle Ages.* New York, 1966.

A   Husa, Vaclav, J. Petran, and A. Subrtova. *Traditional Crafts and Skills: Life and Work in Medieval and Renaissance Times.* London, 1967.

A   Husband, Timothy. "Valencian Lusterware of the Fifteenth Century: An exhibition at the Cloisters," *Metropolitan Museum of Art Bulletin* 29 (Summer 1970), 20–32.

A   Hudson, Noel. *An Early English Vision of Hortus Sanitatis.* London, 1954.

Gv   Hyams, Edward. *The Grape Vine in England.* London, 1965.

Gv   ———. *Dionysus: A Social History of the Wine Vine.* London, 1965.

Ga   Innis, H. A. *The Cod Fisheries.* New Haven, 1940.

Ga   Isaac, Erich. "Influence of Religion on the Spread of Citrus," *Science* 129 (1959), 179–86.

Ga   ———. "On the Domestication of Cattle," *Science* 137 (1962), 195–204.

Gu   Jackson, C. J. "The Spoon and Its History: Its Form, Material and Development," *Archaeologia* 53 (1892).

Gu   ———. *An Illustrated History of English Plate.* London, 1911.

Ga   Jacob, H. E. *Six Thousand Years of Bread.* New York, 1944.

T   Jacobus de Voragine. *Legenda Aurea.* trans. G. Ryan and H. Ripperger. New York, 1941.

A   Janson, H. W. *Apes and Ape Lore in the Middle Ages and the Renaissance.* London, 1952.

T   James, M. *The Canterbury Psalter.* London, 1935.

Tc   James, Margery Kirkbride. *Studies in the Medieval Wine Trade.* Oxford, 1971.

A   Jarry, Madeleine. *World Tapestry.* New York, 1968.

Tc   Jefferys, James B. *Retail Trading in Britain, 1850–1950.* London, 1954.

Ga   Jenkins, J. T. *The Herring and the Herring Fisheries.* London, 1927.

Gn   Jenson, Lloyd B. *Man's Foods, Nutrition and Environments in Food Gathering Times and Food Producing Times.* Champaign, Illinois, 1953.

M   Johnson, Paula. *Form and Transformation in Music and Poetry of the English Renaissance.* New Haven, 1972.

T   Jones, Ernest. "The Symbolic Significance of Salt," in his *Essays in Applied Psycho-Analysis.* New York, 1964, 22–109.

L   Jones, George Fenwick. "The Function of Food in Medieval German Literature," *Speculum* 35 (1960), 78–86.

L   Jones, Gwyn, and Thomas Jones. *The Mabinogion.* New York, 1961.

Tc   Jones, P. E. *The Worshipful Company of Poulterers.* London, 1939.

A   Jones-Davies, M.-T. *Inigo Jones, Ben Jonson et le Masque.* Paris, 1967.

A   Katzenellenbogen, A. *Allegories of the Virtues and Vices in Medieval Art.* London, 1939.

Ts   Kellaway, W., and A. Hollaender, eds. *Studies in London History.* London, 1969.

T   Keller, F. *The Lake Dwellings of Switzerland and other Parts of Europe.* New York, 1963.

T   Keller, Werner. *The Bible as History.* London and New York, 1956.

L   Kelly, Wm. *Notices of Leicester.* London, 1865.

Te   Kelso, Ruth. *The Doctrine of the English Gentleman in the Sixteenth Century, with a Bibliographical List of Treatises on the Gentleman and Related Subjects Published in Europe to 1625.* Gloucester, Mass., 1964.

M   Kerman, Joseph. *The Elizabethan Madrigal.* New York, 1962.

T   Kernodle, George R. "Renaissance Artists in the Service of the People," *Art Bulletin* 25 (1943), 59–64.

Ts   Kimble, H. H. T. *Geography in the Middle Ages.* London, 1935.

G   King, William. *The Art of Cooking in Imitation of Horace's Art of Poetry*. London, 1720.

M   Kinkeldey, Otto. "Dance Tunes of the Fifteenth Century," *Instrumental Music*, ed. David G. Hughes. Cambridge, 1959.

M   Kinsky, George. *Album musical*. Paris, 1930.

Gn Kisch, Bruno Z. "Famine and Food Provision in Numismatics," *Ciba Symposia* 9 (1948), 811–47.

Tc ———. *Scales and Weights*. New Haven, 1965.

A   Kohlhaussen, H. "Der Doppelkopf: Seine Bedeutung für das deutsche Brauchtum des 13. bis 17. Jahrhunderts," *Zeitschrift für Kunstwissenschaft* 14 (1960), 24f.

Gn Kouindjy, Emilie. *Recherches historique sur l'enseignement de l'hygiène alimentaire*. Paris, 1926.

A   Kraus, H. *The Living Theatre of Medieval Art*. Bloomington, Indiana, 1967.

Gn Kroschel, Hans. *Diaetetik und therapie in Konrad von Megenberg's Buch der Natur*. Greifswald, 1920.

G   Küchenmeisterei. Nurenberg, 1490.

A   Kup, Karl. "A Medieval Codex of Italy," *Natural History* 72 (Dec. 1963), 30–41.

A   Kurth, Betty. *Die deutschen Bildteppiche des Mittelalters*. Vienna, 1926.

T   Labarge, Margaret Wade. *A Baronial Household of the Thirteenth Century*. New York, 1965.

M   La Cava, A. Francesco. *La dietetica romana*. Milan, 1947.

G   Lacouperie, T. de. "Ketchup, Catchup, Catsup," *The Babylonian and Oriental Record* 3 (Nov. 1889) and 4 (Feb. 1890).

M   Lacroix, Paul. *Ballet et Mascarades . . . Henri III à Louis XIV*. Geneva, 1868.

Gn Ladurie, E. LeRoy. *Times of Feast, Times of Famine: A History of Climate Since the Year 1000*. trans. Barbara Bary. Garden City, 1971.

Th Lamb, H. A. J. "Sanitation: An Historical Survey," *Architectural Journal* (April 3, 1937).

A   Landwehr, John. *Splendid Ceremonies, State Entries and Royal Funerals in the Low Countries, 1515–1791*. Leiden, 1971.

Ts Langlois, C. V. *La Vie en France au moyen-âge*. Paris, 1925.

G   La Varenne, Francois Pierre de. *Le Vray Cuisinier François*. Paris, 1651.

A   Laran, Jean. *L'Estampe*. 2 vols., Paris, 1959.

M   La Rue, Jan. *Aspects of Medieval and Renaissance Music*. New York, 1966.

Gn Lee, T'ao. "Historical Notes on Some Vitamin Deficiency Diseases in China," *Chinese Medical Journal* 58 (1940), 314–23.

A   Lehmann-Haupt, H. *Gutenberg and the Master of the Playing Cards*. New Haven, 1966.

Ga Lehner, Ernst and Johanna. *Folklore and Odysseys of Food and Medicinal Plants*. New York, 1962.

M   Le Huray, Peter. *Music and the Reformation in England, 1549–1660*. New York, 1967.

Tc Lespinasse, René de. *Histoire générale de Paris. Les Métiers et corporations de la Ville de Paris. Ordinnances générales. Métiers de l'Alimentation*. Paris, 1886.

Tc Lewis, Archibald R. *Naval Power and Trade in the Mediterranean A.D. 500–1100*. Princeton, 1951.

G   Levi-Strauss, Claude. *The Raw and the Cooked*. London and New York, 1970.

G   ———. *Du Miel aux cendres*. Paris, 1967.

Ge ———. *L'Origine des manières de table*. Paris, 1968.

Gv Lichine, Alexis, ed. *Encyclopedia of Wines and Spirits*. London and New York, 1967.

Ts Liger, Louis. *La nouvelle maison rustique . . .* Paris, 1700.

L   Linker, Robert White. *The Story of the Grail*. Chapel Hill, 1952.

Tc Lloyd, Christopher. *The British Seaman, 1200–1860. A Social Survey*. London, 1968.

M   Lockwood, Lewis. "Music at Ferrara in the Period of Ercole I d'Este," *Studi musicali* 1 (1972).

Te Loesch, Ilse. *So war es Sitte in der Renaissance*. Leipzig, 1964.

Gv Longmate, Norman. *The Water Drinkers: A History of Temperance*. London and New York, 1968.

L   Loomis, L. H. *Adventures in the Middle Ages*. New York, 1962.

L   Loomis, R. E., and L. H. Loomis, eds. *Medieval Romances*. New York, 1957.

L   Loomis, Roger Sherman. *Arthurian Tradition and Chrétien de Troyes*. New York, 1949.

L   ———. *Arthurian Literature in the Middle Ages*. Oxford, 1959.

Ts ———. *A Mirror of Chaucer's World*. Princeton, 1965.

A   Longon, Jean, and Raymond Cazelles (Introduction and Commentaries). *The Très Riches Heures of Jean, Duke of Berry*. New York, 1969.

Tc Lopez, R. S., and I. W. Raymond. *Medieval Trade in the Mediterranean World*. New York, 1968.

Ts Lopez, R. S. *The Birth of Europe*. New York, 1967.

Ts ———. *The Three Ages of the Italian Renaissance*. Charlottesville, 1970.

Tc ———. *The Commercial Revolution of the Middle Ages*. Englewood Cliffs, 1971.

Ga Lovet, V. *La Flore pharaonique d'après les documents hiéroglyphiques et les spécimens découverts dans les tombes*. Paris, 1892.

M   Lovarini, Emilio. *Studi sul Ruzzante e la letteratura pavana*. Padua, 1965.

M   Long, John. *Music in Renaissance Drama*. Lexington, Ky., 1968.

Gn Lu, Gwei-Djen, and Joseph Needham. "A Contribution to the History of Chinese Dietetics," *Isis* 42 (1951).

T   Lucas, A. *Ancient Egyptian Materials and Industries*. London and New York, 1962.

Gv Lutz, H. F. *Viticulture and Brewing in the Ancient Orient*. Leipzig and New York, 1922.

Ga Macer. *Floridus De Viribus Herbarum*. ed. L. Choulant. Leipzig, 1832.

M   Mackerness, Eric David. *A Social History of English Music*. London, 1964.

G   Maggs Brothers. *Food and Drink Through the Ages, 2,500 B.C. to 1937 A.D. . . .* London, 1937 [catalogue].

G   Maillant, C. *Les Aphrodisiaques*. Paris, 1967.

A   Mâle, Emile. *L'Art religieux de la fin du moyen-âge*. Paris, 1922.

Ga   Mangelsdorf, P. C. *Plants and Human Affairs.* Bloomington, Ind., 1952.

Ge   *Manners and Household Expenses of England in the 13th and 15th Centuries.* London, 1861.

M   Manifold, John Streeter. *Music in English Drama from Shakespeare to Purcell.* London, 1956.

T   Marco Polo. *Travels.* trans. Robert Latham. Harmondsworth, 1958, 1968.

M   Marcuse, Sybil. *Musical Instruments, A Comprehensive Dictionary.* New York, 1964.

G   Markham, G. *English Housewife.* London, 1683.

G   ———. *Markham's Master-Piece.* London, 1668.

A   Marle, Raimond van. "Iconographie de l'art profane au moyen-âge et à la Renaissance," *La Vie quotidienne.* The Hague, 1931.

Gn   Marouse, Julian. *Diätetik im alterthum.* Stuttgart, 1899.

Ts   Marques, A. Henriques de Oliveira. *Daily Life in Portugal in the Late Middle Ages.* Madison, Wis., 1971.

A   Martin, Kurt. *Minnesänger.* Baden-Baden, 1964.

G   Master Martino. *Libro De Arte Coquinaria.* Italy, 1450.

Gv   Marrison, L. W. *Wines and Spirits.* Harmondsworth, 1957.

G   Massialot, François. *Le cuisinier roial et bourgeois.* Paris, 1691.

Ga   Maurizio, Adam. *Histoire de l'alimentation végétale depuis la préhistoire jusqu'à nos jours.* Paris, 1932.

T   McEvedy, Colin. *The Penguin Atlas of Medieval History.* Harmondsworth, 1961.

T   ———. *Penguin Atlas of Ancient History.* Harmondsworth, 1967.

M   McGowan, Margaret. *L'Art du ballet de cour en France 1581–1643.* Paris, 1963.

L   ———. "Form and Themes in Henry II's Entry into Rouen," *Renaissance Drama* (1968), 199–251.

G   McKendry, Maxime. *The Seven Centuries Cookbook.* London, 1973.

A   McKerrow, Ronald B. *Title Page Borders used in England and Scotland, 1485–1640.* London, 1932.

L   Meagher, John C. *Methods and Meaning in Ben Jonson's Masques.* Bloomington, Ind., 1966.

G   Mead, William Edward. *The English Medieval Feast.* London, 1931.

G   Medlin, Faith. *A Gourmet's Book of Beasts.* New York, 1975.

A   Meiss, Millard. *French Painting in the Time of Jean de Berry: The Boucicaut Master.* London, 1968.

M   Mellers, Wilfred Howard. *Music and Society: England and the European Tradition.* London, 1948.

M   ———. *Harmonious Meeting; A Study of the Relationship between English Music, Poetry and Theatre, c. 1600–1900.* London, 1965.

Ga   Merrill, Elmer D. *The Botany of Cook's Voyages.* Waltham, Mass., 1954.

G   Messisbugo, Christoforo di. *Banchetti compositioni di Vivande.* Ferrara, 1549; ed. F. Bandini, Venice, 1960.

M   Meyer-Baer, Kathi. *Music of the Spheres and the Dance of Death. Studies in Musical Iconology.* Princeton, 1970.

Tc   Miller, J. Innes. *The Spice Trade of the Roman Empire, 29 B.C. to A.D. 641.* Oxford, 1969.

Gn   Milne, Lorus and Margery. *The Nature of Life.* London, 1971.

L   Minor, Andrew C., and Mitchell Bonner, eds. *A Renaissance Entertainment: Festivities for the Marriage of Cosimo I, Duke of Florence, in 1539.* Missouri, 1968.

Tc   Miskimin, H. A. *The Economy of Early Renaissance Europe.* Englewood Cliffs, 1969.

T   Misson de Valbourg, Henri. *M. Misson's Memoirs and Observations in his Travels over England, 1690.* trans. M. Ozell, London, 1719.

Ts   Mitchell, R. J., and M. D. R. Leys. *A History of London Life.* New York, 1958.

A   Mitchell, Sabrina. *Medieval Manuscript Painting.* New York, 1964.

Gv   Monckton, H. A. *A History of the English Public House.* London, 1970.

T   Moorat, S. A. J. *Catalogue of MSS on Medicine and Science in the Wellcome Historical Medical Library.* London, 1962.

Ga   Morettini, A. *Olivicultura.* Rome, 1950.

M   Morley, Thomas. *A Plaine and Easie Introduction to Practicall Musicke.* London, 1597; New York, 1952.

Ga   Moritz, L. A. *Grain Mills and Flour in Classical Antiquity.* Oxford, 1958.

G   Morris, Richard, ed. *Liber Cure Cocorum.* London, 1862.

G   Mourant, A. E., and F. E. Zeuner, eds. "Man and Cattle," *Proceedings of a Symposium on Domestication.* London, 1963.

L   Mourrey, Gabriel. *Les Fêtes Françaises.* Paris, 1930.

Gn   Mullett, Charles F. *The Bubonic Plague and England.* Lexington, 1956.

Ts   Mumford, Lewis. *The City in History: Its Origins, Its Transformations and Its Prospects.* London and New York, 1961, 1966.

G   Murrell, John. *Murrels Two Bookes of Cookerie and Carving.* London, 1631.

M   *Musica Nova.* Vol. 1 of *Monuments of Renaissance Music,* ed. H. Colin Slim. Chicago and London, 1964.

L   Mustard, Helen M., and C. E. Passage. *Parzival.* New York, 1961.

L   Nagler, A. M. *Theatre Festivals of the Medici, 1539–1637.* New Haven, 1964.

G   Napier, Mrs. *Noble Boke of Cookery and Liber Cure Cucorum.* London, 1882.

Gn   Nares. *Haven of Helthe.* London, 1598.

Ts   Needham, Joseph. *Clerks and Craftsmen in China and the West.* Cambridge, 1970.

Ts   ———. *Science and Civilization in China.* Cambridge, 1970.

Gn   Nenquin, Jacques. *Salt, a Study in Economic Prehistory,* Brugge, 1961.

G   *Neues lexikon der französischen, sächsischen, österreichischen und böhmischen kochkunst.* Prague and Vienna, 1785.

G   Nevelière, de la. *Petite histoire d'une très ancienne science.* Paris, 1926.

M   Newcomb, Anthony. "The Musica Secreta of Ferrara in the 1580's," Ph.D. Dissertation, Princeton, 1969.

M   Newman, Joel. *Sixteenth Century Italian Dances.* University Park and London, 1966.

M   *New Oxford History of Music*, vol. 3: *The Ars Nova and the Renaissance, 1300–1540*. eds. D. A. Hughes and G. Abraham. London, 1960.

A   New York. Metropolitan Museum of Art. *The Hours of Jeanne d'Evreux at the Cloisters*. Greenwich, 1957.

A   ———. *Medieval Art from Private Collections*, ed. Carmen Gomez-Moreno. New York, 1968 [catalogue].

A   ———. *The Secular Spirit*. eds. Jane Hayward and Timothy Husband. New York, 1975 [catalogue].

T   Newton, A. P. *Travel and Travellers in the Middle Ages*. London, 1930.

G   Nicolardot, Louis. *Histoire de la table: curiosités gastronomiques de tous les temps et de tous les pays*. Paris, 1868.

L   Nicoll, Allardyce. *Stuart Masques and the Renaissance Stage*. Edinburgh, 1937.

G   Oakley, Kenneth P. "Fire as Palaeolithic Tool and Weapon," *Proceedings of the Prehistoric Society* 21 (1955), 35–48.

Gn   Ogden, Margaret Sinclair, ed. *The Liber de Diversis Medicinis*. London, 1938.

Gv   Okakura, K. *The Book of Tea*. ed. E. V. Bleiler. New York, 1964.

Te   Olivier de la Marche. *Mémoires*. ed. C. Petitot. Paris, 1820.

L   Olschki, Leonardo. *The Grail Castle and its Mysteries*. Berkeley, 1966.

T   Olsen, J. E., and E. G. Bourne, eds. *The Northmen, Columbus and Cabot, 985–1503, in Original Narratives of Early American History*. New York, 1934.

Gu   Oman, Charles. *Medieval Silver Nefs*. London, 1963.

A   Ong, Walter J. "From Allegory to Diagram in the Renaissance Mind: A Study in the Significance of the Allegorical Tableau," *Journal of Aesthetics and Art Criticism* 17 (1959), 423–40.

L   Orgel, Stephen and Roy Strong. *Inigo Jones. The Theatre of the Stuart Court*. London, 1973.

Ga   Organ, J. *Gourds*. London and Newton Centre, 1963.

G   Oxford, Arnold Whitaker. *English Cookery Books to the Year 1850*. New York and London, 1913.

M   Oliphant, Thomas. *La Musa Madrigalesca*. London, 1837.

A   Pächt, O. "Early Italian Nature Studies and the Early Calendar Landscape," *Journal of the Warburg and Courtauld Institutes* 13 (1950).

Ga   Palladius. *On Husbondrie*. London, 1873, 1879.

Ga   Parmentier, A. A. *Traité sur la culture et les usages des pommes de terre*. Paris, 1789.

Ga   Parry, J. W. *The Story of Spices*. New York, 1953.

M   Pattison, Bruce. *Music and Poetry of the English Renaissance*. London, 1948.

L   Payne, Robert. *The Roman Triumph*. London, 1962.

G   Pegge, S., ed. *The Forme of Cury. A roll of ancient English Cookery, compiled, about* A.D. *1390 by the master cooks of King Richard II*. London, 1780.

T   Percy, T. *The Northumberland Household Book or the Regulations and Establishment of the Household of Henry Algernon Percy, The Fifth Earl of Northumberland*. London, 1770.

Th   Perks, Sidney. *Essay on Old London*. Cambridge, 1927.

A   Perls, Klaus G. *Jean Fouquet*. London and New York, 1940.

A   Pevsner, Sir Niklaus. *An Outline of European Architecture*. New York, 1948.

A   ———. *The Buildings of England*. London, 1951.

Gu   Pinto, Edward H. *Treen and Other Wooden Bygones*. London, 1969.

Ts   Pirenne, H. *Medieval Cities: Their Origins and the Revival of Trade*. Princeton, 1948.

Tc   ———. "Un grand commerce d'exportation au moyen-âge: les vins de France," *Annales d'histoire économique et sociale* 5 (1933), 225.

Ga   Pirie, N. W. *Food Resources Conventional and Novel*. Harmondsworth, 1969.

M   Pirrotta, Nino. "Music and Cultural Tendencies in 15th Century Italy," *Journal of the American Musicological Society* 19 (1966).

M   Planyavsky, Alfred. *Geschichte des Kontrabasses*. Tutzing, 1970.

G   Platina, Bartholomaeus Sacchi. *De honesta voluptate et valetudine . . .* Venice, 1475; trans. *On Honest Indulgence and Good Health* by E. B. Andrews, 1967.

T   Pliny the Elder. *Natural History*. trans. H. Rackham. London, 1950.

Tc   Postan, M. M. "The Trade of Mediaeval Europe: the North," *The Cambridge Economic History*, vol. II. Cambridge, 1950.

Gn   Power, (Sir) D'Arcy. "Dining with our ancestors," in his *The Foundations of Medical History*. Baltimore, 1931.

Ge   Power, Eileen, ed. *The Goodman of Paris* [Le Ménagier de Paris, 1392–94]. London, 1928.

Gv   Prakash, O. *Food and Drinks in Ancient India*. New Delhi, 1961.

G   Prarond, Ernest. *Abbeville à table: études gourmandes et morales*. Amiens, 1878.

Gn   Prentice, Ezra Parmalee. *Hunger and History: the Influence of Hunger on Human History*. New York and London, 1939.

Gu   Price, F. G. H. *Old Base Metal Spoons*. London, 1908.

M   Prunières, Henry. *Le Ballet de Cour en France avant Benserada et Lully*. Paris, 1914.

G   Pullar, Philippa. *Consuming Passions. Being an Historic Inquiry into Certain English Appetites*. Boston, 1970.

Ts   Putnam, G. H. *Books and Their Makers during the Middle Ages*. New York, 1896.

G   Pytchley. *The Book of Refined Cookery*. London, 1886.

G   *Queen's Closet Opened*. London, 1710.

Tu   Quennell, M. and C. H. B. *A History of Everyday Things in England 1066–1179*. New York, n.d.

T   Rabinovitch, N. *Probability and Statistical Inference in Ancient and Medieval Jewish Literature*. Toronto, 1973.

Ga   Radcliffe, William. *Fishing from the Earliest Times*. New York, 1926.

T   Rahner, Hugo. *Man at Play*. New York, 1967.

Ga   Ramsbottom, J. *Mushrooms and Toadstools*. London and New York, 1963.

A   Randall, Lillian M. C. *Images in the Margins of Gothic Manuscripts*. Berkeley and Los Angeles, 1966.

A   Randall, Richard. "A Gothic Bird Cage," *Metropolitan Museum of Art Bulletin* 11 (1953), 286–92.

Th   Reader, F. W. "On Pile Structures in the Wallbrook, near London Walls," *Journal of the Archaeological Society* 60 (1903), 137–204.

M   Reese, Gustave. *Fourscore Classics of Music Literature*. New York, 1957.

M   ———. *Music in the Middle Ages*. New York, 1959.

M   ———. *Music in the Renaissance*. New York, 1966.

Gn   Redmayne, Paul Brewis. *Britain's Food*. London, 1963.

G   Renner, H. D. *The Origin of Food Habits*. London, 1944.

L   Rehyer, Paul. *Les Masques anglais*. Paris, 1909.

Gn   *Regimen Sanitatis*. Strassburg, 1513.

Gn   Reynière, Grimod de la. *Almanach des Gourmands, ou calendrier nutritif*. Paris, 1803–1812.

Th   Reynolds, Reginald. *Cleanliness and Godliness*. Garden City, 1946.

T   Rickaby, Joseph. *Aquinas Ethicus: The Moral Teachings of St. Thomas*. London, 1896.

Ts   Rickert, Edith. *Chaucer's World*. New York, 1948.

Te   ———. *The Babee's Book: Medieval Manners for the Young: Done into Modern English from Dr. Furnivall's Texts*, New York, 1966.

L   Rickert, M., and J. Manly, eds. *Text of the Canterbury Tales*. Chicago, 1940.

A   Rickert, M. *Painting in Britain in the Middle Ages*. Baltimore, 1954.

A   Ring, Grete. *A Century of French Painting, 1400–1500*. London, 1949.

L   Robertson, D. S. "The Food of Achilles," *Classical Review* 59 (1940), 177ff.

Th   Robins, F. W. *The Story of Water Supply*. New York, 1946.

Gu   ———. *The Story of the Lamp (and the Candle)*. London, 1939.

Gv   Robinson, Edward Forbes. *The Early History of Coffee Houses in England*. London, 1893.

Gn   Rooche, M. "La Faim à l'époque carolingienne: essai sur quelques types de rations alimentaires," *Revue historique* 251 (1973), 295–320.

Gn   Root, Waverly. *The Food of Italy*. London and New York, 1958.

Te   Roper, John. *Life of Sir Thomas More*. ed. C. Singer. London, 1822.

A   Rorimer, James J. "The Treasury at the Cloisters and Two Ingolstadt Beakers," *Metropolitan Museum of Art Bulletin* 9 (1951), 249–59.

A   ———. "Acquisitions for the Cloisters," *Metropolitan Museum of Art Bulletin* 11 (1953), 265ff.

Ts   Rosenberg, M. V. *Eleanor of Aquitaine: Queen of the Troubadours and the Courts of Love*. Boston, 1937.

G   Rosselli, Giovanni de'. *Opera nova . . . Epulario*, [or, *The Italian Banquet*], Venice, 1516.

Ts   Rowntree, B. Seebohm. *Poverty: A Study of Town Life*. New York, 1901.

Ts   Rowse, A. L. *The England of Elizabeth—the Structure of Society*. London, 1951.

Gn   Rumford, Benjamin Thompson (Count). "Of Food: and Particularly of Feeding the Poor," 1795, in *Works*, vol. V. London, 1876.

G   Rumpolt, Marx. *Ein neu Kochbuch*. Frankfort-on-Main, 1581.

Gu   Rupert, C. G. *Apostle Spoons: Their Evolution from Earlier Types, and the Emblems used by the Silversmiths for the Apostles*. London, 1929.

L   Russell, Joycelyne C. *The Field of Cloth of Gold: Men and Manners in 1520*. London, 1969.

M   Ruzzante. *Teatro*. ed. Lodovico Zorzi. Turin, 1967.

Tc   Sabine, Ernest L. "Butchering in Medieval London," *Speculum* 8 (1933), 335ff.

Th   ———. "Latrines and Cesspools of Medieval London," *Speculum* 9 (1934), 303–21.

Th   ———. "City Cleaning in Medieval London," *Speculum* 12 (1937), 19–43.

Ga   Salaman, Redcliffe N. *The History and Social Influence of the Potato*. Cambridge, 1949.

Gn   *Salerno Regimen*, trans. as *The Englishman's Doctor* by Sir John Harington. London, 1608.

Th   Salusbury, G. T. *Street Life in Medieval England*. Oxford, 1948.

Tc   Salzman, Louis F. *English Industries of the Middle Ages*. Oxford, 1923.

Ts   ———. *English Life in the Middle Ages*. New York, 1960.

G   Sass, Lorna. *To the King's Taste*. New York, 1975.

Gu   Savage, G. *English Pottery and Porcelain*. New York, 1961.

Ga   Savage, H. "Hunting in the Middle Ages," *Speculum* 8 (1933), 30ff.

A   Saxl, F. "A Spiritual Encyclopedia of the Later Middle Ages," *Journal of the Warburg and Courtauld Institutes* 5 (1942).

G   Scappi, Bartolomeo. "Cuoco Secreto di Papa Pio Quinto," *Opera di M. B. Scappi*. Venice, 1570.

M   Scünemann, Georg, ed. *Trompeterfanfaren, Sonaten und Feldstücke des 16.–17. Jahrhunderts*. Cassel, 1936.

Ga   Schafer, Edward M. *The Golden Peaches of Samarkand: A Study of T'ang Exotics*. Berkeley and Los Angeles, 1963.

T   Scheuer, Margaret. *About the Round Table*. New York, 1945.

A   Schiedlausky, G. *Essen und Trinken: Tafelsitten bis zum Ausgang des Mittelalters*. Munich, 1956.

A   Schrade, Leo. "Les Fêtes du Mariage de Francesco de' Medici et de Bianca Cappello." *Les Fêtes de la Renaissance*, ed. J. Jacquot. Paris, 1956.

T   Schroeder, T. H. *Paternal Legislation: A Study of Liberty*. Republished from *Mother Earth*, 1906.

T   Sigerist, Henry. *A History of Medicine*. New York, 1951.

Tc Simon, Andre L. *The History of the Wine Trade in England*. London, n.d.

Ts Singer, Charles. *A Short History of Medicine*. Oxford, 1928.

Ts Singer, Charles, et al., eds. *A History of Technology*, vol. II, *The Mediterranean Civilization and the Middle Ages, c. 700 B.C. to 1500 A.D.* Oxford, 1956.

T   Specht, Franz Anton. *Gastmähler und trinkgeläge bei den deutschen von den altesten zeiten*. Stuttgart, 1887.

Th Smith, Charles C. "Observations on Roman remains recently found in London," *Archaeologia* 29 (1842).

Gn Smith, Joseph Russell. *The World's Food Resources*. New York, 1919.

A   Smith, R. C. *The Art of Portugal: 1500–1800*. London, 1968.

Ga Sokolov, R. "The Drinking Man's Pear," *Natural History* 85 (1976), 86–90.

M   Squire, J. C. *Songs from the Elizabethans*. London, 1937.

Ts Stephenson, C., and B. Lyon. *Medieval History: Europe from the Second to the Sixteenth Century*. New York, 1962.

A   Sternberg, Wilhelm. *Die Küche in der klassischen Malerei*. Stuttgart, 1910.

A   Sterling, Charles, and Helene Alhemar. *Musée national du Louvre. Peintures. Ecole Française XIVe, XVe et XVIe siècles*. Paris, 1965.

M   Sternfeld, F. W. *Music in Shakespearean Tragedy*. London, 1963.

M   Stevens, John. *Music and Poetry in the Early Tudor Court*. London, 1961.

G   *Stir Hit Well. A Book of Medieval Refreshments*. Cambridge, 1972.

Ga Stobart, Tom. *Herbs, Spices and Flavorings*. London, 1970.

A   Stoddard, Whitney S. *Monastery and Cathedral in France*. Middletown, Conn., 1966.

Gn Stohr, August. "Ein beitrag zur geschichte der diätetik," *Festschrift für dritten saecularfeier der Alma Julia Maximiliana*. Leipzig, 1882.

Ga Storck, John, and Walter Darwin Teague. *Flour for Man's Bread: A History of Milling*. St. Paul, Minn., 1952.

Gu Striker, Cecil. "The Evolution of our 'Table'," *Annals of Medieval History* 10 (Dec. 1928).

Ts Strong, Roy. *Splendour at Court*. Boston, 1973.

A   ———. "The Popular Celebration of the Accession Day of Queen Elizabeth I," *Journal of the Warburg and Courtauld Institutes* 21 (1958), 86–103.

L   ———. "Festivals for the Garter Embassy at the Court of Henry III," *Journal of the Warburg and Courtauld Institutes* 22 (1959), 60–70.

Ts Strutt, Joseph. *A Complete View of the Dress and Habits of the People of England*. London, 1842.

Ga Surflet, R. *Maison Rustique or The Country Farme*. ed. G. Markham. London, 1616.

T   Swain, Barbara. *Fools and Folly During the Middle Ages and Renaissance*. New York, 1932.

Gn Talbot, C. H. *Medicine in Medieval England*. London, 1967.

G   Taillevent. *Le Viandier*. Paris, 1375; eds. Jérome Pichon and Georges Vicaire. Paris, 1892.

G   Tancock, A. *Notes and Queries*. Ser. 8, III, 366.

Gv Taylor, John. *Drink and Welcome*. London, 1637.

M   Tegnell, John Carl. *Elizabethan Musical Prosody*. Evanston, 1948.

T   Tennant, F. R. *The Sources of the Doctrines of the Fall and Original Sin*, 1903; New York, 1968.

A   Theophilus, trans. as *On Diverse Arts: The Treatise of Theophilus*. Chicago, 1963.

Ga Theophrastus. *History of Plants*. ed. A. F. Hort. London, 1916.

Ga Thiébaux, Marcelle. "The Medieval Chase," *Speculum* 42 (1967), 260 ff.

Gn Thomas, Gertrude Ida. *Foods of our Forefathers*. Philadelphia, 1941.

T   Thompson, (Sir) Benjamin. *Essays: Political, Economical, and Philosophical*. Boston, 1789–1804.

Ts Thompson, J. W. *The Medieval Library*. Chicago, 1939.

G   Thorndike, Lynn. "A Medieval Sauce-Book," *Speculum* 9 (1934), 183–90.

Th ———. "Sanitation, Baths, and Street Cleaning in the Middle Ages and Renaissance," *Speculum* 3 (1928), 192–203.

Ts ———. *Science and Thought in the 15th Century*. New York, 1963.

G   ———. "Three Tracts on Food in Basel Manuscripts," *Bulletin of the History of Medicine* 8 (1940), 358–64.

Tc Thrupp, Sylvia L. *A Short History of the Worshipful Company of Bakers of London*. London, 1933.

Ts ———. *Change in Medieval Society*. New York, 1964.

Tc ———. *The Merchant Class of Medieval London*. Ann Arbor, 1962.

M   Tielman, Susato. *Danserye*. ed. F. J. Giesbert. Mainz, 1936.

L   Tolkien, J. R. R., and E. V. Gordon. *Sir Gawain and the Green Knight*. Oxford, 1925, 1967.

Ts Tomkeieff, O. G. *Life in Norman England*. New York and London, 1966.

Ga Topsell. *Fourfooted Beasts*. ed. Rowland. London, 1658.

Th Tout, Thomas. *Medieval Town Planning*. Manchester, 1948.

Ts Trail, H. D., ed. *Social England*. New York, 1894.

Ts Trevelyan, G. M. *English Social History*. London, 1942.

Gn Trovillion, Violet. *Recipes and remedies of early England*. Herrin, Ill., 1946.

Ga Tusser, T. *A Hundreth Good Points of Husbandrie*. 1557; ed. D. Hartley. London, 1931.

Ga Ucko, Peter J., and G. W. Dimbleby, eds. *The Domestication and Exploitation of Plants and Animals*. London, 1969.

A   Unterkircher, Franz. *A Treasury of Illuminated Manuscripts*. New York, 1967.

Th Urry, William. *Canterbury Under the Angevin Kings*. London, 1967.

Th Vallentine, H. R. *Water in the Service of Man*. Harmondsworth, 1967.

A   Van Marle, R. *Iconographie de l'art profane au moyen-âge et à la renaissance*. The Hague, 1931–32.

T   Vann, G., and P. K. Meagher. *The Temptations of Christ*. New York, 1959.

Th   Van Veen, J. *Dredge, Drain, Reclaim: The Art of A Nation*. The Hague, 1962.

A   Velmans, Tania. "Le Parisinus Grecus 135 et quelques autres peintures de style gothique," *Cahiers archéologiques* 17 (1967), 209–35.

G   Verdot, C. *Historiographie de la table . . .* Paris, 1833.

Gn   Vickery, Kenton Frank. *Food in Early Greece*. Urbana, 1936.

T   Villena, Don Enrique de. *Arte Cisoria* [1423]. Madrid, 1967.

Gu   Viollet-le-Duc, E. E. *Dictionnaire raisonné du mobilier français*. Paris, 1871.

A   Volpe, Giocchino, et al. *La vita medioevale italiana*. Rome, 1960.

T   Wagner, A. *Heralds and Heraldry in the Middle Ages*. London, 1956.

T   Waley, Daniel. *The Italian City Republics*. London and New York, 1969.

Gn   Walford, Cornelius. *The Famines of the World: Past and Present*. London, 1879.

M   Walker, Ernest. *A History of Music ·in England*. Oxford, 1952.

A   Warburg, Aby. "I costumi teatrali per gli intermezzi del 1589," *Gesammelte Schriften* I Leipzig, 1932.

G   Warner, Richard. *Antiquitates culinariae: Tracts on Culinary Affairs of the Old English*. London, 1791.

A   Washington, D. C., Smithsonian Institution. *Dürer and his Time*. Berlin, 1965–66.

G   Wason, B. *Cooks, Gluttons & Gourmets: A History of Cookery*. New York, 1962.

Ts   Watteville, H. de. *The British Soldier: His Daily Life from Tudor to Modern Times*. London, 1954.

Gn   Way, Arthur, trans. *The Science of Dining: A Medieval Treatise on the Hygiene of the Table*. London, 1936.

G   Wegener, Hans. *Küchenmeisterei in Nürnberg*. Leipzig, 1939.

T   Weiss, R. *The Renaissance Discovery of Classical Antiquity*. Oxford, 1969.

A   Weitenkampf, Frank. *The Fifteenth Century and the Cradle of Modern Book Illustration*. New York, 1938.

L   Welsford, Enid. *The Court Masque*. Cambridge, 1927.

L   Weston, Jessie L. *From Ritual to Romance*. New York, 1957.

M   Weyler, Walter. "Documenten betreffende de Muziekkapel aan het Hof van Ferrara," *Vlaamsch Jaarboek voor Muziekgeschiedenis* 1 (1939).

Ga   White, Kenneth D. *Roman Farming*. London, 1970.

Ts   White, Lynn. *Medieval Technology and Social Change*. Oxford, 1962.

A   Widmann, H. *Geschichte des Buchhandels vom Altertum bis zur Gegenwart*. Wiesbaden, 1952.

A   Wilshire, William Hughes. *A Descriptive Catalogue of Playing and Other Cards in the British Museum*. London, 1876.

Th   Willis, Robert. "The Architectural History of the Conventual Buildings of Canterbury," *Archaeologia Cantiana* 7 (1868), 1–207.

T   Wilson, Frank Percy. *The Plague in Shakespeare's London*. London, 1963.

T   Wilson, Violet A. *Society Women of Shakespeare's Time*. New York, 1924.

M   Winternitz, Emanuel. *Musical Instruments and their Symbolism in Western Art*. New York, 1967.

G   Withals, C. *Ompharium*. London, 1556.

Ts   Withington, Lothrop, ed. *Elizabethan England*. New York, 1902.

M   Withington, R. *English Pageantry*. Cambridge, 1918; London, 1920.

A   Wood, D. T. B. "Tapestries of the Seven Deadly Sins," *Burlington Magazine* 20 (1912), 210–22, 277–87.

M   Woodfill, Walter L. *Musicians in English Society from Elizabeth to Charles I*. Princeton, 1953.

Gn   Woodforde, John. *The Strange Story of False Teeth*. New York, 1970.

G   Wooley, Hannah. *The Gentlewoman's Companion: or A Guide to the Female Sex*. London, 1673.

T   Wright, A. R. *British Calendar Customs*. London, 1940.

Th   Wright, Lawrence. *Clean and Decent: the Fascinating History of the Bathroom and Water Closet*. New York, 1960.

G   ———. *Home Fires Burning: the History of Domestic Heating and Cooking*. London, 1964.

Ts   Wright, Louis B. *Middle Class Culture in Elizabethan England*. New York, 1965.

Ts   Wright, Thomas. *A History of the Domestic Manners and Sentiments in England During the Middle Ages*. London, 1862.

Ts   ———. *The Homes of Other Lands*. London, 1871.

Ga   Wynne, Peter. *Apples*. New York, 1975.

Ga   Yarrell. *History of British Fish*. London, 1841.

L   Yates, Frances A. *The French Academies of the Sixteenth Century*. London, 1947.

A   ———. *The Valois Tapestries*. London, 1959.

L   ———. "Elizabethan Chivalry: the Romance of the Accession Day Tilts," *Journal of the Warburg and Courtauld Institutes* 20 (1957), 4–25.

M   ———. "Poésie et musique dans les 'Magnificences' . . . ," *Musique et poésie au XVIe siècle*. Paris, 1954.

M   Yonge, N. *Musica transalpina*. 1588 and 1597. *Metropolitan Museum of Art Bulletin* 26 (June 1968), 441–54.

Gv   Younger, William. *Gods, Men and Wine*. Cleveland, 1966.

Gn   ———. "The Pools of Healing," *Natural History* 68 (Dec. 1969), 578–91.

T   Yule, (Sir) Henry, and A. C. Burrell. *Hobson-Jobson. A Glossary of Coloquial Anglo-Indian Words and Phrases, and of Kindred Terms, Etymological, Historical, Geographical, and Discursive*. London, 1886.

Ga   Zambrini, F., ed. *Il Libro di cucina del secolo XIV*. Bologna, 1863.

Ga   Zeuner, F. E. *A History of Domesticated Animals*. London, 1963.

T   Ziegler, Philip. *The Black Death*. New York, 1969.